ANSWER THE CALL

ANSWER THE CALL

*Virtual Migration in
Indian Call Centers*

AIMEE CARRILLO ROWE, SHEENA MALHOTRA,
AND KIMBERLEE PÉREZ

UNIVERSITY OF MINNESOTA PRESS
MINNEAPOLIS • LONDON

Portions of chapter 1 were previously published as "The Rhythm of Ambition: Power Temporalities and the Production of the Call Center Agent in Documentary Film and Reality Television," in *Critical Rhetorics of Race,* edited by Michael G. Lacy and Kent A. Ono, 197–213 (New York: New York University Press, 2011).

Published by the University of Minnesota Press
111 Third Avenue South, Suite 290
Minneapolis, MN 55401-2520
http://www.upress.umn.edu

Library of Congress Cataloging-in-Publication Data
Carrillo Rowe, Aimee.
    Answer the call : virtual migration in Indian call centers / Aimee Carrillo Rowe, Sheena Malhotra, and Kimberlee Pérez.
    Includes bibliographical references and index.
ISBN 978-0-8166-8938-5 (hc : alk. paper)
ISBN 978-0-8166-8939-2 (pb : alk. paper)
1. Call centers—Social aspects—India. 2. Call center agents—India. 3. Intercultural communication—India. 4. Group identity—India. 5. Transnationalism—India. I. Malhotra, Sheena. II. Pérez, Kimberlee, 1962– III. Title.
HE8789.I4C37 2013
381'.1420954—dc23
                                        2013030776

Printed in the United States of America on acid-free paper

The University of Minnesota is an equal-opportunity educator and employer.

20 19 18 17 16 15 14 13   10 9 8 7 6 5 4 3 2 1

Contents

Preface

On the Ground

Laveena pulls up in her black Land Cruiser in front of Sheena's family home in Bangalore. Laveena is the chief financial officer and one of the founders of I2U, a call center across town in the new Technology Park. Laveena has arranged for us to conduct interviews at I2U and was generous enough to pick us up from Sheena's house on her way to work. We exchange hellos as we make our way to Tech Park, located on the outskirts of the city. Laveena's driver maneuvers quickly and efficiently through crowded streets, the large vehicle bobbing and weaving as cars communicate through frequent honks. Laveena calmly talks on her BlackBerry to someone in Germany as we pass makeshift housing. Small markets line the road; venders push carts and hawk their goods.

The signs to I2U begin to appear about five miles before we reach the call center as the business of the street life gives way to swanky glass buildings, which have sprung up to house multinational corporations like Dell and AOL. High-end housing complexes in various stages of construction are mushrooming along Bangalore's I.T. corridor, adjacent to numerous matchbox apartments. Billboards promise safe, luxurious living conditions—American style—for I.T. professionals. Even though we are getting further from the center of the city, these apartments are already priced out of the range of most of the agents who work in Bangalore's numerous call centers. The billboards serve as images of aspiration that might capture agents' imaginaries, not a reality they might actually attain. Although agents won't live here, the industry's middle and upper management will, as will high-end American and other Western employees, who will use these company flats during their stints in the country.

We pull up to the I2U building. Its exterior is made of glossy blue glass that deepens as it reflects the cloudless sky. The building opens out onto large manicured lawns, well watered by automatic sprinklers. This building could be transplanted into the cityscape of a midwestern American city: the sprawling lawn, the outward expanse of the building, its relative isolation from other buildings. It is a four-story office building with seven other business operations taking up the rest of the building space. This is a very different scenario from Bangalore's central business district, where buildings crowd each other out on Commercial Street, barely an arm's length between their exteriors. The luxury of lawns and the expansive architecture of the building signifies a remove from the crowded Bangalore streets we have left behind. It is another space, another world.

As we walk through the foyer to the stairs, the building's glossy first world exterior gives way to less polished innards. Through a veil of blue tarps, we glimpse construction in adjoining offices. Several lean-bodied workers meander through bamboo scaffolding carrying bowls of cement on their heads. The building's hasty construction reverberates with the sound of loud machinery—jackhammers, electric saws and drills, a cement mixer. The building's interior is being pieced together as we enter. The forms of labor being done here are divided by the permeable boundary of blue tarps: the informatics labor is cordoned off from this unfinished, behind-the-scenes manual labor. The tarps serve as a veil, demarcating an uneven division of labor taking place on the ground, even as this site is just one of countless centers that are designed in service to the West. Laveena guides us away from the loud, messy construction. "We just moved into these new offices," she offers by way of an explanation. "I'd hoped the construction would be completed soon because it's so noisy."

Laveena is a study in paradoxes. Her handshake is firm, but her voice is soft. She dresses in trousers and a *kurti*, a mix of Western and Indian traditional wear, presenting a deliberately cultivated professional look, but not one that is too concerned with the latest fashion. Of medium height and average build, she has a quick smile and talks at a fast pace, as if her mind runs faster than her mouth. Her ambition to be the best at what she does is anything but average. She is as much at ease negotiating on the phone with clients from all over the world as she is speaking the local language with the parents of one of her agents to put them at ease about where their daughter is working. She often plays mother to the agents at her firm, calling them her kids when she speaks about them, yet, she prides herself on discipline and her no-nonsense approach to managing them. She sees herself as being on a mission to help the lower-middle-class Indian access the global stage, setting up a new training and education project to get them the skills they will need to succeed. And yes, she expects to make a fortune along the way.

As we follow her deeper into the building's interior, the noise begins to fade, the sound dampened within soundproofed rooms. We peek into plush offices that branch off from a large central room, then pass through the main room, which is divided into symmetrical cubicles peopled with agents wearing headsets, nodding as they look into computer screens and speak to unseen callers. Laveena ushers us into her corner office. She draws our attention to the view out the large windows that frame half the office space, pointing out various buildings of Tech Park. She tells us she knows the CEO at AOL in case we wish to talk to folks there. It is apparent she is well connected in the industry, even though hers is a relatively small-scale operation that concentrates on delivering quality.

Laveena calls for Suraj, a team manager. After a brief introduction, he gives us a tour. Suraj walks us around the call center floor, where call center agents, wearing Indian and Western clothes and I.D. cards around their necks, sit in gray cubicles and talk into headphones or to each other. They peer at their computer screens, some reading from scripts and others tracking the data in front of them. Their animated tones and attention to detail convey a sense of intimacy with the customers on the other end of the line, half a world away. In our interviews, we will learn that the easy banter between agents and their callers is a highly cultivated craft designed to include discussions of the regional and cultural goings-on in the everyday lives of their customers: the score of last night's game, the weather in Texas, or plans for the upcoming holidays. Agents' fluency in these details allows them to establish familiarity with their distant callers. This knowledge and practice ease the flow of business. It anticipates and reroutes the otherwise expected communication gaps, mistrust, and awkward silences and offers agents the ontological experience of spatial proximity and cultural fluency. Agents often adopt Western names to ease the exchange for the customer, who may be put off by long names that sound foreign to them. These performances of sameness grease the wheels of the interaction, setting the customer at ease to share the sometimes personal and financial information that the agents have access to or need to gather.

In contrast to the intimacy of the call, the physical space is covered with signs of call center life: a poster congratulates agents for a contract renewal from Microsoft; desks are decorated with photographs of families and friends; the bulletin board features a photograph of a young woman, bold letters proclaiming her Agent of the Week. There are six prominent clocks on the walls, each set to a different time: New York, Chicago, Los Angeles, London, Hong Kong, New Delhi. The one labeled New Delhi is set off to the side, just a bit. Though this call center is in Bangalore and all of India is in the same time zone, time in the call centers is marked by the capital city that the rest of the world uses.

Suraj leads us to a clean, quiet office, where we seat ourselves around a small table and check our recorder. Over the next several hours, he sends us, one by one, a long line of agents to interview. At twenty-seven, Suraj is on the fast track to success. He selects the company's best and brightest for us to interview. One of the agents he sends along is Pavitra. In a quiet voice and with an easy smile, she tells us about moving to Bangalore from Goa. She has a law degree but was getting paid only 3,000 rupees (about $75) a month to work in a law office in her hometown. She heard you could start out making between 7,000 and 10,000 rupees a month in the call centers—more than double her salary as a lawyer. She decided to make the move. She misses her sister, her parents, and the slow-paced life of her beachside hometown. Here at I2U, she averages six hundred calls a night. She spends long hours talking to strangers in America. "I put on an accent and use a name that's not mine," she explains. But they are starting to become hers. She steps into an alternative personality under the name Roxanne—a woman who can speak to anyone across the globe. She forgets after awhile where Pavitra ends and Roxanne begins. Night after night, she explains, she repeats the same words: "Hi, thank you for calling. My name is Roxanne. How may I help you?"

Pavitra/Roxanne likes working at the call center. What she likes best is the friends she has made here. Because they do the same work, they really understand her. She does not know how to reconcile the cultural toll this work takes—the loss of family, home, a previous self. The regimented job produces stress. She feels the continual pressure of round-the-clock monitoring and measuring of her performance. She and other workers have had some health issues: insomnia, nausea, nightmares, sore throats; sometimes they cough up blood. In spite of all this, by the end of the interview, she insists this job has remade her. It has given her the confidence to talk to anyone in the world. Her story is one of many that reveal the shifting dynamics of home and family, work and love; the industry is changing everything.

Relationships between parents and children, men and women, workers and employers, call center agents and non–call center agents, agents and the callers across the globe—nothing will ever be quite the same. What we will encounter over the course of six years of interviews with close to fifty call center agents, managers, owners, and trainers are the ways that the rhythms of the call center workers' body clocks have begun to tick to different time zones, as have their desires. We will find, as we immerse ourselves in their words and their worlds, that these call center agents—who work the night shift answering innumerable phone calls, primarily from Americans—feel they are losing touch with their Indian families and friends. They express a longing for these Indian intimacies and a nostalgia for an India that felt somehow more tangible, more immediate, more real. Many feel more connected to Americans, whom they do not see but whose needs they serve, than to the Indians living right down the street. Others describe the odd ways their lives have become defined by their daily orientation toward the happenings in the United States. They have become fluent in talking about things they have never experienced. Working with Americans makes agents feel empowered, yet they are sometimes subjected to American racism in ways they find difficult to comprehend.

What we will learn in writing *Answer the Call* is that call center labor creates its own world. We have come to theorize this world as a virtual borderlands in which nations, disparate time zones, and faraway people are brought together to create messy lifeworlds for Indian call center agents. The borderlands have been conceptualized as a physical space where different people come together and as an imagined psychic, relational, and political space generated in response to uneven power relations. Likewise, Indian call centers generate a new borderlands out of uneven economic, communicative, and material relations between nations. Call center labor creates a borderlands between Indian call center agents and American consumers that is simultaneously porous and impermeable, an invisible yet tangible site of ontological and relational becoming. The borderlands of Indian call center labor are both someplace in particular and no place we can actually go. Agents spend a great deal of time migrating through a virtual borderlands, where their sustained and mediated contact with American consumers recasts the landscapes of their own subjectivities. The stories of these agents, whose lives are not merely their own, reveal intimate faces of globalization and the complex sensibilities it generates.

Acknowledgments

The authors wish to thank individuals and institutions that graciously supported *Answer the Call: Virtual Migration in Indian Call Centers* over the years we have been working on the book.

We are thankful for the institutional support we received for our project. We thank the College of Humanities as well as the Office of Graduate Studies, Research, and International Programs at California State University, Northridge. Generous support through various grants funded travel to gather interviews for our project and awarded release time to complete sections of this book.

We thank the University of Iowa Obermann Interdisciplinary Research Center, the Center for Ethnic Studies and the Arts (CESA), the Project on Rhetoric of Inquiry (POROI), and the South Asian Studies Program (SASP) at the University of Iowa for support of our project over the years.

Many individuals have been important to this project's completion. Aradhana Seth's early video documentation of Indian call centers was the initial inspiration for our work. Our project has been informed by many conceptual conversations with her around the "migration of the mind" she observed in her early shoots at Indian call centers. We thank Aradhana for her generosity in providing the cover image for the book and granting us permission to utilize transcripts from her documentary project as needed.

Gaining access to call centers (especially in the early years) was never an easy task, and we thank all those who helped facilitate access and shared their insights along the way. Lathika Pai, Pavitra Rajaram, Wasim Sheikh,

Roy Sinai, and Vikram Subramaniyam were instrumental in helping us attain access to call centers and enabling the interviews we conducted.

We are especially grateful to Naomi Greyser, Daniel Gross, Meena Kandhewal, CESA faculty (Corey Creekmur, Deborah Whaley, Miriam Thaggert), POROI faculty (David Depew, Russell Valentino, Les Margolin) at the University of Iowa, Kent Ono, Kristin Langellier, Eric Peterson, and Mazie Hough, who provided careful readings and insightful feedback on various chapters. Thank you to Danielle M. Kasprzak of the University of Minnesota Press for helpful feedback and support of this project. We also thank the anonymous reviewers for their careful readings and comments.

We thank all our participants, who were generous with their time and their insights about their work. We dedicate *Answer the Call* to those who continue to labor at call centers across India. Their voices are the foundation of this book.

Introduction

Answering the Call

I'd say a lot of the older values that have come down from previous generations are being ignored. A lot of us are moving toward the Western culture, [the] Western state of mind. I think those things are taking the biggest impact as we get more exposure to the American culture.

—SUNITA, I2U, 2003

Sunita has worked at I2U for about a year, and like a good ethnographer, she has observed call center life carefully. She sits across from us at a small table in a quiet office, sharing thoughtful insights in a soft, clear voice: call center labor is changing India's values; call center life takes its toll; there are costs to modernizing India. Agents are becoming Westernized, she explains, her tone and gaze remaining steady, as though she's accustomed to the upheavals she describes. Sunita maintains an embodied sense of tradition: full-bodied, with long, straight hair, she dresses in muted colors and casual Indian attire: a *salvar kameez*,[1] scarf, and flat sandals. Sunita spends most of her waking hours talking to Americans, primarily working the night shift and sleeping during the day. Her schedule leaves her little time to spend with family and friends. She earns more money than her parents and lives with two other agents in a small apartment near I2U. Sunita does not appear to be sentimental about India's loss of tradition. As an account manager, she recognizes this loss as part of the call center territory. As she puts it, the "older values" of their parents' generation "are being ignored" as agents find themselves "moving toward the Western culture, Western state of mind." Not just any Western culture, but the "exposure to the American culture," in particular, seems to capture agents' imaginations. Some agents take to partying, dressing in Western clothes, and purchasing status commodities like mobile phones, iPods, designer clothes (both American and Indian), and cars. They use credit cards that the call center agencies make available upon hiring them to make these extravagant purchases.

1

Call center labor gives agents a sense of being oriented toward the West. The accent and cultural training they undergo and the American clients they serve create a sense of movement toward America. Raja explains that he feels he is, in a sense, in America, or moving between India and America: "Maybe you can say I am living on the edge between the worlds," Raja explains (365-Call, focus group interview, 2006). "I have to be what I am here and I have to be what I am there." Raja finds America compelling, but he loves his country, even as he finds himself navigating the liminal space between worlds. Although America has a piece of his heart, India has the fullness of his soul. Raja's presentation reveals his outward investment in the West: he dresses his short, thin frame in smart blue jeans, Dockers, and an Izod sports shirt. His outward display collides with Raja's internal code: deep down, Raja values tradition. He respects his parents, he loves his wife, and he wants a traditional family. For instance, although his wife aspires to work in a call center, Raja prefers she keep the home, like his mother still does in their intergenerational household. In these ways, Raja sees himself as irrevocably Indian. Yet Raja simultaneously feels an imagined sense of belonging to America. He spends countless hours talking to Americans, and now he trains and leads twenty agents who must learn to do the same. These experiences have Westernized his business, cultural, and aesthetic sensibilities. He likes the modicum of power his work as a team lead provides, and he uses it to bring younger agents up, just as his managers have brought him up. Raja thrives between worlds; he doesn't really mind being on the fringes of the West. He never wants to actually immigrate to America because in India, he says, he can live like a king.

What is at stake in Sunita's sense of Westernization? How do we account for Raja's experience of living between worlds, of his sense of continually tacking between here and there? *Answer the Call* explores these questions and the dynamic new conditions of subject formation that inspire them. Call center labor is part of an emerging form of mediated transnational labor that connects workers in India to corporations and consumers in the United States through high-speed satellite and cable links.[2] Although related industries like body shopping move workers across national borders (Xiang 2006),[3] in the call center industry, the labor, not the body, is transported across national boundaries. A. Aneesh calls this form of labor—in which Indian workers remain in India but their labor is exported to the United States—virtual migration.[4] Information technologies bridge the here and there in daily, psychic, and immediate ways, connecting agents to faraway customers in real time. The new time-space relations generated by this virtual contact create unprecedented conditions for these workers to undergo a form of global migration from India and to America, even as their bodies remain bound within the national homeland. *Answer the Call* builds on and departs from Aneesh's study of Indian workers, who, he argues, "still retain a single, unambiguous national identity" (2). As Sunita and Raja's accounts suggest, Indian call center agents retain no such single or unambiguous national identity.[5] Rather, their identities are recast, dislodged, and remade through the global virtual movement that animates their labor.

Call center agents' identities split and then split again as they move toward America—a point of arrival they never tangibly reach. The virtual migration that agents undergo has no geographically distant point of arrival, yet their experience of moving between here and there, between India and America, is not merely imagined. Something is happening to agents' sense of place and time. This something falls somewhere, as Raja explains, in between: between India and America, migrating and remaining within the homeland, diasporic subject and Indian citizen; between experience and imagination; between class mobility and consumption; between here and there, then and now, past and future, tradition and modernity. Call center agents live and work between these multiple cracks of material culture. Their existence blurs the lines. We engage and analyze their stories to unpack the dense cultural lives agents live as they dwell in the potentiality of virtual migration that affords them spatiotemporal, class, and citizenship mobility. However tangible and elastic their mobility might be, it is simultaneously suspended in the confines of the very boundaries that they migrate across.

Answer the Call draws on interviews collected between 2003 and 2012 with forty-five agents, trainers, managers, and CEOs to attend to the time-space rearrangements and cultural implications that call center labor entails. These conversations have attuned us to the ways that call center agents occupy an inverted temporal and spatial world in which they immerse themselves in American culture. Agents consume American images and products; their labor requires them to internalize and perform Americanness for Americans and for each other. Call center labor's temporal inversion and India's checkered geographies collude with the industry's compulsory Americanization to produce call center labor as a virtual migration. Indian agents are variously assimilated, incorporated, and rejected in a virtual

U.S.–India borderlands. Scholars are beginning to track the tremendous impact call center labor has on its workers in India and other developing global zones.[6] Reena Patel's *Working the Night Shift* (2010) explores the gendered dimensions of call center labor as night shift employment challenges traditional "gendered norms of mobility" as women populate the nightscape (11). Kiran Mirchandani's *Phone Clones: Authenticity Work in the Transnational Service Economy* (2012) interrogates the ways agents perform "authenticity work," "an elaborate set of largely invisible activities" through which agents "emulate an ideal as imagined by their employers and customers" (4). Shehzad Nadeem's *Dead Ringers: How Outsourcing Is Changing the Ways Indians Understand Themselves* (2011) argues that globalization incorporates workers in developing countries through a process of inclusion and marginalization: They are included through the "spatialization" of jobs and work and "simultaneously excluded from core and creative activities, thereby ensuring their vulnerability, if not expendability" (4). Other scholarship explores the globalization of technospace, telecommunications, and informatics (Sassen 2000; Shome 2006; Sridharan 2004; Freeman 2000). Our study extends this work through our explicit attention to the communication processes through which these new technologies are recreating time and space for Indian agents. We also focus on the performance of identity that constitutes agents' subjectivity. Finally, we attend to the simultaneity of time and space formations to account for the virtual migration of Indian call center agents.

To do so, we argue that agents migrate through time, checkered geographies, and virtual space. Movement across space, nation, and culture, as many culture critics have argued,[7] produces diasporic and (post)colonial subjects marked by their hybridized identities. But call center agents' movement lacks the concrete materiality of physical migration. If agents migrate—and it is our position that they do—their movement is temporal, psychic, virtual, and communicative. This virtual migration functions through three layers of movement: agents migrate through time; through the checkered geographies of first and third world zones; and through the virtual spaces generated between agents and their American customers over the course of the phone call. The first component of call center agents' virtual migration is a movement through time. Nadeem (2011) conceptualizes the transnational temporal structure that makes call center labor so compelling to Western corporations as time arbitrage. Although outsourcing has traditionally been driven by labor arbitrage, which enables first world corporations to cut costs by shifting employment to less expensive parts of the world, call center labor additionally exploits the "time discrepancies between geographical labor markets to make a profit this operates on two scales" (75). Although time arbitrage benefits transnational corporations by creating a twenty-four-hour work cycle, the implications of this work on agents' sense of (trans)national belonging has yet to be fully theorized.

To accommodate the U.S. workday, Indian agents often work the night shift and sleep during the day, leaving them little time for family, friends, and cultural events like weddings, celebrations, and shared meals. "It's only in the weekend or whenever you have your two days off," Ekaraj explains, "that you really have three meals with your family" (I2U, personal interview, 2004). Although agents may have previously been accustomed to extensive family time—sharing meals, holidays, and leisure time—this time is eclipsed by the demands of call center work, in the interest of labor and capital. Families, events, and celebrations remain the same, but the agents migrate away from them—sometimes while still living under the same roof, and sometimes by moving into apartments in other areas of the country. This temporal dynamic displaces them from the daily rhythms of Indian life, generating in agents a diasporic sense of loss, longing, and nostalgia for an India they cultivate from a sensibility of distance. The synchronicity that time arbitrage generates between Indian and American rhythms in turn creates a sense of global belonging—of moving toward America and becoming modern subjects. In this sense, temporal distance becomes remapped as a spatial one, for agents live as if they were far from India, even as America feels quite close.

The second layer of agents' virtual migration is a spatial one marked by their daily movement between first world and third world zones—what we call checkered geographies.[8] India's uneven development marks its geographies through distinct yet closely proximate zones: slums nestle up against tech parks; the local-trade, open-air markets that line dusty roads give way to glassy malls with guards, fountains, and escalators; and the high walls of gated communities insulate members of the rising classes from the crowds of people and animals populating the streets. These new geographical developments, which include the physical spaces housing the call center industry, are modeled after American architecture and often are run and owned by transnational conglomerates. So agents travel through expansive time and contracted space to create new forms of migration: they migrate between first and third world zones within the national space—and so do their identities. Indian by day and American at work during the night shift, the call center agent straddles multiple worlds within a condensed amount of time and space. Call center agents travel tremendous psychic, cultural, and temporal distances just by showing up for work. The route we travel in the preface is one agents might travel from home to work. Although they may have only commuted from Bangalore's city center to Bangalore's Tech Park, or migrated from Goa to Bangalore to join the call center industry, in psychic, cultural, and temporal dimensions, they have migrated to the other side of the globe. Although globalization theorists have begun to mark out the emergence of such zones of distinction, we have little sense of the daily ways in which people move in and out of such zones and what this movement between first and third world spaces and cultural practices might mean for how we think about migration and diaspora. Agents migrate through virtual space as they reorient their attention, communication practices, and affective labor toward their American callers. This reorientation reconfigures their subjectivities as they recast their sense of self within global and American frameworks.

The third component of Indian call center agents' virtual migration is their migration through virtual space. Bram Dov Abramson's (2002) notion of network geography[9] explains that globalization theorists must account for the ways that transnationalism remakes physical space and generates network spaces layered throughout material spaces. This concept emphasizes the distinction between physical and virtual space to underscore the layering of networked spaces atop physical places, and the ways that such layerings complicate even critical notions of socially constructed space. Network geography accounts for alternative mediated spaces, like virtual chat rooms and telephone-mediated labor, that profoundly remake people's lives. Indian call center agents' continual immersion in a virtual setting, generated within telephonic space, becomes a prevalent mode of experience through which agents exist. "It [call center work] has an impact," Ganesh explains. "You know, 'cause you start talking like them. Nine to ten hours you're there. You're there with your friends all the time, so you start thinking like them as well" (TechNow, personal interview, 2007).

Where is the "there" and who are the "them" to which Ganesh refers? Certainly at one level we might read him to mean the physical "there" of the call center. But that "there" is also a layered space through which agents travel elsewhere for "nine to ten hours." When considered as a network geography, the "there" in Ganesh's account signals forms of migration that happen through virtual, as opposed to material, space. The "them" populate the site of "there" and occupy the relational dynamic to which Ganesh orients himself. Here we see the kind of fractured identity/subjectivity that call center agents experience in their virtual migration. He and his call center friends are spending so much time with "them" and are talking like them, yet are not them. Call center labor is thus organized through these multiple manifestations and reconfigurations of time, space, and relations. To understand the ways the Indian call center industry generates conditions for virtual migration, we turn our attention to the history of the industry.

The Indian Call Center Industry

The call center industry is a component of U.S. corporate outsourcing to India. Indian call centers and BPOs[10] supply customer service support and other labor-intensive services to U.S. consumers. This controversial, multimillion-dollar business has grown since the late 1990s to generate a rapidly growing workforce of over one million twenty- to thirty-year-old Indian call center workers, both men and women. Call center agents are trained to fluently perform American culture and accents.[11] Although agents live and work in India, their bench might offer customer service and/or sales operations for U.S. corporations such as Dell, Citibank, Delta Airlines, AOL, and Microsoft. The cost-effectiveness of outsourcing for U.S. corporations is facilitated by the combination of lower overhead operational costs[12] and the significantly reduced labor costs of Indian workers.[13] India has been among the top customer service outsourcing sites since the inception of the industry and has been the preferred destination of U.S. corporate outsourcing since 2007.[14]

The Indian call center industry emerged in the late 1990s as a perfect storm of component parts that began with the liberalization of the Indian economy in 1991. The increased flows of culture and economic processes made Western products, story lines, and images—like Coca-Cola, Levi's, and Nike as well as popular television programming like *The Bold and the Beautiful* and *Friends*—familiar sights in India. U.S.-based corporations such as Citibank set up shop in India not only to minimize costs, but also to cultivate markets in the growing Indian economy. Intangible goods like credit cards and car and home insurance, uncommon before this time, became popular. Tech industries like Dell and Hewlett-Packard sought markets for selling advanced technology.

Simultaneously, Indian foreign nationals in the United States—who were experts in industry, finance, and the dot-com boom and who were familiar with the educated and English-speaking Indian labor pool—returned to India to help get these American business ventures off the ground. One such person is Ronit. Ronit's reflections on the call center industry are retroactive, as we met him only after his departure from the industry to pursue a life in the arts. A well-connected background coupled with his success as an industry leader enabled Ronit's career change in his early forties. Ronit brought a U.S. Ivy League education to the industry. His global mobility is reflected as much as in his easy and contemplative narratives as it is in his favored long *kurta*[15] and jeans. His salt-and-pepper hair and tall, trim, solid build lend substance to his self-appointed position as the head of the family in the call center he led. Ronit believes call centers can function as a site where college grads can continue to develop their character and transcend the possibilities available to their parents. In the following excerpt, Ronit recalls the high-level discussions he had with CEOs of Fortune 500 companies and what it took to pitch the idea of outsourcing work to India:

> So a lot of our time was spent pitching to clients, demonstrating our capabilities, entertaining them, taking them to the five-star hotels, exposing them to our people, demonstrating what we're capable of. A lot of these young people, the good ones, were fully co-opted into the sales game. And they knew exactly when to grumble and when to put on a face, brilliantly again. At that level, at that strategic level, the discussions are mainly business and blue-sky, sort of, "We're creating jobs, what is the potential here. . . ." There was a focus on the quality of talent that India has. And those kinds of levels of discussions were very high. (Ronit, former BigBank executive, personal interview, 2012)

Familiar with the labor arbitrage that brought Indian workers to the United States, as well as the outsourcing trend in the manufacturing world, these Indian foreign nationals built partnerships with Indians and Westerners who had the capital to finance these industries. This constellation quickly set into motion the infrastructure that would allow for service operations outsourcing to India. Ronit remembers that at the start of the call center boom, there were different possibilities being explored for what shape the industry would take. As he explains, "There were all kinds of models being explored. Build and deliver? Do you just outsource the work to me? Do you want to outsource the work to me temporarily and then later have your own shop? The people that you train, do you want to keep them forever?" (personal interview, 2012). His comments suggest the degree of latitude and creative power those like Ronit had in the early years of shaping the industry. Global mobility and ties to those in elites both in the United States and India positioned cosmopolitan subjects like Ronit and Laveena to build the industry from the ground up—or, perhaps more aptly, from the "here" to the "there" and back.

In its earliest incarnation in the late 1990s, the call center industry operated under a cloak of secrecy designed to conceal the contentious fact that the industry was housed in India. Agents were instructed to act as if they were stationed in the United States: they were required to take pseudonyms, speak with American accents, and deny their geographical and social locations as Indians. U.S. and multinational corporations insisted on such measures because they feared customer backlash for outsourcing their service operations. As call center CEO Iqbal explains: "Some companies go to the extent, they actually—if the customer asks the rep where they're based, they tell them they're based in North America." This practice may continue, as Iqbal says, in "some companies." Initiated by corporate training and repeated—and apparently internalized—by the agents we interviewed, the practice is justified as facilitating the "ease of business." To accommodate the aural sensibilities of American callers and to minimize call times, agents explain, they strive to neutralize their accents and shorten their names to those familiar to U.S. customers: Rekha becomes Rachel, Sita becomes Stacy, and Ekaraj becomes Elvis.

This secret was paramount to the effort to manage American anxieties over outsourcing, such as American job losses and third world workers handling their personal information (social security numbers, medical records, credit card balances). The practice indicates the degree to which complex historical and contemporary relations of (neo)imperialism continue to animate the industry. American sentiments recirculate an underlying Orientalist fear of the faraway East. Agents describe encounters with customers who express fear and anger over outsourcing. For instance, several agents—many of them Hindu—explain how American callers directed anti-Muslim sentiment at them in the wake of 9/11. Others report how callers benevolently comment on their good English. The distance between here and there is filled with countless images through which the West comes to imagine the East, and in turn itself.[16] Although the Indian diaspora continues to grow in the United States, the familiarity of many Americans with India is fairly limited and largely mediated through the repeated circulation of Orientalist tropes.[17] As the call center industry grew and became more visible, it would become a significant point of contention and debate in the presidential elections of 2004 and 2008—and remained so in 2012, when President Obama received cheers from the audience by attacking Romney's job tour as a foreign visit. In chapter 3 we discuss agents' efforts to make sense of the racism to which they are subjected, and chapter 1 explores in greater detail what happened when U.S. media broke the story of the Indian call center industry's long-standing secret in 2003. Although the exposure of the industry's secret revealed the offshore nature of the Indian call center industry, agents continue to strive to create a seamless encounter for their American callers.

The task of masking of operations and the agents' location was institutionalized in rigorous screening and training methods, which still permeate the industry. First agents must pass an entrance exam during which they are evaluated on the thickness of their accent and their fluency in English. Next agents engage in training processes that last between two and six weeks[18] and vary according to the process or service agents need to provide. Some companies provide in-house training sessions, while others hire external organizations that specialize in providing voice, accent, and cultural training for the industry. Techniques vary, but immersing agents in the culture and accent with which they will engage customers is paramount. For the agents we interviewed, fluency in an American accent and internalization of U.S. American culture were emphasized. Training occurs in classrooms that are set up to emulate a fairly traditional model of education with agents, like students, sitting at desks or in pairs at tables facing the head of the classroom. Most instructors gain expertise from years spent in the industry or in other service-oriented industries, such as hotels, where they come into regular contact with a U.S. clientele. Others are actors who are trained in voice and diction; a few are Americans who relocate to India. Although the initial goal of this training was to facilitate efficiency in business transactions, the practice has evolved to foreground the cultivation of agents' identity, voice, and knowledge. Training content emphasizes U.S. culture and history, as well as distinctions among regions and geography. Training processes focus on language and diction to train agents in the embodied performance of American aural aesthetics. These combined tactics are designed to help agents pass as American.

Agents must learn to speak American English, which differs from the British English most English-speaking Indians learn in school and speak in everyday life. Agents report that they are encouraged to listen to and mimic American actors; several agents emphasize the importance of watching the TV show *Friends* as the best model of American accents and culture. Trainers encourage agents to loosen and manipulate their tongues through acting exercises, tongue twisters, and sing-alongs to popular U.S. songs. For example, Aradhna Seth's footage of a training session shows agents singing and moving to Sugar Hill Gang's 1979 hit "Rapper's Delight." Seth's footage also shows trainers and agents singing along to Billy Joel's "We Didn't Start the Fire." One trainer uses this song to teach language and U.S. history. In one scene an agent struggles to work her mouth and tongue around the word *Arkansas*. The trainer pauses, highlights Arkansas on a map, and repeats, as the agents mimic, "Arkansas, drop your jaw," as she drops the end of the word. The use of repetition is linked to lessons in geography, history, and pronunciation to enable agents to locate the knowledge of American culture firmly in their bodies. In this way, training is designed to generate tangible touchstones for agents imagining themselves into U.S. spaces.

Agents are also taught to mold their bodies to accommodate American-style standards of office work. Because agents are assigned to cubicles and headsets that might be shared among agents, training discourages the common practice among Indian women of oiling their hair. Agents are advised in normative standards for U.S. hygiene, which emphasizes the use of deodorant, closed-toed shoes, and not eating at one's desk. Such forms of discipline function simultaneously to create a spectacle of agents' Americanization for the benefit of U.S. corporate executives, who on occasion visit the centers to see operations in practice, and to generate among agents an embodied sense of participation in American business culture. Training stages the grounds for agents' immersion into a narrow slice of American culture—which foregrounds consumption, entertainment, accent, and hygiene—to stand in for the messy mix of U.S. Americanness.

CALL CENTER WORK AND A
CULTURE OF ACCELERATION

A host of cultural, economic, social, and technological forces collude and collide to generate a sense of acceleration in the Indian call center industry. The industry has grown rapidly, attracting young twenty-something college graduates who earn an average of ten thousand rupees per month (roughly equivalent to $200 to $250 per month in the time span of our interviews)—two to three times the beginning salaries in many other service industries. This capital affords call center agents a high degree of sociocultural, class, and consumption mobility. Call center agents often earn more at the start of their careers than their parents do at retirement, enabling them to participate in a modern way of life that threatens to displace the traditions associated with the previous generation. "You get more money at a young age," Anila explains. "Maybe your dad would have got it after his thirty-five years. You are getting it now" (I2U, personal interview, 2005). Anila is ambivalent about her work at the call center. As a team lead, she has some authority, and she likes the financial aspects of the work, even though she worries about what it will mean for Indian families. Agents earn more than their fathers—and they get their money now, while they're young. Anila feels a tremendous sense of loss: of family, home, and what once was a sense of temporal normalcy. Her account provides a sense of the acceleration that permeates the call center industry. Although it might take her father "his thirty-five years" to earn this wage, agents are "getting it now." Time is compressed, life cycles accelerated. Call center agents live time differently than their parents, differently from so many other Indians—differently, even, from the Indians they were before their immersion in call center life.

These accelerations of time and space converge to create a rift between agents and those of their parents' generation. Agents' earning potential gives these young workers the consumer power to cultivate Western life-styles without reverting to their parents' wishes or demands. This generational rift is not merely about young angst and the loss of parental control. Rather, it taps into deeper issues of tradition and modernity as India is increasingly permeated by the consumer practices of the West. The generational rift is compounded by the gender dynamics of call center labor. The industry employs men and women at a ratio of about two to one, although women's participation is growing exponentially and is expected to nearly match men's very soon.[19] For instance, organizations like NASS-COM[20] encourage diverse hiring practices by showcasing companies with the best record in the gender and diversity arena. Reena Patel (2010) points to the gendered components of call center labor, with her concept of the nightscape productively conjoining critical theories of time and space to account for women's vexed relationship to occupying public space at night.

Radha Hegde's (2011) critical analysis of feminist and mainstream responses to the rape and murder of a Bangalore call center worker further demonstrates the centrality of women in contestations over tradition and modernity.[21] As Patel and Hedge argue, the presence of women in the industry raises concerns over gender roles as women's safety and purity come to stand in for a loss of tradition. Because of time arbitrage, in which agents work the night shift to accommodate the American day, many call centers provide door-to-door shuttle service. Although this service was designed to ease the movement of workers and to alleviate parents' concerns over women's propriety, shuttles often run late and do not necessarily secure agents' safety.

As the industry matures, agents build intimate ties, sometimes even marrying one another and having children together. Such intimacies are an ambivalent aspect of call center life because they gesture toward a future in which Indians will lose touch with tradition, a theme we explore more fully in chapter 4. Although intraoffice and intraindustry relationships are often encouraged and facilitated through social events sponsored by call centers, these intimate ties raise questions for agents, managers, and CEOs over the industry's threat to Indian culture. Call center workers often express ambivalence over the generational divide, the shifting class status, and American cultural adaptations the industry produces. This ambivalence is exacerbated by the prospect of children. As Harish, a mid-level manager within the outsourcing industry, explains:

> I don't have to go and ask my dad for money to go to a pub. To go and blow up a few thousands [rupees] on the weekend, throwing a party for my friends in a pub or something. I don't have to ask my dad, so you know, I have the money. So that freedom is what they look for. And that is the concern. It's very interesting to closely watch what happens to the society. Not now. Ten years from now. If this continues, you know? They are going to be the parents of the next generation. They're going to have kids. They're going to [pause]. So how that influence works is something that we'll have to kind of wait and watch. (Harish, Premier Accounting, focus group interview, 2005)

Harish finds he must navigate the anxieties and benefits of call center life. Clicking his ballpoint pen as he speaks, he worries about details that other call center workers might gloss over. He worries about call center kids making more money in their first year out of college than their parents did at retirement. He worries about agents living together before marriage. And he worries about what all this will mean for India's future. In spite of his fears, he is loyal to his company and his workers, strategizing to boost agent retention to improve the bottom line. As a midlevel manager, he sees himself as a father figure to many of the young agents; he tries to guide them through the accelerated maze of call center culture. In the above excerpt, Harish exclaims, "They're going to have kids. They're going to. . . ." He trails off as if unable to name an unspeakable future for agents and the families they might build. He doesn't actually know what these freedom-seeking agents might do; he cannot imagine India's future safely resting in their life choices. So like others of his generation, Harish will have to watch and wait.

The anxiety registered in Harish's account centers around issues of class, culture, and generation, all of which are changing so fast that life seems to be accelerating for call center workers. This acceleration generates a host of anxieties for the nation within transnationalism: India's future is at stake. The call center industry, with its generous salaries and high-class buildings, represents, in ways both material and metaphorical, a new kind of India: modern, Americanized, first world. Call centers are often housed in buildings large enough to accommodate two thousand workers per shift. The architecture of call centers emulates high-tech campuses in the United States, such as Microsoft. Centers are cordoned off from India's thoroughfares by fences and guards, who monitor and record the comings and goings of employees and visitors. The dailiness of call center life not only alters agents' class status, but also shifts agents' subjectivities in relation to Indian, American, and global culture. With complementary industries like food trucks and chai carts right outside the door, agents could spend their entire shift—and the time before and after—within the walls of the center. Call centers are designed to accommodate agents' needs so that they can maintain a busy work schedule without having to leave. For example, many centers offer cafeterias, lounges, recreation rooms, and gyms. Cafeterias offer Indian fare but are just as likely to offer food-themed days featuring American staples such as pizza. Gyms and lounges provide spaces to socialize and get away from the monotony and repetition of phone labor. Many centers provide ATMs and banks, and they offer their employees credit cards. Most offer company-sponsored social mixers that reinforce practices of competition and company belonging. These mixers are designed to cultivate agents' identities as workers: agents are recognized through honors such as employee of the month, and they receive awards for the most calls or most income generated. Such practices cultivate identification with the industry as something more meaningful than just a place of employment. Although call centers are not what Foucault would describe as a total institution,[22] they do function to redirect agents' social, temporal, and physical locations within Indian culture. They produce alternative subjectivities that take agents away from their families' day-to-day lives and interrupt familial and cultural relations.

Another factor contributing to the sense of acceleration in call center life is its high attrition rate, which ranges from 20 to 30 percent, with an average turnover rate of two years.[23] So although U.S. corporations extract their labor for a low wage (by U.S. standards), agents constitute a mobile workforce, which tends to shun efforts at labor organizing. Because call centers seek to recover their investments in training workers, they are highly motivated to retain their workers. I2U owner Laveena explains that there is a "gap" between what call centers need "on the job" and "what was taught in the [college] curriculum"—a gap that call centers must fill by training workers to "type, [speak] basic grammatically correct English, e-mail etiquette, professionalism" (2009). The cost of this investment is "extremely high," Laveena explains, as is the "cost of retention of talent . . . because you, you know, just train them and in three, four, five months, just when they are about ready to start producing for you, they have moved on to someone else" (2009). The economic trick call centers face, then, is to keep agents long enough to turn a profit on the investments required to fill the gap in their training. Agents like Ekaraj, who occasionally jumps from one call center to another to avoid burnout, are well aware of the power of their labor in the global economy and use it to their advantage to remain on the go.

One strategy call centers deploy to retain their mobile labor force is to create what Aiwha Ong (2006) would call first world zones in the third world. As cultural geographers and critical communication scholars have argued, space and identity are mutually productive.[24] The production of such spaces provides a context for call center life to take on its own social and subcultural force as agents immerse themselves in the capitalist logics and affective ties that animate the industry. Like the Barbadian women of Carla Freeman's (2000) ethnographic study, who cultivate pink-collar identities as both workers and consumers within the global economy,[25] call center agents cultivate modern, Westernized, and Americanized identities, both through the production of their labor and through their increased capacity to participate in globalization as consumers.

As with the informatics industry Freeman investigates, call centers actively cultivate consumer identities in their workers. We see this trend in our conversation with Ganesh. As a middle manager, Ganesh (TechNow, 2007) gravitated from the hotel industry to call centers early in the game, when the industry was young. Ganesh portrays a sense of class and tradition, dressed in checkered shirts and black trousers, his shoes polished to a shine. He seems self-conscious about his age of thirty-something and his small belly in this youth-dominated industry. His upward mobility has allowed Ganesh to abandon his old scooter in favor of the slick Honda City automobile in which he loves to drive his family around. He is grateful for the material benefits his years in the call center industry have brought, but he constantly seeks a change in process and job responsibility so he can keep himself engaged. With regard to the cultivation of agents as worker/consumers, Ganesh explains that companies strategically retain agents by creating spaces and social activities designed to create a sense of modern community: "They [the companies] say, 'Take them out. Let them have a drink. Let them have a good time.' Once a month we used to have a good party in a good five-star hotel, where there used to be a disco and all that. You can dance and drink your way to glory." The activities that cultivate in agents a sense of freedom, community, and Westernization also produce a sense of anxiety in folks of the previous generation like Harish, described above. These vexed identities and the spatial, temporal, and community practices that produce them are no mere accident. They are actively cultivated by the industry itself. The glory such activities are designed to engender is fleeting, offering moments of intense embodiment[26] and sociality (dancing and drinking) to puncture the mundane dailiness (nightliness) of call center labor.

BETWEEN HERE AND THERE: VIRTUAL BORDERLANDS AND VIRTUALSCAPES IN INDIAN CALL CENTERS

In our conversations with women and men who work at various levels in the call center industry, we gained a sense of their communication practices and the sense of liminality and fragmentation agents experience. How do we account for the form of migration agents undergo, in which they leave without leaving, and arrive without arriving? What do agents' experiences of in-between-ness tell us about the boundaries between here and there, India and America, us and them? The compelling force of agents' experiences of being caught between India and America invites us to rethink what and where is India, America, and the expansive yet compressed border that divides them. We refer to this mediated space as a virtual borderlands.

As with previous theorizations of borderlands identities,[27] call center agents' subjectivities are forged at the crossroads of a host of uneven global flows. Yet these flows are located not in a geographically bound border zone. Rather, they are forged within the virtual space of the call center exchange. The ongoing communication between agents and American callers, coupled with the intensive training and work schedules that structure their labor, reorient agents' sense of time, space, and belonging. As we note above, some agents experience their labor as a form of virtual migration—as "moving toward the Western culture" (Sunita, I2U, 2003) without necessarily arriving "there." Some agents experience this communication-based movement between India and America as a rupture, producing a fragmented identity: "Working in the call center industry," Elijah cannot reconcile his split lives. He explains that the agents' business persona "was pretty much like a mask. You see, you go to the center, you wear your mask. But when you come out, you put it all away and hang it by the door" (2004). Like Anzaldúa's (1987) mestiza, Elijah bridges the disparate lives he leads inside and outside of the call center: the business persona must wear a mask to cover the sensitive, shy, and overly responsible young Indian man he is at home, where he lives with his parents and helps raise his four younger siblings.

For other agents, such as Jaffer, the borders between work life and daily habits become blurred, especially, as his story illustrates, when talking on the phone:

> I remember one incident when I called my friend and he wasn't there. It was his dad who answered the phone and he was like, "Who is this?" And I was so used to saying the script that we used to do pseudo names, I used to tell: "I am Marc calling on behalf of so and so." And when my friend's father asked, "Who is this?" I am like, "It's Marc calling on behalf of—" and then I am saying, "Sorry, actually this is Jaffer." (Jaffer, 365-Call, focus group interview, 2006)

Jaffer's reference to the mask he wears while working the phones marks out the performative quality of call center labor. As agents repeatedly

answer the telephone calls of American customers, these ongoing mediated communication interactions create new social conditions in which
agents cultivate an entirely new identity—one that is unfamiliar or inauthentic, like wearing a mask. Yet Jaffer, who is a Muslim in a predominantly
Hindu country, finds that here in the call center, his religion doesn't matter because everyone has to take on another identity. At work, Jaffer is
Marc. He lives in virtual borderlands—somewhere between India and
the United States, never fully a part of either. Jaffer shares his concern over
the consumerism of the call center culture: "In this industry, money matters over culture." For him, the border space generated by the phone call
places him in a space of alterity. Such a mundane task as calling a friend
becomes unsettled as he slips, uncannily, into a virtual borderlands. The
global continually animates and interpenetrates the local. India is no
longer just India but is also intimately inhabited by America.

Our reading of call center labor productively extends Arjun Appadurai's
([1996] 2000) notion of the various scapes—media, ethno, techno, ideo,
and finance—that enable massive new global connectivities within late
modernity.[28] Agents, as with many young Indians of their generation, begin
their immersion in American culture long before working in the industry.
When India opened its economic and media markets to the West in 1991,[29]
the distribution of Western images, narratives, and cultural values permeated what Appadurai calls the mediascape of India's media markets. What's
different in call center labor is that agents watch American sitcoms, movies,
and television dramas not merely to consume these images. They watch
to become fluent in American culture and accent. Consuming American
media, Pavitra explains, such as "watch[ing] the series of *Friends*," is one
way agents learn to emulate American culture: "That's the way the customers would speak to us and that's the right way of what we need to
know." As we explore in greater detail in chapter 2, the call center industry
mobilizes mediascapes through the technoscapes and financescapes of
virtual labor to generate new ethnoscapes within India. Call center labor
generates an interactive, mediated process in which agents perform Americanness for Americans. This interactivity distinguishes the conditions for
agents' subject formation from those in Appadurai's account. Call center
labor places agents in a virtual relationship with customers in which call
center agents not only consume America but must also be consumed by
America: they must proactively cultivate their performance of self in ways
that are intelligible to Americans, as if they had migrated to the United

States. We refer to this process of moving from consuming to performing American culture as a virtualscape.

Call center labor, then, reorients the ways in which we theorize globalization within the interactive virtual context generated by telecommunications. Although globalization theorists have attended to the transnational connectivities that link social subjects across global space, the communication phenomenon of call center labor—interactive, immediate, and, most importantly, demanding an assimilated performance by the call center agent—generates new conditions for subject formation for these workers. As Sunita puts it:

> It is a little bit different because when you are watching TV, you are just watching TV. Agreed . . . you hear the ideas, you watch the way they live, but it is just TV. Over here [in the call center], when you are constantly interacting on a daily basis, you start thinking—you have to think along their wavelength. That's what you know to do for customer support. (Sunita, I2U, personal interview, 2004)

As agents answer the call countless times over the course of the night shift, they are also responding to the hailing of U.S. power and global capital.[30] The repetition of this hailing—as agents answer call after call, night after night—creates a social, cultural, and labor condition that reorients the psyche of the call center agent, quite tangibly directing his or her gaze, energy, and affective labor toward America. As the agent responds to this hailing, he or she cultivates a sense of being American in India. The formation Inderpal Grewal (2005) dubs transnational America[31] is extended by call center agents, who move beyond merely consuming American culture to performing American identities to serve American consumers. Assimilation in the virtual borderlands marks a new moment in the ongoing formation of transnational America.

For the agents who are immersed in these virtual borderlands, a new form of global citizenship becomes available as they find they can speak with "people from all over the world" (Pavitra, I2U, 2004), a theme we explore in chapter 3. Their capacity to speak to and fulfill the needs of faraway others converges with India's recent emergence onto the global stage as a trillion-dollar economy ("India Becomes Trillion Dollar Economy," 2007), an economic growth miracle that could soon result in India becoming a global superpower (Luce 2007; Bhandare 2007). Thus national and neoliberal forms of inclusion dovetail in the formation of agents' hybridized global, located, and transnational subjectivities, especially as the performance of modern identities for Americans takes on increasing significance in India.[32]

Agents' accounts of their experience of dwelling in this virtual borderlands is vexed—both empowering and degrading. Agents such as Samir explain that "meeting people from all over is the best part of the job": "I always enjoy connecting to various cultures and everything even across distances. So that's the best part for me. I get to meet a lot of people from all over. I get to talk to some strange people here" (U.S. Computers, personal interview, 2005). Samir is a hip trainer for U.S. Computers, handsome and well dressed in black jeans and a fitted T-shirt, straddling the worlds of American and Indian sensibilities. What makes the virtual borderlands Samir occupies so compelling, he explains, is the people he meets there. His account underscores the affective power and sense of global belonging he gains from this virtual, intercultural, and interpersonal communicative sphere. But agents also underscore the pain they experience when their efforts to perform Americanness for Americans fail.

Raveena is reluctant to claim her participation in the rapid changes sweeping Indian culture and initially redirects our questions about her life to her frustration with the Westernization of other agents. In spite of her contempt for the shallow aspects of call center life, Raveena also breaks with tradition. She is inevitably part of the Indian call center generation, moving from her parents' house not to a spouse's, but to a flat with other call center agents. Although she enjoys the company of others in the industry, she misses the rhythms of her tight-knit extended family. She negotiates the industry with a tense hybridity, citing the incompatibility of Indian names with the ease and efficiency of business. The racism Raveena has experienced at the hands of her American callers may be one reason she bristles at the suggestion she's become Americanized. "'I don't want to speak to you,'" Raveena says, emulating an American caller. "'Transfer the call immediately.' So they won't let us speak as well." A new form of oral/aural racism emerges as American callers seek to patrol the virtual borders of the nation, an argument we develop in chapter 3. The call center industry generates a virtual borderlands between India and America, a contentious site in which competing claims to neoliberal, global, and national citizenship are played out.

THE UNEVEN DISTRIBUTION OF
TIME-SPACE RELATIONS

Above we initiate the argument that agents migrate through time, checkered geographies, and virtual space. Here we develop that claim that agents migrate through time and space in ways that extend current theorizations of global migration. Our concept of virtual migration works through two intertwined processes: the temporal inversions that structure call center labor and the virtual geographies through which it circulates. To maximize the workday through time arbitrage, Indian call centers organize their hours to accommodate the needs of the U.S. workday. As Aneesh (2006) argues, "Since the U.S. and India have an average time-zone difference of twelve hours, the client may enjoy, for a number of tasks, virtually around the clock office hours: when America closes its offices, India gets ready to start the day" (2). Back-office duties—such as transcription, accounting, and software applications—are forms of labor that do not require Indian workers to directly communicate with American clients. In such cases, the twelve-hour time difference between the United States and India enables a twenty-four-hour-a-day work regime in which Indian workers pick up where American workers left off the night before.

What distinguishes call center labor from the back-office duties Aneesh analyzes is that call center labor requires real-time interactions between American callers and Indian workers. As such, agents generally work the night shift. Call center labor is organized through what we call a temporal inversion that requires agents to spend long hours during the night speaking to American callers and sleeping during the day. This temporal inversion places a heavy psychic and cultural burden on agents as their labor demands their fluency in American culture, while their down time occurs at a time when local others are at work. Sanjana is an agent who personifies the ideal of a good traditional Indian woman. She inhabits a professional setting with ease; tall, she dresses gracefully in a dark-colored *salwar kameez* (pyjama-style pants, long, loose flowing top, and scarf), sandals, and a *bindi* (a red dot on her forehead, signifying that she is married). Sanjana was brought up in a small-town, middle-class Indian family with patriotic values. She relished the Indian celebrations and singing the Indian anthem in grade school, and now she cheers India's progress as the world's largest democracy and fastest growing economy. Yet the long nighttime hours she must work leaves her feeling cut off from her community and family: "Right now, I am sleeping and people are all working and when I am awake everyone just sleeps. There is no interaction at all" (I2U, 2005). Sanjana's lack of interaction, coupled with the intensive interactions agents have with American customers, constitutes one of the most compelling implications of call center labor's temporal inversion: agents virtually migrate between India and America.

On one hand, temporal inversions produce a sense of cultural and affective loss: community, family, and cultural events such as weddings and Indian holidays, agents explain, feel faraway. I2U agent Anila explains what this temporal inversion means for her social life:

> And you are also not off on Saturday and Sunday. It's on any two days, which means that none of your friends are around in those two days. You don't get to see your parents because if your dad goes in the morning and comes home late at night, you probably will be seeing him once a week, hopefully. All your social life wrecks down. (Anila, I2U, 2005)

Call center life heavily rearranges the rhythms of workers' lives—working the night shift, taking days off in the middle of the week, working during Indian holidays (such as Diwali[33]), and getting time off for American holidays (such as Christmas and Thanksgiving). "Culturally it is going to effect us," Raja explains. "We're doing things now that we were not doing earlier. Now we're aware of Valentine's Day!" (365-Call, focus group interview, 2006). This schedule—with its daily rhythms displacing agents' relating with intimate others and its annual rhythms synced to American holidays that have no basis in Indian culture—creates a sense of distance between agents and those who work outside of the industry. As Anila puts it, her "whole social life wrecks down."

This "wrecking down" of their social lives also distances agents from those cultural events through which their Indianness is produced, performed, and imagined. As an American citizen of Indian descent who's returned temporarily to oversee the development of his call center, Armaan is especially attuned to the loss of culture. He expresses his American identity in his dress: blue jeans, a polo shirt, and dark leather boat shoes. Like second-generation Indians in the United States, Armaan is concerned about how fast the country is becoming Westernized. He worries that agents are unable to attend family and cultural events—and worse that they may no longer even be missed. He grew up in America learning about

Indian culture, and now that he's actually in India, he bemoans the loss of a culture he knows only as a powerful myth. Coming into the industry as a manager, the rapid changes feel exaggerated to Armaan. He's simultaneously an insider and an outsider, sent to the country for precisely his borderlands identity. Armaan is nostalgic for Indian tradition, even as he appreciates the Western corporate structure and all of the values that accompany it. As Armaan explains, call center work distances agents from their families and Indian culture:

> Indian families are fairly tight and connected. They do things together. And now it's become acceptable within a family to have a son or a daughter who works different shifts, which means that there's ceremonies or parties or something that happens where it's acceptable that that person is not there anymore. (Armaan, Premier Accounting, focus group interview, 2005)

The generational divide that often preoccupies call center workers like Armaan marks more than just a loss of familial intimacy. It also signals a significant cultural shift in which agents become estranged from India, even as they become increasingly immersed in America. The reality that the person is just "not there anymore" evokes the increasing distances and the psychic migrations produced by call center labor. The agent is absent—no longer found in India because she is temporally removed. She has virtually migrated to America. This observation informs a theme of a diasporic population that doesn't physically leave the homeland, which we examine in chapter 4.

Even as these temporal inversions give agents a sense of distance from India, they also engender a sense of proximity to America. As we detail above, the call center industry evokes a sense of distance from India and a movement toward America as agents find themselves moving "between worlds" (Raja) and "toward the Western culture" (Sunita). This convergence between an intense virtual immersion in American culture and an embodied temporal distance from India is most clearly a function of the organization of call center labor's working rhythms. Virtual migration provides a window through which to theorize new time-space relations under globalization—those global processes that seem to accelerate the experience of time and reduce the significance of distance.[34] David Harvey (1990) refers to these new time-space relations as characterized by their compression: "It has also entailed a new round of what I shall call 'time-space compression' in the capitalist world. . . . The time horizons of both private and public decision-making have shrunk, while satellite communication and declining transport costs have made it increasingly possible to spread those decisions immediately over an ever wider and variegated space" (147).

Call center labor is certainly produced within this dynamic as new information technologies and modes of virtual contact enable its circuits of communication that facilitate agents in India to serve customers in America in real time. But the notion that time and space are compressed in any uniform way universalizes the perspective of the privileged global subject, whose experience of time and space may well be accelerated by such global processes. For call center agents, who spend countless hours servicing the needs of American callers, time is not only stretched out but is also decoupled from its embedded dailiness. Time becomes inverted. "In those kind of [night] shifts," Sanjana explains, trying to invite her interviewers to imagine her experience, "you don't get to do anything. You are so, like, exhausted that you now imagine you reach home by 1 [A.M.], your eyes are like dragging you to get some sleep." Thus time and space are not compressed for privileged global subjects in any passive or immaterial way. Rather the time-space compression privileged subjects experience is a function of a time-space inversion and displacement for others, whose labor is predicated on such inversions and displacements. The universalizing "we" through which such theoretical claims are often expressed[35] underscores the erasure of the immense labor that such compressions entail. This "we" certainly does not include call center agents; rather, as we argue in chapter 2, call center agents carry the freight of the time-space compression on their backs.

Although we agree with theorists such as Harvey (1990), Giddens (1990), and Castells (1989) that such shifting time-space relations and spaces of flows mark a fundamental shift in capitalist relations of production, it is equally important to attend to the unevenness through which such shifts are distributed. Do such transformations, Vincent Mosco (1996) asks, "reflect, as some argue, a fundamental transformation, a remapping of capitalism, brought about by fundamental shifts in the space of flows of fundamental labor and capital resources (Castells 1989)? Or is this just the latest way of thinking about patterns put in place in the earliest days of commercial capitalism?" (14). We respond to Mosco's provocative questions through the specificity of agents' accounts of time, space, and virtual migration. The transnational force of time arbitrage inverts time for agents. Attending to such temporal inversions and the communication processes they entail allows us to rethink the relationship between time and space, virtuality and corporeality.

Call center labor is also organized through a host of spatial realignments. The industry relies so heavily on virtuality, the spaces it joins must also be reconceptualized. This dynamic generates a virtual geography,[36] or what Manuel Castells (1989) describes as the culture of real virtuality.[37] In such a system, "people's material/symbolic existence" is "fully immersed in a virtual image setting . . . in which appearances are not just on the screen through which experience is communicated, but they become the experience" (404). Such virtual geographies enable what Zygmunt Bauman (2000) describes as a postpanoptic arrangement[38] in which the ruled and the rulers are spatially removed from one another, generating a context for the formation of virtual disciplinary practices. Call center workers are disciplined to manipulate their bodies, not only to be awake during the U.S. workday, but also to assimilate to American communication and cultural expectations. They immerse themselves in American culture and accent training to neutralize any oral markers of Indianness (such as Indian intonations, sequence, and word usage, as well as expressing appropriate sensibilities about the details of American life). Thus space and the bodies that inhabit it are reconfigured by the intense virtual contacts of call center labor.

To the extent that their labor is exported through communication processes, we agree with Bauman (2000) that postpanoptic power is enabled through the industry's liquidity. Yet the agents' body marks the limits of Bauman's metaphor: there is "some vomiting" as people "find it difficult to adjust" (Iqbal), and often agents report sore throats, coughing, even coughing up blood. Sleeplessness, exhaustion, nightmares, depression—these are some of the hazards of Indian call center labor. The virtual processes that mediate call center labor may well be fluid, constituting certain postmodern and hybridized subjectivities and geographies. But as agents may carry the brunt of time-space compressions on their backs, the body can only be stretched so thin.[39] We excavate this argument in chapter 2.

METHODOLOGY

Ethnographic interviews with Indian call center workers serve as the basis for this project. Above we explore how the communication practices through which the call center industry operates generate psychic, temporal, and spatial migrations for Indian call center agents. On the basis of our interviews with call center workers, we explore how call center agents describe these transformations as constituted within communication processes. This approach provides new insights into the ways in which transnationalism circulates as a communication phenomenon.[40] The hybridity through which the call center agents are reconstituted occurs largely by and through the communication practices in which they engage. The call center phenomenon provides a productive site to attend to the communication processes through which global belongings and forms of citizenship are imagined.

To undertake such an exploration, we conducted individual and focus group interviews with forty-five call center workers between 2003 and 2012. During this time, we made multiple trips to Bangalore and Mumbai, India, to engage call center agents, trainers, managers, and CEOs in personal interviews and focus groups. Interviewees hail from a range of call center industry structures, including two of the first and largest call centers in India, several renowned multinational corporations, and two small-scale Indian call centers. Our interviewees represent a range of positionalities within the call center industry: we interviewed agents, team managers, trainers, COOs, CFOs, and CEOs. We have changed the names of the call centers and given pseudonyms to agents to conceal the identities of the workers we interviewed. Further, in an effort to retain these workers' privacy in a public industry, the descriptions of the agents' lives are composite representations based on multiple agents. Informed by the rhetorical and performative turns in anthropology and communication studies, our aim is not to offer a transparent representation of call center life, but rather to ground our theorizing and analysis in workers' lived experience.

Studying our conversations with this diverse group of call center workers allows us to apprehend the processes through which the industry globalizes communication as they are produced and imagined from multiple perspectives. We have also spent significant time traveling in India, hanging out in the new malls, subways, airports, and call centers, following local and national news, reading popular novels, and watching the latest Bollywood films. All of these activities provide us with a rich sense of the rapid pace at which India is modernizing and becoming increasingly recognized as a global player. The influx of American cultural products and practices into India builds off, even as it displaces, British imperialism as the privileged axis of imperialism within India at this historic moment. Our interviews and the theorizing they inform, therefore, focus primarily on call centers in India that service clients in the United States.

Our interviews relied on loosely structured questions that changed over the nine years of our study. We tape-recorded, transcribed, and thematized interview materials, which served as the basis for the chapters that follow. In order to tease out the ways in which globalization is communicated, we approach our interview materials and the meanings we make from them as rhetorically produced.[41] We actively explore the ways in which meanings are contingently constructed within particular contexts and by rhetorical actors in order to meet certain psychic, cultural, historical, and rhetorical needs. Inspired by the reflexive turn within ethnographic inquiry,[42] we do not view interviews as transparent interactions, providing us with unmediated access to agents' experiences in particular or call center life more broadly. Rather, we view such encounters as rhetorical situations in which subjects self-stage, generate mixed meanings, and seek to work out the challenges to their senses of self created by call center labor.

This approach, for instance, attunes us to the fact that agents are accustomed—indeed trained—to perform Americanness for Americans. The interpersonal and global dynamics of call center labor might ironically have been played out over the course of our interviews as agents were once again interpellated by those in positions of power to answer the call—this time of the Westernized researcher. There is no outside to these global power relations, even in our best attempts to neutralize inequities and build meaningful alliances with call center workers.[43] It is difficult to assess how the layering of these interview dynamics with those of call center labor animated our exchanges with agents. Might agents feel the need to perform their Americanized identities for us? Was the Americanization we perceived really there, a stable identity persisting beyond the context of the interview? Might agents have tailored their narratives to accommodate the potential perceptions of the managers for whom they work and who often arranged our interviews? Such questions are productive to the extent that they reveal the limits of ethnographic inquiry, not because we could actually ever really find their answers but because they reveal that ethnography is never innocent and that the knowledge it generates is always dangerous.

Thus the themes we drew out of these conversations are not meant to portray the real call center agent but rather to infuse key concepts in cultural studies, communication studies, transnational feminism, and globalization studies with the rich and textured meanings generated by this labor force, which imagines itself as global through its labor as communication workers. To this end, we place the accounts of agents, managers, and CEOs in conversation with important dialogues within critical theory, cultural studies, and transnational feminism. We build theory inductively, from workers' words up, and deductively, from theory down to lived experience. Some readers may find this approach unsettling, as it may seem that we fail to represent agents' real lives or that we appropriate workers' voices in order to advance academic debates. But we find that call center workers have tremendous expertise in articulating the pressing issues facing globalization theorists, particularly the underexamined area of virtual migration because they are the ones living it. Our rhetorical approach allows us to examine theoretical categories as dynamic, rhetorically generated formations, which in turn allows us to theorize these categories as sufficiently pliable. Drawing on agents' voices, our theorizing seeks to accommodate the new time-space and communication-based relations that animate the texts and contexts of this study. These voices serve as the material out of which such interventions are generated. The specificity of these accounts productively exposes the ways in which globalization scholars may risk reifying the very categories and privileging the very identities they seek to displace.

Our rhetorical approach leads us to critically examine U.S. representations of the call center industry in chapter 1. This intertextual reading places agents' voices in conversation with the representations of them that those of us situated in the West tend to consume. Reading one set of representational practices against another exposes the racist, developmentalist, and imperialist assumptions that circulate in the West as actively produced. It also seeks to counter these narrow representations by centering call center agents' lived experiences and critiquing the conditions that produce them. Chapter 1 provides critical reading of U.S. documentary film and reality television of the call center industry to denaturalize the vantage of the American viewer vis-à-vis the figure of the Indian call center agent. Intertextuality exposes the multiple vantage points and power relations through which the call center industry, and the agents upon whose labor it depends, emerge across cultural, national, and temporal contexts. For example, although popular U.S. media represents the figure of the call center agent as an economic threat, our personal and focus group interviews allow us insights into how workers negotiate the American racism to which they are subjected.

The nine-year period of our study, from 2003 to 2012, marks a crucial moment in the development of the call center industry. The time span of our research allows us to access different moments in the trajectory of the industry's unfolding. The early U.S. corporate practice of requiring agents to use aliases and Americanize their accents required the agents to perform a large degree of emotional labor to conceal their Indian identities from the U.S. consumer. This practice later shifted to a simultaneous avowal and disavowal of the Indian body as outsourcing became public knowledge in the United States. Regardless of the practice, as chapter 4 underscores, the emotional labor that agents must perform does not evaporate but rather shifts as the industry does. More recently, the industry is constructed in the United States as transparent, as India is framed as an emerging economic superpower. And finally, as we detail in the conclusion, the call center industry is becoming increasingly consolidated as the disciplinary practices of neoliberal subject formation that were developed in the industry are becoming increasingly democratized.

Chapter Outline

Chapter 1, "The Rhythm of Ambition: Power Temporalities and the Production of the Call Center Agent in U.S. Popular Culture," offers a rhetorical criticism of ten reality-based documentary television shows that were released over the course of several years (2004–2011). Our readings of these texts allow us to develop the concept of power temporalities, which informs the remainder of the book. We explore the anxieties through which these U.S. representations depict agents' virtual migration to the United States and the inverse of this process: the migration of U.S. jobs to India via outsourcing. These representations mediate a whole host of anxieties surrounding call center labor and its cultural effects in the United States. Our reading exposes the efforts to contain those anxieties by fixing time and space within predictable progress narratives that effectively recenter the United States.

Chapter 2, "'I Used to Call Myself Elvis': Suspended Mobilities in Indian Call Centers," turns to the voices of call center agents in an effort to apprehend the (non)experience of agents as they strive to transport their consciousness to America. Indian call center agents become estranged from their immediate surroundings as they stretch their imaginations and identities to meet American customers in the virtual space of the telephone call. This chapter considers the implications of the particular demands of their transnational labor for agents' sense of embodied being. How are we to assess what constitutes the experience of the call center agent? The communication-based and time-space contours of virtual migration create a host of forces that displace, defer, and decouple the conditions of experience, affect, and consciousness that theorists often associate with subject formation.

The temporal inversion of call center labor, in which agents orient their work life to accommodate the rhythms of the American workday in order to communicate to Americans, displaces these workers from the local events through which Indianness is often experienced and imagined. As agents miss family gatherings, time out with old friends, and downtime with their parents, they describe feeling displaced from the affective anchors that gave meaning to their lives before their immersion in call center life. Agents find that their communication practices must be remade to accommodate the affective needs of their American callers; becoming fluent in American cultural life enables them to feel successful at attending to the affective needs of their customers. This affective labor, however, compels them to gain intimate knowledge of a whole host of events that they have never experienced, such as watching the Super Bowl, surviving a tornado, or driving a car. Our close readings of the voices of call center agents allow us to consider what this convergence of experience, deferred and displaced, means for the call center agent's subject formation. It affords us insights into the paradox of a suspended mobility, which simultaneously maintains the illusion of movement and possibility, as agents may imagine literal migrations, or class migrations for themselves, even as they are actually stuck or suspended in the *Twilight Zone*–like atmosphere of night shifts that are designed to evacuate their own experience in order to privilege the realities of the consumer at the other end of the line.

Chapter 3, "'I Interact with People from All Over the World': The Politics of Virtual Citizenship," explores the competing and converging forces of citizenship that emerge through virtual migration. Although India imagines its national identity through its emergence onto the global stage, the call center agent emerges as a contested figure—as both a global citizen and an Indian. Interpellated by discourses of nation and transnation, the subjectivity of the call center agent is constituted through a new politics of recognition. Agents describe the vital role that being acknowledged or rejected by American consumers plays in their sense of self, marking a shift in the national orientation of the gaze that confers recognition. The communication interaction between agents and customers is an aural/oral performance in which neoliberal and national citizenship are negotiated.

Agents place tremendous importance on the recognition of the American consumer as providing them with a new sense of themselves as global players: "I can talk to anyone around the globe."

American consumers, often immersed in discourses and material conditions marking the declining status of U.S. citizenship, sometimes reject Indian call center agents, subjecting them to racist and xenophobic remarks. We argue that such moments mark a policing of the virtual borderlands, where these callers leverage their consumer status to mobilize a broader U.S. backlash against the perceived neoliberal privileges of Indian agents. In this sense, the call center interaction becomes a site of intense negotiations over the parameters of competing and converging sites of citizenship: neoliberal and transnational, U.S. and American. The picture we sketch in this chapter places U.S., Indian, and neoliberal modes of citizenship in conversation with one another as the call center exchange serves as a productive site for such comparative analyses. On one hand, agents' accounts of American racism underscore the resurgence of U.S. remasculinizing and nativist rhetorics within new conditions of virtual migration enabled by call center labor. On the other hand, agents perceive themselves as gaining power, both within circuits of neoliberal exchange and within the Indian nation-state.

Chapter 4, "'I'm Going to Sing It the Way Eminem Sings It': India's Network Geography," considers the implications of virtual migration for agents' lives outside the call center. The ways in which their virtual assimilation spills over into public spaces are a source of tremendous anxiety for agents and their parents, as well as for call center CEOs and managers. Although it has been convincingly argued that Indian cultural life is undergoing tremendous economic shifts, how is the new Indian middle class mediated by questions of national and transnational citizenship? And how does the Americanization of Indian cultural life permeate these shifting economic circumstances? This chapter argues that the reconstitution of communication practices and class boundaries generated within the call center industry enables agents to imagine their class mobility as a form of virtual migration. We consider the ways in which call center agents narrate the checkered geographies that they span as they move between/across class and national zones and as they migrate between/across boundaries of class and nation, zones of poverty and wealth, borders of India and America. We analyze agents' accounts of the new cultural identities that they take on within the call center industry to consider the limitations and possibilities of the category of diaspora. The specter that such slippages evoke is one of temporal rupture in which India's future might become severed from its past—a rupture various subjects continually work to suture.

Finally, in the conclusion, "Returning the Call," we draw connections between the most recent changes in the call center industry and continually morphing global relationships. Because the call center industry is such a dynamic formation, "Returning the Call" draws on a closing interview we conducted with a former call center owner, Laveena, to examine what she has learned from her experience with the industry, where she sees its future, and its impact on Indian and global culture more broadly. We conclude *Answer the Call* with this forward-looking observation: India's global future has been deeply informed by the call center industry. The industry retains its economic force through consolidation, but perhaps more compellingly, business leaders like Laveena seek to democratize its training practices to generate a more widely available pedagogy of neoliberalism.

1 The Rhythm of Ambition

Power Temporalities and the Production of the
Call Center Agent in U.S. Popular Culture

"Welcome to customer care. Welcome to customer care." Indian call center agents sound out each syllable in careful U.S. American accents to greet their customers with a well-honed professionalism. So the 2006 PBS WideAngle film *1-800-INDIA* introduces the Western viewer, perhaps for the first time through a visual medium, to the Indian worker at the other end of the line. The verbal "welcome" repeats as a disembodied voice-over against a barrage of disparate images: headset-wearing Indian agents sit in sleek office cubicles and nod conversationally; a crowded, narrow street market is peopled with cycle rickshaws, pedestrians, scooters, and vendors; women in brightly colored saris pass before the camera, their heads covered. "In this dusty suburb of India's capital, New Delhi," a narrator's voice informs us, "old traditions are colliding with new opportunities."

This chapter orients the Western reader to the politics of representation through which the figure of the Indian call center agent is rendered intelligible in the West. We rhetorically analyze the truth-telling genre of documentary film, which serves as the primary genre through which the West comes to know the Indian call center industry. We chart the formation of this highly mediated call center figure through competing discourses of time and space and of nation and globalization. Our intertextual reading of popular documentaries and reality television shows reveals how these texts manage Western anxieties over outsourcing by recirculating familiar relations of race, gender, and heterosexuality. Our reading situates these power relations within developmentalist notions of time, or what we call power temporalities. Power temporalities attend to the uneven structuring force of time on the lifeworlds of differently located global subjects. As globalization theorists have argued, time and space have become acceler-ated and compressed under late capitalism. Attending to the unevenness of such realignments requires a careful examination of how space and time are constructed. Building on Doreen Massey's (1994) notion of power geometries, which examines how globalization generates uneven mobilities for differently located subjects, power temporalities extend her insightful concept to critique the global production of time. Our focus on power temporalities is not meant to decouple examinations of time from those of space, but to more fully theorize the intersection between these inter-twined forces.

Our reading of documentary films reveals how U.S. documentary and reality television productions naturalize developmentalist notions of time—notions of time that privilege the West and construct the developing world as always already inferior, out of step, behind. Difference is produced and managed through a familiar developmentalist script, written onto the bod-ies of differently located global subjects: Indian women in call centers stand in for progress, or a movement toward development, while white men sig-nify a temporal point of arrival, or a telos of progress. These figures are linked through an implicit heteronormative bond that overcomes, even as it reinscribes, spatial and temporal distance. Thus heterosexuality is the condition of possibility for imagining a (trans)national future and the hinge that sutures previous colonial discourses to current imperial relations. Our reading reveals how U.S. anxieties about globalization and outsourcing are managed through a developmentalist rhetoric, or power temporalities. While the call center industry is quickly developing India, India's growth is outstripping America's, and the Indian call center agent is modernizing; India is always safely behind America. Depictions of agents who strive to emulate Americans reassure the U.S. viewer that he or she, like the white male hosts and protagonists of these shows, will always represent the ideal of development and thus can never be surpassed.

The geography of call center labor was a tightly held secret in the early years of the industry. Secrecy was said to maximize operational efficiency: accents were neutralized, long Indian names gave way to Johns and Janes, and, most importantly, those in the West never saw who was doing the laborious, monotonous work "over there." So when NOW with Bill Moyers aired the first television news magazine segment on outsourcing in August 2003, the entire industry—and how viewers in the West would imagine it—was radically transformed. The call center agent quickly ascended as a global spectacle, an embodied marker of an impossible collapse of time and space under globalization, as the anticipated truth behind global capital's latest smokescreen: outsourcing. From this moment forward, the call center agent became a heavily mediated figure rendered intelligible in the West through multiple global flows: capital and mediated images, emerging notions of worker and consumer, and unprecedented relationships of time and space that would fall heavily on their bodies, now constructed as global players (Friedman 2004).

The outsourcing discourse is bound up in America's vexed relationship to late capitalism, often expressed as both an unwavering commitment to the myth of progress and a host of anxieties about American decline. The rising Indian worker and the emergence of India as a global player have become common tropes in popular discourse, constructing India (along with China) as a threat to U.S. global standing. Developments in telecommunications technologies enabled an increasingly flexible[1] relationship between multinational corporations and offshore workers by accelerating communications, overcoming distances, and leveling the differences. The resurgence of anti-Muslim sentiment in the wake of 9/11 fueled these U.S. anxieties, ushering in a host of recirculated Orientalist imagery.[2] These anxieties are organized through newly converging and conflicting relations that effectively reorganize space and time in the service of free market neoliberalism.[3]

The topic of outsourcing that saturated public discourse reached heightened attention during the 2004 and 2008 presidential debates and remained a point of contention and accusation in the 2012 election. Democrats and Republicans alike rallied the American worker by denouncing outsourcing as undermining American jobs. The rhetoric focused on the struggle over America's future standing in the world, employment, and purchasing power.[4] These debates marked a particular historical shift between globalizing forces and nation-state politics. The kinds of jobs that were outsourced inflamed the previous outrage over *maquila* cross-border outsourcing of lower-end work. This new outsourcing trend exported sought-after, middle-class, service-sector and high-tech white-collar jobs. These anxieties were produced through rhetorics of American downsizing and diminishment, discourses that run counter to the American superpower sensibility of bigness.

Globalization theorists and critical geographers have productively theorized critical concepts to grasp the complexity of these shifts, while others like Massey (1994, 149) have productively critiqued the universalizing tendencies in this work. Massey urges scholars to conceptualize compressions of time and space through their differentiated effects on social groups and individuals, who are "placed in very distinct ways in relation to these flows and interconnections." If space must be differentially understood, we argue, so too must time—as well as the work of compressing or expanding it. Indeed, temporal disparities are vital to the uneven flow of information services in the call center industry. We refer to the uneven compression of time as a function of power temporalities. Power temporalities attend not only to the distinct ways in which groups and individuals are placed in relation to emerging spatial relations, but also to increasingly disparate global temporalities. What kinds of temporal relations generate sites of affinity and difference within shared geographical space? How does the globalization of the service industry generate temporal pressures on differently situated global subjects? How are emergent temporalities unevenly distributed, so that some subjects gain time at the expense of others? And how are normative notions of time (re)asserted to manage U.S. anxieties over outsourcing?

This chapter traces the power temporalities at work in reality programming produced in the United States and India between 2003 and 2007, which have largely shaped U.S. perceptions of the call center industry. We limit our archive to documentary and reality-based television news programs because these productions circulate supposedly neutral, unmediated, and "real" constructions of the industry. First we analyze two news magazines, which were the first to break the outsourcing story to the United States: *NOW with Bill Moyers* and *60 Minutes'* "Out of India" (2004), and a documentary produced for the Discovery Channel entitled *The Other Side of Outsourcing* (2004). *The Other Side of Outsourcing* features journalist Thomas Friedman, who lends the documentary an ethos of fair and balanced expertise on outsourcing. Friedman's documentary focuses on the global structures that shape the lives of Indian call center agents and their families in the wake of this burgeoning industry. We also analyze PBS's *1-800-INDIA* (2006), which explores the empowerment of four newly working and increasingly Westernized women in Geckis, one of India's first call centers. We include a reading of *30 Days'* "Outsourcing" episode (2006), which follows a U.S. worker, Chris, who loses his job to outsourcing, then goes to India to get it back. Chris lives and works with call center agents at 24/7, one of the giant call centers in Bangalore. Finally, we include independent productions, *Nalini by Day, Nancy by Night* (2005); *Destination Bangalore* (2007); and *John and Jane Toll-Free* (2005). We emphasize *John and Jane Toll-Free*, which was produced in India and aired by HBO in the United States. It provides an intimate depiction of the ways the industry affects workers' lives, relations, dreams, and imaginaries.[5] These films attest to the "stubborn parochialism" of the reality form[6] to recast the global through the national. In the following sections we tease out the distinctions and convergences among these texts to unpack the power temporalities that produce Western conceptions of the call center industry.

The first section maps the temporal structures that organize documentary cinema as a genre; we discuss how this genre organizes the power temporalities through which viewers apprehend the Indian call center industry. Next, we offer rhetorical readings of the documentaries and television programs to theorize what we call the checkered geographies of late capitalism.[7] This section reveals uneven development as a spatial and a temporal arrangement, which confounds India's unfettered alterity to the West as the "here and now" converge with the "there and then." Modernity's progress narrative is mobilized to alleviate the unsettling temporal collapse that India's rapid modernization represents to the United States. The rhetorical force of these texts reasserts a tradition/modernity binary in which the United States stands in for India's future and so is always and necessarily just beyond the reach of India. The final section explores raced and gendered heteronormative time as what M. Jacqui Alexander (2005) calls a pivot around which practices of colonialism and neocolonialism link to neoimperialism.[8] Heterosexuality yokes disparate temporalities together to advance the interests of transnational capital and U.S. neoimperialism.

DOCUMENTARY FILM GENRE: POWER TEMPORALITIES AND THE PRODUCTION OF "THE REAL"

The visual technologies of documentary film generate a truth effect that shapes and manages U.S. anxieties over globalization. Documentary film draws on Hollywood film techniques to suture[9] viewers into a certain vantage point from which to make sense of the action in the film. That vantage point, as we detail below, is structured through a white male American gaze. The gaze of the viewer, embodied in the white male protagonist, is also situated in present time, while the object of the gaze, the Indian woman, is situated as temporally behind the viewer. Documentaries fetishize the brown female body that strives to catch up to the American worker, situating the

Indian call center industry within a linear temporal structure based on the inevitable myth of progress. The female call center worker symbolizes India's progress: she becomes a modern Indian woman through her labor as a call center agent. While her progress may threaten American viewers, the threat she poses is contained through power temporalities. The Indian woman is framed through a temporal lag: in seeking to emulate the accent and culture of the viewers, she is always already behind. This power temporality confirms the viewers', and by extension America's, superiority. The films organize time in this way through suturing techniques. These filmic techniques use camera angles and cuts to create viewer identification with the white male gaze to position viewers in the present and the Indian woman in the past.

Our reading of the viewing practices that animate the reality genre allows us to tease out the power temporalities at work in these representations of Indian call centers. We read the recurring themes in these films to explore how they fix normative sensibilities of time and space. These themes include the following: day for the U.S. customer is night for the agent; India's future is America's past; multiple modernities uneasily coexist and collide; Indian tradition is both repudiated and longed for; checkered geographies generate new forms of time travel; and national belonging is temporally mediated. The documentaries organize time in ways that reassure American viewers that India, while developing, is still safely behind America. This reassertion of temporal distance frames the newly mediated intimacies that call center labor generates as it joins American callers and Indian agents across time and space. While such intimacies may make India feel close, power temporalities compound the reassertion of spatial distance to reassert distance and difference. These documentaries serve a pedagogic function: they teach American viewers how to view their relationship to Indian agents. In this chapter's opening vignette, agents eagerly welcome the American caller, and they do so in carefully honed American accents. This warm, familiar welcome interpellates viewers into a position of power over Indian agents as American viewers are invited to (visually) consume their own (oral/aural) consumption of call center agent's labor.

Documentary film produces a truth regime about the Indian call center agent, seemingly allowing the discerning viewer in on the industry's secret. The agent's body is a visual spectacle, suddenly and shockingly coupled with the voice the U.S. consumer had only previously decoded through sound. Seeing the agent's body through the viewing practices of the reality genre enables the viewer to temporally and spatially locate the agent. The films depict agents' extensive efforts to neutralize their accents in order to sound more American. The repetition of such images and story lines recenters American viewers, reassuring them that although call center labor bridges distance, agents are still far away and far behind. The shows deploy an us/them binary through the frequent use of collective pronouns such as "us," "we," and "our": our casualties, our lost jobs, our loss of control. The genre constitutes the audience as a collective "we" through a discourse of caring and responsibility, as reality programming is designed to generate a sense of "having done something" by virtue of seeing—of being "somehow part of the solution, because they've watched and cared."[10]

The programs rhetorically construct temporal and spatial difference and distance to manage U.S. anxieties over outsourcing and the broader time-space compressions that animate the industry, linking older discourses of imperialism to more recent manifestations of neoimperialism. Alexander (2005) attunes us to the layered quality of time, noting that previous historical events mark subsequent moments through the hazy outline of their imprint, what she calls palimpsestic time.[11] When the "then" is not so easily contained in the "there" and the "now" is no longer the exclusive terrain of the "here," the colonial order of time and space becomes scrambled. The virtual migration of call center agents, then, scrambles the there and then of India vis-à-vis the United States. The industry's time-space disruptions are managed in these films through the resurgence of the tradition/ modernity, here/there order of things.[12] Globalization theorists such as Massey (2005) have attuned us to the spatial complexities of late capitalism, but less attention has been given to its temporal components—the power temporalities of the time-space compression. Although recent theorizations of queer and feminist temporalities[13] have productively problematized the relationship between heterosexuality and temporal normativity, they have yet to attend to globalization. Our reading of documentary and reality programming seeks to fill this gap.

The documentaries under investigation retrace familiar (palimpsestic) temporal relations to reduce the complexity of time-space upheavals generated by the call center industry. To do so, they suture viewers into familiar time-space logics through the confident gaze of a benevolent white male figure: Thomas Friedman in *The Other Side of Outsourcing;* an anonymous male voice-over in PBS's *1-800-INDIA;* Greg Spotts in *American Jobs* (2004); the two corporate leaders of *Office Tigers* (2005); and host Martin

Spurlock and American worker Chris Jobim in *30 Days*. The audience is structured into the narrative action through the eyes of these male figures, who cultivate their authority to speak for Indians through their courageous ventures to the "there and then" of India. The reality genre deploys a decoupage of film techniques (cuts, shots, reverse shots, voice-overs) to suture the viewer to the films' narrative through the vantage of the white male gaze. The white male figure establishes authority over and against striving third world women: he is all knowing, benevolent, worldly, and fully in the present. The positive affects associated with these white male authority figures is in turn transferred to the audience through the identification that suturing creates. These techniques, characters, and story lines converge to organize time, situating viewers firmly in modernity and its attendant forms of authority.[14] For instance, in one scene in *The Other Side of Outsourcing*, Thomas Friedman challenges a group of call center workers to a series of challenging tongue twisters. His American accent is idealized against their hybrid Indian, British, and American English accents. Their speech is portrayed as slightly lacking, although in a good-natured manner. This exercise positions Friedman, and by extension the audience, as more advanced than the agents who emulate him.

The *30 Days* "Outsourcing" episode further illustrates the ways this suturing function also organizes time and space.[15] The opening scene features the show's host, Morgan Spurlock, providing a brief lesson in history, geography, and culture designed to orient the viewer to the "problem of outsourcing." Spurlock's authoritative voice-over plays over images of India, call centers, and agents. The narration goes something like this: while Americans benefit from the cheaper labor that outsourcing makes possible, they risk "going too far" in the direction of the "free market," potentially working against their own economic interests through job losses. The Indian worker on the other side of the world, who is willing to work for "peanuts," is both a resource and a threat. Spurlock's authoritative summary invites the viewer to trust Spurlock, who pares down the complexities of globalization to a simple question of the viewers' interests. As the narrative voice-over continues, we see animated flow charts and maps charting the West's "discovery" of India, depicted through cartoons of Indians in turbans leading elephants. By locating India in space and time (then and there), this sequence also locates the viewer in space and time (here and now). The sequence recycles a narrative of discovery and preindustrial tropes to affix India as distant—faraway in both time and space. The opening sequence thus establishes two significant vantage points: the viewer is sutured to the action through Spurlock's authoritative vantage and situated through a sense of distance (spatially, temporally) from the agent.

As the opening sequence comes to a close, we see Spurlock sauntering down a busy Indian street, approaching the camera. "Ultimately, are we all replaceable? What about me?" Spurlock earnestly entreats the viewer. "My job's not that hard. Should I be worried about getting replaced by someone who's cheaper, and just as charming?" At this cue, the camera cuts to an anonymous Indian man of similar build, walking down the same street toward the camera. The Indian fills the imprint left by Spurlock's absent body with a new and different form, visually replacing him. The Indian host picks up the dialogue at the point in the script where Spurlock left off: "We'll find out as a disgruntled, displaced American worker travels all the way to India to find his job for the next 30 days." The merging of these two figures is established through the convergence of camera work, eye contact, and scripted cues. These techniques suture the viewer into the anxious location of the displaced American worker: the subject of the gaze (Spurlock), who has temporarily been replaced by a charming but anonymous Indian host. The anxiety this replacement generates is immediately relieved through a humorous differentiation: as soon as the Indian man steps into the place of the white man, Oriental music strikes up, marking Indian masculinity through its time-bind to tradition.[16] The slippage between U.S. and Indian masculinities and the anxiety of replacement/displacement that it signals are temporally and spatially organized. The fleeting convergence of whiteness and brownness is quickly followed by the temporal subordination of India as tradition—as spatially and temporally distant. The audience must fill in the unspoken enthymeme that America, and by extension the viewer, are realigned in a normative here and now that is part and parcel of an imperialist progress narrative.

This marking of temporal difference is simultaneously an unmarking of the implicit telos of progress: the United States is implicitly centered as an invisible norm. The viewer's identification with Spurlock both unites the audience as Americans and reasserts the global space-time of America as an unmarked coordinate toward which other nations and workers will always strive but never reach. The show's sardonic representations of Western displacement both evoke and dislodge a mimetic ambivalence,[17] marking the impossibility of the Other outperforming the Western self and the naturalness of the performance of this idealized self-over. Sequences like this contain the anxieties created by the scrambling of time generated by call center labor. They reestablish India's distance from America—a distance threatened both by the virtual proximity the call center industry establishes between callers and agents and by America's exportation of jobs to India. The Western audience is well versed in the suturing work of Hollywood film. The filmic techniques establish a sense of familiarity that permits identification with a reliable white male narrator, thus relieving anxieties over shrinking global distances. With Spurlock's gaze serving as the point of view through which the viewer decodes India, the anxiety of the camera's limited scope is overcome and the broader anxieties of globalization are worked out.

While seven of the documentaries under examination rely on such a white male figure (either as host, main character, or voice-over persona) to do this kind of suturing work, the other documentaries—*Nalini by Day, Nancy by Night; Destination Bangalore;* and *John and Jane Toll-Free*—depart from this narrative and viewing structure. These films do not feature a reassuring white male figure but rather offer a more critical, complex, and empathic view of the call center agent. For example, *Nalini by Day, Nancy by Night* provides historical footage of the industry's origins: viewers see the installation of telephone cables and satellites that enable President Lyndon B. Johnson to take an overseas call, which, he announces, will enable us to "conquer airspace and build global connectivity." This footage offers the viewer a visual touchstone that exposes the manifest destiny that laying the cable so long ago anticipated. Alternatively, *Destination Bangalore* addresses concerns over cultural changes that the global industry imposes on Indian youth, family, and creativity. This film inverts the gaze to attend to the intimacies of India's anxieties of globalization's accelerations, inviting viewers to identify with Indian workers. In spite of its more critical vantage, the film ultimately does similar cultural work to its American counterparts to contain U.S. anxieties through the reassertion of India's tradition. The dizzying effects of globalization are temporally juxtaposed with the Gandhian values of community care that industry management seeks to perpetuate through philanthropic pursuits. Although sympathetic, the film contains the anxieties of time-space compression through a backward temporal gaze, thereby managing these anxieties by tethering India to a glorious past.

John and Jane Toll-Free counteracts the accelerations of time and space of call center labor not through reversion to white male authority but through the production of a dreamy aesthetic in which time lags. The film works through a temporal juxtaposition: the industry's accelerations are depicted through extremely slow-moving camera work and edits. Originally produced for an Indian audience, the documentary's temporal orientation and rhythm lull viewers into a dream state oddly punctured by the painful and anxious struggles of the agents it depicts. The camera in *John and Jane* lingers for unusually long moments on call center agents in their most intimate moments: lying face down in bed, rolling a joint, swaying in a spiritual trance, working with tremendous patience and kindness to accommodate elderly or irate American callers half a world away. Such depictions humanize agents, inviting viewers to identify with agents' struggles, anger, and mundane dailiness. So although *John and Jane* relies on suturing work to organize its message, its surreal temporal aesthetic fails to deliver the kind of temporal reassurance of progress, linearity, and U.S. temporal supremacy made available by its more mainstream counterparts. Even so, the lingering camera allows the American viewer to visually consume the agent. Viewers are invited to feel sympathy for the characters, but they are also invited to feel pity and distance from the agents. So while *John and Jane* departs from other reality programming by centering the vantage point of agents, once it circulated beyond India to an American audience, its function shifted. In the United States, its enduring gaze indulges viewers' desire to visually consume India's long-kept secret: its call center agents.

The filmic structure of the documentary, then, performs a tremendous amount of cultural work in establishing and ordering the identities in relation. The call center industry's new technologies generate newly mediated intimacies that unevenly connect U.S. consumers and Indian workers across disparate time-space relations. These films serve an affectively charged pedagogic purpose, telling viewers who they are in relation to agents. The gaze that the films engender situates the U.S. viewer in relation to the Indian call center agent, containing the threat posed by agents, outsourcing, and India's rapid development. It does so not only by reasserting the familiar temporal and spatial distance that call center labor disrupts, but also by organizing difference through a reliable temporal structure in which America is figured as development's telos. Yet this temporal point of arrival is also a receding spatial horizon for the Indian worker, whose labor may be exploited to benefit the U.S. consumer but whose body remains safely beyond the territorial bounds of the U.S. nation-state.

In the next section we build on the suturing work begun here to explore the production of India's checkered geography. We consider the ways in which checkered geography, where first world zones increasingly permeate third world zones, are also a temporal arrangement.

"Money, Money, Money, Money:" Nation, Transnation, and Neoliberalism's Spatialized Logics

In this section we offer rhetorical readings of reality programming to examine the production of what we call India's checkered geography. The images featured in these programs tack between third world and first world representations, between slums and skyscrapers, allowing the viewer to travel between the first world and third world zones in India. Call center agents, who travel through checkered geography in the course of daily life, are depicted as upwardly mobile and ambitious, and thus a potential threat to the American worker's employment. Yet the films' treatment of India's checkered space serves to alleviate that threat by reassuring the viewer that India's progress remains temporally behind and spatially distant from the United States. The representation of checkered geography, in which poverty is juxtaposed in close proximity to affluence, positions the viewer to judge the viability of the industry and India's rising middle class. The hypervisibility of Indian slums signify a recurrent colonialist trope of backwardness and a lack of civilization to (re)secure the distance that modern buildings threaten to encroach. Such visual juxtapositionings organize space and time to realign India and the United States in a familiar power temporality.

The 60 Minutes "Out of India" outsourcing segment provides U.S. viewers with a rationale for the unsettling phenomenon it names: "Money, money, money, money." The repetitive claim relies on a tautological logic to generate a grand narrative of global employment and migration, with the opening voice-over recalling Spurlock's: "It may have cost hundreds of thousands of American jobs, but it's made American products more affordable." Other documentaries, like NOW with Bill Moyers, emphasize American job losses, claiming that three million middle-class jobs will be lost in the United States over the next fifteen years to students in India. These programs expose the viewer to a dangerous possibility: India is poised to catch up or even exceed the United States as a global economic superpower. The claim that recursive reference to money splits viewer loyalties between neoliberal logics of meritocracy and American exceptionalism, positioning the viewer to draw the line between good and bad versions of development. This superior positioning invites viewers to assess the viability of the call center agent as neoliberal citizens, thus posing implicit questions: Which agents have earned the right to upward mobility? Which Indians should belong to the global economy? These questions—and the viewers' capacity to answer them—(re)assert a sense of Western moral superiority to the up-and-coming Indian call center agent.

These programs widely depict the exportation of America in the forms of local geographies (malls, upscale shops, well-known American establishments), buyers with cash in their pockets, and a hearty consumerist sensibility. As the narrator in *1-800-INDIA* observes, "Shopping malls, previously unknown in India, are Gurgaon's temples to this new prosperity. And the cash registers are ringing up the purchases of the industry's young affluent employees." The narrator's voice is placed over shots of shopping malls with shiny floors and neon signs, peopled with young women toting large purses and browsing racks of merchandise. These images suture the figure of the call center agent as consumer into such first world zones in India. As Geckis CEO Pramod Bhasin explains, "These are young people, they're twenty-two to twenty-five. They're earning often more than their parents did. And these people are spending money. Unlike many other older employees who will necessarily save, this crowd goes out and spends everything it can." The young generation of call center agents is marked by their consumerism—and the labor that enables it—against the previous generation of the Indian laboring class. This class-based generational divide is dramatized to give a sense of India as temporally fractured as viewers are invited to identify with young agents through the shared cultural and classed terrain of consumption.

The generational divide Bhasin references is a repeated marker that distinguishes between two Indias, the new and the old. New India is aligned with the needs of transnational capital, the logics of neoliberalism, and the sensibilities of American consumerism; old India is aligned with outmoded economic practices that work against the needs of capitalism, which seems to naturally create excessive poverty and backwardness. The viewer is invited to discern between two Indias—both spatially distant (both Indias are "halfway around the globe"), but new India is temporally close. New India is marked by global accelerations and a sense of modernization that accompanies its Americanization, depicted through the camera's treatment of modern spaces and subjects marked by class privilege, youth, and hard work. The camera travels through spaces of poverty and wealth, positioning

the viewer as a visual tourist of faraway places—to an India that is temporally and spatially distanced. Yet the visual tour also helps viewers overcome
that distance by bringing new India into American living rooms as the
camera lingers on those faraway sites that resonate with American sensibilities. This visual tourism equips the documentary format to wedge open
time-space discontinuities, reassuring and confirming the viewers' privilege
to arbitrate the worth of the contemporary Indian worker/consumer.

In one scene, Osmond, a call center agent depicted in *John and Jane Toll-
Free*, speaks directly to the camera, earnestly engaging the viewer in a conversation about his deeply held desire to become a billionaire. The film
marks the contradictions and impossibilities that saturate his desire: imaginatively directed toward America, but spatially and temporally contained
within India and by his meager employment as a call center worker. The
camera cuts from Osmond's face to scenes of the hefty young man moving
around his cramped apartment, listening to motivational tapes. He hangs
clothes to dry, makes himself a breakfast of eggs and bacon, hums an Elvis
Presley song, and optimistically talks about his dream of becoming a billionaire. His voice-over unfolds over cuts to a series of images that symbolize U.S. class privilege: wide freeways flowing with fast-moving cars, the
Hollywood sign, upscale hotels and parks. Osmond speaks with a steady
confidence:

> So I do picturize myself as a billionaire. And that's very strong. But yes,
> you have to be [pause] in America. Indians, you know? Certain parts of
> India, they're not quite civilized. America has always been ahead of all the
> nations. Anyone and everyone who goes to the States [pause] becomes rich.
> That has registered in my mind.

As Osmond speaks, the camera lands on various inanimate objects in the
apartment, which become visual referents for viewers. The camera work
locates the viewer inside of Osmond's home as a "participant in his visual
coercion," as Silverman (1983) would describe it. "By privileging the point
of view of an inanimate object," this filmic technique makes the viewer
"acutely aware of . . . the absent one—i.e. of the speaking subject" (208).
Unlike traditional suturing techniques wherein the gaze is directed at its
object through the eyes of another human, the gaze in this sequence is organized from the vantage of the inanimate objects in Osmond's apartment.
This view seemingly "remains unmediated, unsoftened by the intervention

of a human gaze," exploiting the viewers' awareness of the cinematic apparatus to "play on the viewing subject's own paranoia and guilt" (208). The film's structure implicates the viewer in Osmond's impossible desires, exposing the material limits of meritocracy and the promise of the American dream. Osmond's ambition for the bright future he insists—against all odds—that he *"will* acquire" and the notion that such opportunities are available to "everyone and anyone who goes to the States" resonate with American anxieties about India's development. This anxiety is managed, however, as the viewer gazes back at Osmond from his or her idealized spatiotemporal destination. Because viewers occupy his point of arrival, they are positioned to judge the viability of his desires. So while Osmond insists upon the bright future that he *"will* acquire," the viewer—who gazes back at him from the future he seeks and who can assess his ambition through the camera's excavation of his lived experience—knows better.

Indian poverty is the object of Osmond's (self-)hatred, but is also a necessary condition of the outsourced industry that employs him. India's poverty is simultaneously a condition of possibility for American investors and consumers and a source of pity for the U.S. viewer. India is portrayed as a deeply divided economic zone, at once approaching America in its modernity and consumerism and yet always, reassuringly, on the brink of chaos and collapse. *60 Minutes* features a voice-over over images of poverty, traffic, and chaos:

> India epitomizes the new global economy—a country that often looks on the edge of collapse, a background of grinding poverty, visually a mess, and yet [here the images switch to U.S.-style, corporate spaces], whether you know it or not, when you call Delta Airlines, American Express, Sprint, Citibank, IBM, or Hewlett-Packard technical support numbers, chances are, you'll be talking to an Indian.

The voice-over narrates the specter of India's checkered geography, placed over visual evidence of the uneasy commingling of first world and third world zones through the legible markers of American and capitalist normativity (Delta, American Express, Sprint) at the edge of markers of third world chaos.

In *The Other Side of Outsourcing,* host Thomas Friedman takes the viewer on a tour of Bangalore's slums, just around the corner from the shiny Western-style call centers. Gazing at the camera, Friedman asks his viewer how a nation with such disparity can participate in the world economy. In sequences such as these, viewers are interpellated into the role of India's judge and jury, empowering them to adjudicate India's viability under neoliberalism. This theme resurfaces in a scene in *30 Days* in which an uprising breaks out in Bangalore when Indian actor Raj Kumar dies. The upheaval leaves the episode's American protagonist, Chris, stranded at the call center. When Chris calls home to find out what's going on, his Indian "brother," Ravi, tells him, "It's like big chaos." "Big chaos, like what?" Chris asks. "They are burning tires, burning cars," his brother replies, urging him to get home to safety. Viewing the action from Chris's vantage, the scene submits the viewer to the agency asserted by the poor from whom our hero, Chris, is no longer safely distanced. The thrill of Chris's escape consolidates the fraternal bond between brothers as Ravi helps Chris escape to the safety of their shared family home.[18]

The next day, Chris and Ravi tour the torn urban landscape, providing the viewer with an intimate vantage of the destruction: overturned cars, burning tires, large American buildings with windows shattered by the rocks the protestors threw. Chris and Ravi interpret the destruction for the viewer. At first they acknowledge that the act gives voice to the anger of the city's poor inhabitants, but Chris's identification quickly shifts from the poor to multinational capital: he wonders how many millions of dollars American companies lost during the two-day upheaval. He warns Ravi that American corporations won't put up with losing that kind of money for long. The sequence demonstrates India's instability; it is always on the brink of "big chaos," here initiated seemingly irrationally, because of the death of an actor. Its titillating production of a fraternal bond between Chris and Ravi invites the viewer to participate in its homosocial affect (Sedgwick 1985). The bond between brothers affectively charges the sentimental encounter with the poor, providing a fleeting intervention into global capital's production of poverty, only to be quickly contained as Chris realigns his sympathies with the interests of transnational capitalism.

India's zones of checkered geography, in which transnational corporations generate spaces of hypercapital alongside zones of neglect by both capital and the state, underscore the ambivalent quality of America's mimetic function. These representations provide viewers access to the spectacle of the call center industry's proximity to the Indian slum. Such depictions reassert American supremacy by exposing India as both an economic success (at the very sites of its capitulation to transnational capitalism) and as an economic failure in the slums. These representations in turn mark India's economic conditions and limited possibilities for success. The extensive attention the films give to India's checkered geography—in which transnational corporations generate spaces of hypercapital alongside zones of neglect by both capital and the state—underscores the ambivalent quality of the rhetorical and economic force of America in India. The failure crystallized in the trope of the Indian slum registers as a sign of moral degradation assigned to the backward Indian nation, even though neoliberalism's checkered geography relies on "diverse categories of human capital" that generate "patterns of noncontiguous, differently administered spaces" (Ong 2006, 7). As viewers are invited to visually tour these checkered zones of uneven development, they also tour a range of affectively charged temporal arrangements that they are empowered to assess as a result of their secure temporal placement in the now and spatial location in the here. Thus the audience gains control over the uneven formation of neoliberalism's noncontiguous spaces through the production of America's normative temporal placement in relation to India's striving to emulate it. This position empowers the viewer to assess the viability of India's development from the point of arrival toward which that development is directed.

The reality programming under investigation here both animates and manages the anxieties that accompany outsourcing. As the boundaries of America become increasingly spread out, the films reassure the viewer that India remains spatially and temporally bound through its difference and distance from America. The films work through a neoliberal logic of American exceptionalism to intervene on behalf of the U.S. worker/ consumer, inviting the viewer to adjudicate India's place in the global order of things.[19] The viewer's positioning in the present—as the telos toward which India and its call center agents are moving—warrants his or her moral authority to do so. The films' temporal suturing is thus reassuring. Because the viewer consumes the action from the vantage of the telos referenced within the films, the viewer is depicted as well suited to evaluate India's development and the viability of the call center agent as an emergent/ infantile global subject. This positioning empowers the viewer to navigate a series of ongoing U.S. American anxieties: migration and the racialization of the population at home, globalization and an increasingly borderless world, and free market neoliberalism's uneven economic effects. These anxieties are condensed in the outsourcing debate around a central tension. On the one hand, middle-class American workers are at risk of displacement/replacement within a global society. On the other hand, they stand to gain from the trickle-down benefits of multinational corporate cost cutting enabled by outsourcing. It is the viewer, empowered through the gaze of the benevolent white male figure, who decides.

The viewer's position of power is established through the reassertion of spatial and temporal distance. This move (re)fortifies the American nation against the perceived incursion of outsourcing. This reassertion of difference and distance allows the viewer to safely consume the benefits of the faraway Indian worker, who is safely located outside of the territorial boundaries of the United States. While the transnationalization of America unevenly permeates particular transnational zones of Indian national space, the territorial landscape of the United States remains protected from unwanted migrants seeking national belonging from within its increasingly militarized borders. Thus the formation of transnational America, contained safely outside of the bounds of the United States, extends the global reach of U.S. hegemony even as it secures the nation's borders. Viewers are reassured they can reap the benefits of cheap third world labor without ever having to encounter the materiality of the workers' racialized bodies back at home. America hence dematerializes precisely through its use of transnational labor outside its borders.

The call center industry is depicted through a host of power temporalities as agents work long nights to accommodate and reaffirm the supremacy of American neoliberalism. Clocks in Indian call centers are set to U.S. time. The extent to which agents conform to these temporal demands serves as the basis for such determinations. Agents' temporal flexibility represents the rhythm of their ambition—the tempo by which the viewer will judge the agent as fit for the market and for America. The rhythm of ambition (re)aligns the viewer with the forces of global capitalism through a presumed moral superiority conferred by the very alignment that this logic in turn confirms. Thus the tautological claim that money is the basis for outsourcing is replayed through the films' interpellation of the viewer through an alignment of neoliberal logics and American exceptionalism. The market and the American viewer are allied in determining the viability of the call center agent as neoliberal citizens, which is, in turn, to determine the extent to which Indians might become Americans.

"GEOGRAPHY IS HISTORY": NEOLIBERALISM'S POWER TEMPORALITIES

In this section we attend to the ways that power temporalities are constructed in and enacted through documentary films. Reality programming reasserts the tradition/modernity temporal binary in which the United States stands in for India's future. This future is embodied in the ambitious, hard-working body of the call center agent. The documentary films on Indian call centers work through an ambivalent convergence of colonial mimicry with emerging global temporalities and spatial relations.[20] The Indian call center agent emerges as a figure of colonial mimicry, articulated through temporal and spatial shifting: by day, a dutiful son or daughter; by night, the girl or boy next door. That the agent is figured simultaneously as spatially and temporally distant *and* immediate marks this figure through a vexed ambivalence. The immediacy that developments in global technologies make possible between such disparate geographical locations and temporalities is brought into viewers' living rooms through documentary film—an immediacy that creates social conditions in which the politics of passing take place.

This time-space displacement compels us to rethink Homi Bhabha's ([1994] 2003) claim that "the visibility of mimicry is always produced at the site of interdiction" (89). Here it is the anxiety that the American consumer might not know to whom he or she is speaking. "And yet, whether you know it or not, when you call Delta Airlines, American Express, Sprint, Citibank, IBM or Hewlett Packard's technical support number," a *60 Minutes* voice-over alerts viewers, "chances are you'll be talking to an Indian." Thus the visuality of the popular discourse serves to render the call center agent intelligible by creating a visual spectacle of the agent's previously concealed body, placed within an ambiguous time/space: here and there, now and then. The authoritative voice of the journalist is coupled with the agent's visual spectacle to provide a temporal arc to the narrative: while the dutiful son or daughter and the boy or girl next door both establish a familial relation of the laboring youth, duty is a concept linked with tradition. The fracture of the Indian agent's familial and labor identities functions to place him or her in a liminal temporality that is neither fully here nor there, now nor then. The films entreat the viewer to consume the agents' formerly concealed bodies, labor practices, and shifting cultural identities and to assess the threat the agent potentially poses through the normative time-space placement the films generate. If colonial mimicry is marked by its inherent ambivalence, progress narratives that define the West over and against the third world reassure the viewer of his or her superiority. As we argue above, the films' suturing practices reassure the viewer through his or her time-space placement in the developed world over and against India's status as developing. Thus the logics of mimicry and ambivalence must be thought through those of time and space, particularly as the politics of passing becomes increasingly mediated through new telecommunications.

"Geography is history," explains Raman Roy in *60 Minutes*, considered by many to be the father of Indian outsourcing and favorably compared to Bill Gates as one of the most significant global players of our time. His bold and simple claim characterizes the contemporary collusion of time and space in which the materiality of space itself becomes swallowed by time within the logic of a linear progress narrative. Roy's depiction resonates with Bauman's (2000) liquid conception of time, as opposed to the solid quality of space within modernity:

> In modernity, time has *history*, it has history because of the perpetually expanding "carrying capacity" of time—the lengthening of the stretches of space which units of time allow to "pass," "cross," "cover"—or *conquer*. Time acquires history once the speed of movement through space (unlike the eminently inflexible space, which cannot be stretched and would not shrink) becomes a matter of human ingenuity, imagination and resourcefulness. (9)

For Bauman, technology expands time's "carrying capacity," which loosens its correspondence to space. These new time-space relations, in turn, usher in a host of power relations marked by what Bauman refers to as their postpanoptic quality. Within such contexts, power becomes extra-territorial as rulers and ruled are no longer spatially bound in shared space-time. What distinguishes postpanoptic power relations is rather that rulers may escape into "sheer inaccessibility" (13). How does a postpanoptic view of power get played out in documentary film about Indian call centers? Raman Roy's claim that geography is history provides a point of entry into examining how reality programming represents new space-time relations to shape American viewers' imaginary of India. Roy's claim that geography is history produces a relationship wherein time overcomes space, destabilizing the temporal placement of India in the past as Indian and American modernities commingle. The films in turn work to overcome the anxieties such displacements create by (re)centering the U.S. customer's temporal and spatial location.

"We service the globe. We service all parts of the world irrespective of what time it is here or there," Raman Roy offers the viewer as way of an explanation of his claim that geography is history. Thus service is framed outside of time—as "irrespective" of its constraints on the body. Such claims produce Indian labor through its temporal subordination to the needs of the customer. Geography becomes irrelevant for those multinational corporations that outsource their business processes to India and other third world outposts and also for leading third world business leaders. These two subject positions are rendered coeval and spatially proximate. Cosmopolitan third world subjects like Roy have technology at their fingertips: they can ride global capital's forceful wave of neoliberalism to attract U.S. foreign investment. Such moves level space and time, positioning the United States and India on equal time-space footing—a source of tremendous Indian national pride. Of course, it is the agent's body and his or her capacity to accommodate such power temporalities that enable such time-space compressions.

Friedman's documentary takes the audience into the video conferencing room of a call center, Infosys, where another high-ranking executive describes technology's capacity to overcome distance. He explains that he has the world at his fingertips through the forty digital screens that surround him, dwarfing his body as the camera reveals the control room that connects him to counterparts and clients all over the globe. The United States and other first world countries become spatially unbounded,[21] extending their tentacles to extract outsourcing service sectors at half the cost of conducting business at home. According to *60 Minutes*, the Indian corporate elite gain a renewed sense of national identity that becomes articulated through transnational labor: "There is a huge amount of nationalistic pride," Roy claims. "Because we want to show that as a work force, as a labor pool, we are equivalent to, if not better than, anybody else. Anywhere in the world." Indian national identity is mediated through the nation's capacity to serve transnational capitalist interests by providing the immediacy of well-trained agents. The call center agents live temporally inverted lives in order to create these immediacies—to be positioned as America's dutiful sons and daughters by day and the boy or girl next door to U.S. consumers by night. India remains spatially and temporally tied to its territorial boundaries, even as its competitive edge is secured through the subordinated status of its workers.

This ambivalent national pride circulates through a hierarchy of simultaneous yet uneven modernities. Reality programming shows the viewer how technology eradicates space, while the Indian bodies conducting this labor are scrutinized according to their capacity to accommodate the industry's temporal inversions. By doing so, the films reinscribe the politics of passing and the threat of commingling American and Indian modernities within a familiar and visual register. This theme arises when Chris from *30 Days* arrives at the call center for his first day (night) as a call center agent. "Since daytime in the U.S. is nighttime in India, prime time in the call center is from 6 at night till 3 in the morning," Chris explains, gazing into the camera. "The good shifts at the call centers are the night shifts. They're the busy shifts. They're the ones that pay more. So people who are ambitious work the night shifts." Chris sees himself as fit to judge the quality of agents' labor on his first day on the job. He defines their ambition as workers' willingness to forego their immediate, local, and national temporalities in favor of one that is organized around daytime in the United States. Thus Chris invites the viewer to assess the ambition of the call center agents and their fitness as neoliberal subjects to the extent that they comply with the power temporalities of the industry.

"Schedules, calendars, time zones, and even wristwatches are ways to inculcate . . . forms of temporal experience that seem natural to those whom they privilege," Elizabeth Freeman (2007, 160) writes, exposing the multiple forms of technology through which dominant notions of time become naturalized. The power temporality produced within *30 Days* centers the U.S. workday over and against the Indian night shift. Neoimperialism's uneven power relations, then, are naturalized through a "specific regime of asymmetrical power into seemingly ordinary bodily tempos and routines" (Freeman 2007, 160). The temporal inversion entailed by call center labor and its implications for the tempos and routines of its workers are *30 Days'* absent subtext. This erasure presumes and privileges the ordinary tempos and routines of the American consumer-viewer. Thus national identities are hierarchically arranged through power temporalities. The films help naturalize a sense of global time that privileges the temporal location of the U.S. viewer, while Indian time clocks must scramble to keep up. As we shall see in the following section, the temporal inversions that structure call center labor fall unevenly on the bodies of Indian women.

"IT'S LIKE 1950S AMERICA": GENDER,
HETEROSEXUALITY, AND NEOLIBERAL CITIZENSHIP

The Indian woman in need of a white male savior is a well-worn narrative of colonial modernity (Spivak 1988). This gendered trope justifies Western incursions based in a host of interrelated relations and identities: the presumed superiority and benevolence of the white male savior in relation to the worthy, victimized brown woman in relation to the uncivilized brown man. The reality programming under investigation circulates this familiar colonial narrative. In this section we read this narrative to attend to the temporal and interrelated (hetero)sexual logics that underwrite it. As we outline above, many of these films feature a white male figure who serves as a point of identification for viewers (Chris in *30 Days*, Thomas Friedman in *Outsourcing*, Greg Spotts in *American Jobs*). As with the production of whiteness more broadly, these white male figures are unmarked.[22] Although many have commented on the notion that whiteness as a social location is invisible, theorists have yet to account for the temporal privilege of whiteness. The white male figures featured in reality programming escape bodily and temporal contours over and against the gendered and racialized specificities of the Indian women the films they depict. The Indian woman, alternatively, is feminized, embodied, and historically situated within the linear trajectory of development's progress narrative. In this section we draw on M. Jacqui Alexander's (2005) argument that heterosexuality serves as a pivot[23] that yokes disparate temporalities to the rubric of colonial time.

These texts deploy heterosexuality and its attendant desires to mediate the Indian woman's Westernization, and in turn her intelligibility to the Western viewer. Through these affective structures, the female call center agent is represented as like us—or rather, like how we used to be some fifty years ago.[24] The white male gaze enables this reading: their often detached and rational commentary about the progress of brown women helps viewers interpret Indian women as sympathetic figures. The temporal lag through which Indian women are figured contains the threat of outsourcing within a sympathetic affect. In this sense, the films help American audiences apprehend their relationship to the call center industry affectively through the gendered and heterosexed figure of the Indian woman, whose relationship to the viewer is in turn mediated through her relationship to the white male gaze that apprehends her. Because the white male figure sutures the viewer to the film's narrative within the normative moment of the present, the progress narrative that mediates the relationship between this figure and the Indian woman temporally orients the audience in relation to her. The call center discourse traffics heavily in the figure of the Indian woman, whom the films privilege as the preferred marker of Indian development. Her movement toward Westernization is the measure of her individual progress while it also stands for India's modernization. This figure grounds India's development within the moral authority of late capitalism's reformation projects: neoliberalism and Americanization. Indeed, the Indian woman represents the nexus of transnationalism's disparate temporalities and spatialities. Especially in relation to white and brown men, the female call center agent yokes together difference and distance within the affect of gendered and heterosexed desire. Her gendered, racialized, and post-colonial positionalities unfold vis-à-vis her relations to white and brown men. These relations are mediated through her presumed heterosexuality, which situates her among the competing and converging needs of nation, transnation, and empire. These intimacies get played out through narratives familiar to young American audiences: marriage, dating, moving out, becoming adults, negotiating new relationships with parents.

The pedagogic function of documentary film traffics in the potent figure of the third world woman as the marker of progress. In one sequence Friedman echoes his female interview subjects, who refer to India as a mini-America. The diminutive ascription frames neoliberalism's checkered geography in relative terms, positioning India's development as subordinate to America's. That such an ascription spoken by female call center agents marks a host of convergences: her voice speaks for India; her development stands in for India's; and perhaps most importantly, her diminutive status contains the threat her nation represents. The Indian woman functions in this and other scenes as a marker of Indian progress. In relation to Friedman and other white men, female call center agents frame progress within previous savior narratives. The uplifted figure of the third world woman is positioned as a desirous figure in whom audiences can safely invest their emotions. The threat of outsourcing is contained through a progress narrative in which America resurfaces as the unmarked telos toward which India (mini-America) will presumably develop. Friedman's authority as an acclaimed American journalist, known for his expertise on global issues, authorizes the truth-value of the Indian woman's claim. Friedman stands in for the real America, while the Indian women stand for mini-America;

the generational divide between Friedman and the young Indian women underscores the claim to India's diminutive national status.

In *30 Days* the gendered dynamic of time gets played out through the intimacies of traditional and modern family building. Chris's progressive modern family is constructed as the standard by which Ravi's traditional family is framed as less civilized. The show begins and ends with Chris having dinner with his girlfriend, newborn son, and parents, these familial intimacies serving to bookend its narrative structure. This frame invites a modern heterosexual audience in the United States (especially middle-class whites) to identify with the show's protagonist and thus to view Ravi's relationship through Chris's normative gaze. The erasure of Chris's body at key moments in the film is significant because it allows the viewer to seamlessly enter the lives of Ravi and his wife, Soni. His movement in and out of the screen sutures the viewer into the action in his place, positioning Chris, and by extension the viewer whose gaze his figure frames, as placeholders for modernity. The viewer can then decode the actions, intentions, and capacity for modernity of the Indian woman, who vacillates between tradition and modernity.

30 Days leverages the affective appeal of the relationship between Chris and his Indian host family to provide a sentimental point of entry into the tradition/modernity conflict the show recirculates. Chris is hosted by a young couple, Soni and Ravi, who live with Ravi's parents in a joint family home. Ravi works long hours in a call center, and Soni, who desires to spend more time with her husband, is training to become an agent herself. But Ravi wants a traditional wife. Soni's desire is animated both by familial love and female empowerment, not merely by obligation. Soni's vexed desires thus map onto different and uneven space-time registers that get played out in India's private and public spheres. For instance, Chris associates Ravi's domestic arrangement with tradition against the rapidly modernizing public sphere: "When you go out, you're entering Americanized India, and when you enter the door, you're entering old India," Chris explains. His account is laid over scenes of Soni and other women dressed in heavy saris performing a *pooja*[25] ceremony—holding *diyas* (earthen candles) and dancing around the living room before their male audience. In this sequence Chris's disembodied voice provides a rational account for the visual spectacle of the Indian women's intimate, private-sphere activities. His commentary maps India's checkered geography, while the women's dress and dancing marks their exotic otherness as temporally distant from the viewer. Chris visually disappears as he speaks, rendering his voice omniscient: he is both inside the home and outside of it, liberated to traverse tradition and modernity. The Indian women's hypervisibility underscores Chris's invisibility and in turn positions the viewer as voyeur, studying the action from a suspended filmic no place and looking back on the intimate action as if looking into the past. *30 Days* recalls Partha Chatterjee's insights into Indian anticolonial nationalism. For Chatterjee, the feminized inner sphere serves as the repository of India's refusal to fully take up the imperatives of Western nation building. Yet this protected inner sphere also symbolizes India's spiritual superiority over the West. By contrast, Westernized nation building take places in the realm of the outer sphere of public life.

Soni's "liberation," marked through her increasing capacity to move between the domestic and the public spheres, serves as *30 Days'* primary narrative device to join and distinguish the disparate time-space relations at stake in the film. These logics become localized on the contested site of Soni's body as it moves between the public and private dimensions of the international division of labor. The slippage between Soni's gendered labor and broader discourses of (trans)nation emerge most explicitly in the following sequence. On the second day of his stay, Chris begins to express in asides to the viewer critical commentary on the gendered relations he observes in the home. "When I watch Soni, she's always trying to get something for somebody or taking care of the house or cleaning something," Chris says over shots of Soni serving the men breakfast. As the men eat, Chris asks Soni if she prefers working "inside or outside of the home." Breaking an awkward silence Soni admits that she likes to work outside the house but that she cannot "manage such a big family and work outside." Ravi, decoding the critical subtext of Chris's question, interrupts, explaining:

> When you have this kind of arranged marriage, you know that your wife [a twang of Oriental music begins] is going to come into your home. And she's going to take care of the rest of the family. It's not an obligation actually, but you do that because that's how it has followed.

This domestic scene abruptly cuts to a voice-over designed to orient the American viewer to India: "India's rich culture dates back tens of thousands of years," the narrator explains,

But in the mid-1800s, India was colonized by the British, and all government business was conducted in English, and today India has the third most English speakers in the world behind the United States and the United Kingdom. Although a lot of Indians speak English, if they want to sell products to Americans, they're going to need to hone their accents.

This sequence underscores how gendered heterosexuality serves to bridge disparate temporalities in order to resuscitate colonialism's rescue narrative for the contemporary moment of empire. Here the intimate sphere of Soni and Ravi's home is mapped onto a condensed progress narrative spanning "tens of thousands of years," beginning with "India's rich culture" and moving toward an American telos. The sequence broadly urges Indians into assimilated subject positions, as "honing their accents" and "selling products to Americans" become the emphasized imperatives of nation and empire.

The sequence positions Soni as the implicit object of this honing. This imperative appears as an answer to her expressed desire to be released from the domestic sphere into the public sphere. Her individual movement thus reads as metonymic of Indian women's empowerment within the imperial progressive narrative (from India's rich tradition to British colonization to U.S. and U.K. neoimperialism) the narrator provides. The twang of music that underwrites Ravi's speech—coupled with the flow of the sequence from the home to the world, then to now—render colonialism's trace palpable within empire. These articulations affix the heteropatriachal domestic spectacle to tradition, enabling Chris (and the viewer) to occupy modern time. The film recapitulates the economies of neoliberalism, affixing them seamlessly to former colonialism through the relations of ruling affirmed within a heterosexual frame.

This time-space trajectory (from the ancient to the modern, from colony to postcolony, from home to the world) finds its telos in Chris's white male heterosexuality and modular American family building. His tender phone calls to his girlfriend and infant son domesticate his colonial masculinity, infusing his character with a benevolent affect. His sympathetic character is developed through his emotional displays: he kisses his girlfriend and newborn son good-bye; he worries about his downward mobility, household responsibilities, and ability to provide for his new family; he longs to "give [his son] the safe haven [he] had." As he moves from his home to the world, his sentiment is reaches out to touch toward hardworking others. In one sequence, Chris takes a tour of the slums, just a few blocks from the call center where he works. He learns that many of the call center janitors live with extended families in cramped quarters. Chris cannot make sense of the poverty he encounters here—that working people, even managers, could live in "hovels." Meeting these meritocratous others gives him pause. Shaking his head in disbelief, he recants his earlier complaints about job losses in America: "I don't know what to make of that." Visibly undone by the scene, Chris suddenly longs for home, so he calls his girlfriend on his car ride out of the slums. Just as his girlfriend answers, a woman holding a child knocks on the window, gesturing toward him with her upturned hand. He jumps back almost imperceptibly from the window, averting his gaze. "OK, there's just some beggar lady with a little baby knocking on the window," Chris says solemnly into the phone. "It's killing me. I want to take them all home. After having David, the colors of children are brighter."

Chris's encounter with the woman and child provides a narrative turning point to the critique of capital that he was on the verge of expressing. His slum tour rendered palpable for Chris, and by extension his viewer, the underbelly of the international division of labor, the failure of neoliberalism's promise of upward mobility, and his own implication in the struggles of the slum dwellers. The thrust of this story line suddenly shifts when Chris calls his wife and expresses a paternalistic sentiment to save the children of India. His benevolent and heartfelt desire to save children salvages not children but Chris's privileged self-concept from the discomfort of his incipient recognition of exploitation. His flight of fancy liberates Chris from his unsettling revelation as he can safely imagine himself as savior to India's brightly colored children. Chris's salvation narrative is reassuring because it reestablishes spatial—and by extension affective—distance: in his fantasy Chris removes the kids from India and takes them home to America. His hollow and fleeting affect redirects the show's building critique back to the intimacies of the American private sphere, intensifying his longing. The tearful display generates what Naomi Greyser describes as an "affective geography," a structure of feeling enabling an imagined interchange among disparate subjects.[26] Time becomes palimpsestic in this scene as the there and then and the here and now touch, making visible "the ideological traffic between and among formations that are otherwise positioned as dissimilar" (Alexander 2005, 190). Palimpsestic time suggests that affective geographies are not only spatialized, but also temporalized. The "touching register" (Greyser 2007, 277) of sentimentalism bridges subjects across space and time. The audience looks out from the car window over Chris's shoulder as the woman moves her closed fingers toward her mouth, a gesture that marks her incapacity to feed herself and the child slung over her hip. Chris's abundant body is juxtaposed against her small, dark frame, marking the woman's failure within neoliberalism and her displacement from modern time. Her displacement is the necessary subtext to Chris's sympathetic outburst and the containment it enables. This fleeting time-space rupture is thus quickly contained through the (re)insertion of the here and now as distinct from the there and then: salvation entails removing the children from the abject space of India (there and then) and relocating them in U.S. America (here and now).

Thomas Friedman serves a similar rhetorical function as Chris in *The Other Side of Outsourcing*. Friedman embodies benevolent white masculinity, providing the viewer with an intimate vantage on Indian femininity, and by extension an assessment of India's progress. Friedman maps time through his commentary on the generation gap. The younger generation is depicted as Westernized by virtue of their call center employment, while their parents are shown holding firmly to traditional Indian culture. As with *30 Days*, progress narratives are animated by the intimate dynamics of domestic life. And as with *30 Days*, this temporal narrative pivots on heterosexual relationships—dating and marriage, family duty and loyalty, spiritual purity and loose morals. "Girls were before not working. They were getting married, but now they're working, socializing more," call center agent Sophia Ross explains. "Girls working," Ross offers, accounts for the "growing generation gap"—particularly each group's relationship to India. Friedman mediates the intergenerational tensions, imploring agents to "balance new and old" by "taking the best of both worlds." This move positions Friedman as the arbiter between contested generations and in turn the uneven temporalities and (trans)national identities produced by outsourcing.

Friedman's call for balance resonates with Inderpal Grewal's (2005) argument that the global circulation of the American dream produces multiple and fragmented Indian identities (immigrant, Indian, ethnic, and American). American multiculturalism, Grewal argues, permeates consumer culture and discourses of American exceptionalism. Friedman's call for tolerance extends pedagogies of American multiculturalism to India, framing India's uneven modernities as failing to approximate an American moral imperative through a "civilizational discourse that identifies both tolerance and the tolerable with the West" (Brown 2006, 6). Intergenerational rifts generated by outsourcing are thus recast through a discourse of tolerance in which America yet again is positioned as more civilized than India.

Such generational and gendered contestations permeate *The Other Side of Outsourcing*. In one scene, two call center agents who are sisters, Cynthia and Sophia, invite Friedman into their multigenerational home, where they serve him pizza for lunch. Their parents bemoan the declining values symbolized in their daughters' gesture and wax nostalgic for the old India. Cynthia expresses her enthusiasm for the new India through the film's refrain: "It's going to be a mini-America!" Friedman prompts discussion about intergenerational tensions, asking Cynthia if she idolizes "Bill Gates or the yogi." "Bill Gates," she replies. "He made lots of money!" The mother rebuffs her daughter's preference, countering that "God is a model" for her. The scene recalls and updates Chatterjee's (1993) account of the feminized inner sphere as the foundation for Indian national identity. Cynthia's preference for Bill Gates recasts Indian national identity through a host of transnational frames: American, high tech, wealthy. The inner sphere of the home—previously imagined as pure, feminine, and untainted by the West—becomes the very site in which transnational America is cast as the primary site of identification for the new Indian woman. Cynthia's identification with Bill Gates confirms the viewers' suspicion that white masculinity serves as the telos toward which the young Indian generation is moving against her mother's preference for old India.

Intergenerational conflict is managed through spatial differentiation in another sequence. Call center agent Nitu Somaiah takes Friedman on a tour of the apartment she shares with her two friends, Devika and Afreen. Nitu's living arrangement symbolizes her newfound freedom because of the heterosexual intimacies it enables: the young women "go out with guys" but keep their trysts a secret from their parents. The domestic sphere shifts in this sequence to an entirely separate home space, resembling, for Friedman, the young women's Americanization. "As they showed me around," he tells the viewer, "I couldn't help thinking of the hit TV show, *Friends*." The intimacies that animate the domestic sphere are structured by shifting roles of heterosexual belonging vis-à-vis (trans)nation. When Friedman compares Nitu's life to *Friends*, he invites the American viewer to draw on his or her cultural literacy to identify with the young women. Friedman's comparison evokes a cultural reference familiar to American viewers, inviting them into a privileged insider position. Nitu and her friends are thus depicted as more closely resembling the American youth depicted in the popular show than Cynthia and her sister, even as *Friends* sets the standard by which Indian women's modernity is assessed. Indian women strive to emulate American women, reaffirming modern U.S. intimacies as the telos of their progress.

In one scene, Friedman attends a voice training session, where he is invited to the front of the room to lead the class in a tongue twister activity. Friedman flawlessly performs the tongue twister, highlighting his American accent, and receives enthusiastic applause from his students. Such scenes mark and then erase the bodily contours of the standard assumed and produced within the text as the telos toward which agents strive to move as Friedman's performance sets the standard for normative whiteness. His body then quickly disappears, displaced by the affective display of the agents' applause. The camera lingers on the earnest faces of agents striving to emulate Friedman. Friedman's body thus emerges to mark the sound of normative whiteness, then recedes from view. The mock voice-training activity, cast onto the temporal structure of the film, locates Friedman in the present and the agents who mimic him as lagging—however earnestly—behind. The show treats viewers to intimate scenes of the Indian girl next door as a modernizing woman, striving to be like them yet always safely behind.

The genre's preoccupation with Indian women's development also permeates *1-800-INDIA*. This documentary features the success stories of female call center agents, figured through tropes of individualized feminist empowerment: confidence, economic security, "being someone." Renuka Chibber Khot was a doctor, but now she works at Gecis, a voice-over explains. At Gecis she "makes more money . . . than she did in medicine." Renuka's empowerment is both economic and intrapersonal: "It has given me so much confidence," she enthuses to her viewers. "I was a girl who used to stammer. I have never stood up in front of ten people and spoken. Now, they look up at me. That's a great feeling!" For Renuka, confidence is mediated through such recognition, signaling a shift in Indian social status from occupation (she was a doctor) to class status and global, or neoliberal, intelligibility, which circulates through the figure of the empowered woman. As one female agent featured in *1-800-INDIA* claims: "I have a good job to show that Santosh Kohli is also someone." The slippage between her employment and her intelligibility as "someone" signals the extent to which gendered neoliberalism serves to render intelligible the very status of the human. Here the figure of Indian woman comes to stand in for India's progress and emergence onto the global stage, as the telos of this emergence is safely located in the West. As filmmaker Ann Carter describes her sense of the project: "When describing this film to friends, I found myself using terms like 'women's liberation' and 'gender equality' to describe the gains these women in India are making—terms which today in the West seem old-fashioned, harking back to an era twenty to thirty years ago."

This affective work of liberation and rescue resurfaces in *Office Tigers* as the American CEO and COO, as well as head trainers, guide Indian women in various intimate capacities. In one scene, the white male COO helps his assistant find a "good man." The shy assistant reluctantly discusses her unsuccessful love life outside of the call center. The COO, though unmarried and admittedly uninterested in finding a wife in India, offers his employee a modern perspective on what men want from women as he instructs her to invite men to dinner and to offer to pick up the tab. While the COO admits that only a "loser" would actually accept such an offer, he convinces her that such displays of assertiveness say "something" about her. That something promises to place her in the category of a modern, compatible, and competitive partner. As she acquires this education on romance within the public space of the call center, the woman becomes modernized through the COO's domesticating mentorship.

John and Jane Toll-Free is the only documentary that fails to display the white male body as telos. While the gendered dynamics of modern India's progress narrative permeate the film, the absence of an imagined outcome for such progress leaves the viewer a bit unsettled. For instance, Osmond, the agent who listens to self-help tapes and intends to own a mansion, explains to the viewer his plans to pursue his American dream by securing employment in Amway. Osmond invokes the viewer as his confidant, confessing that although he's lost both of this parents, Amway is his mother now: "My mom expired when I was just eight. And my dad expired last year. You could say that Amway is a kind of provider for me. You know? It's a kind of a motherly figure. Mother cares. Mother builds you up." Osmond's candid admission sutures the viewer into a familial script of the gendered dynamics of global displacements, mediated through the figure of the mother—not through traditional maternal figures like nation or home (Osmond rejects India as uncivilized). Instead, Osmond finds maternal sustenance in Amway, a corporate and pyramid-driven company. His confession enlists the audience on sympathetic grounds to consume his emotional and physical needs that emerge in the background images of him making breakfast, a reversal of traditional gender norms.

Scenes such as these represent the domestic sphere as a hypervisible forum providing viewers a window into a host of indulgent gendered and heterosexed intimacies. These representations organize the convergences and tensions between the postcolonial and national production of space and also of time. Gendered heterosexuality at the nexus of the domestic and public spheres hinge multiple and contested time-space formations: tradition and modernity, colonialism and imperialism, India and America, nation and transnation, home and world.[27] Heterosexuality serves as the pivot around which narratives of colonial modernity are linked to and through those of contemporary American Indian neoimperial relations, yoking together disparate temporalities through a reliable narrative that decodes the Indian woman.

CONCLUSION: POWER TEMPORALITIES AND GLOBALIZATION

This chapter examined U.S. American outsourcing in popular reality programming to trace the contours of time, space, race, gender, and heterosexuality. These principles organize contemporary configurations of nation and transnation, empire and neoliberalism. Within this sphere of representation, Indian national identity emerges as inseparable from America, which serves as the ideal toward which India strives. America and India are produced as simultaneously national and transnational discursive formations. This suggests that transnationalism does not displace but rather works with and through national formations. Our readings also point to the power temporalities through which these national formations are organized. The reality programming we examine suggests that power geometries are inseparable from the power temporalities that organize U.S. representations of the Indian call center industry. U.S. representations organize time in ways that normalize American subjectivities and sensibilities as inhabiting the here and now, and while India strives to catch up, America's temporal normativity ensures that such efforts only reinforce U.S. hegemony. Our reading reveals how these shows invite U.S. American viewers to see the call center agent through a frame of temporal subordination—as potential global/American subjects. These productions reinforce viewers' investments in global capital's spread and simultaneously in the American supremacy that is confirmed as its most highly cultivated manifestation. The shows draw on Hollywood suturing techniques to achieve this effect as the audience is sutured into the call center drama through the figures of a white male authority. The white male gaze provides both a vantage through which to judge agents and serves as the telos toward which the Indian woman's development strives. Thus the films not only orient viewers spatially but also position the audience temporally within the present, inviting them to gaze back in time at the call center agent.

These time-space forces are configured through raced and gendered heteronormativity. Heterosexuality serves as a temporal hinge, recirculating previous tropes of white masculinity and Indian femininity to conjoin disparate temporal registers of Indian imperial rule. If the white male figure functions as a telos in reality programming's progress narrative, the figure of the Indian woman marks India's movement toward that telos that is America. The camera sutures audiences to the action through the vantage of the white male hero. This structured gaze follows Indian women as they move between home and the world, providing audiences with an inside view gained by the white male adventurer. This orientation provides the relational ground on which intimate heterosexual struggles are staged in relation to Indian women's progress: her responsibilities to keeping a home or capacity to work outside of the home; to date or to build a family in an arranged marriage; to live in extended family homes or in apartments. The white male figure, in turn, establishes his ethos through his affective ties to nuclear, heterosexual family building. These ties domesticate the man, recalling previous narratives of benevolent imperial masculinity. Thus heteronormativity serves as the pivot around which disparate temporalities are conjoined: British imperialism is evoked as the precursor to American neoimperialism through the well-worn narrative of "white men saving brown women from brown men" (Spivak 1988, 297). As such, heterosexuality provides leverage for the American viewer to adjudicate the Indian woman's capacity for neoliberal inclusion. Domesticated heterosexuality provides moral authority to the white male gaze that decodes her social positioning. Heterosexuality provides an intimate meeting ground, establishing the shared, although temporally distinct, relational terrain of domestic intimacies.

2 "I Used to Call Myself Elvis"

Suspended Mobilities in Indian Call Centers

> When we [call center agents] see friends, normally we tend to
> talk the way we used to. But when we wear the headset, we
> hear a customer—the way they talk—probably what we do is
> that we mirror and we try to put on an accent to match
> their tone.
>
> —YADAV, 365 Call, focus group interview, 2006

> Out of the eighty-seven people [working on the auto process],
> eighty-five have never driven a car! But they talk about auto
> figures. And they talk like they're pros. And they do it really well.
>
> —GANESH, Tech Now, personal interview, 2007

This chapter draws on phenomenology and theories of governmentality to account for the politics of experience that shape Indian call center agents' subject formation. We explore how agents negotiate disparate time and space locations as their identities are pulled and tugged by virtual migration. Ekaraj's claim, "I used to call myself Elvis," demonstrates how agents resist, deploy, and internalize the pressure of call center labor like taking pseudonyms. The use of pseudonyms, accent training, and displays of cultural proficiency in the daily experiences of American callers are all necessary practices that agents perform in their jobs. In the basis of our conversations with agents, we explore how these activities shift the ground of agent's lived experiences from the immediate to the faraway. Those daily activities that animate agents' lives—those events that we might think of as experience—are hollowed out through the production of their labor. Their consciousness, their modes of speech, the names they go by, and the intimate knowledge that they must display of mundane details are not based in the space-time of their own lived experience. Rather, these activities are directed toward someone else's experience. If the category of experience is a formative activity of who subjects are becoming, what does it mean when these attentions are oriented elsewhere? The previous chapter explores the construction of power temporalities in documentary programming. One implication of our reading is that whiteness is constructed through the convergence of the visual (white male body) with the aural (American accented voice). In this chapter we extend this reading through a critical examination of our interview material, where the production of whiteness and racial difference are played out in an oral/aural register. As agents strive to accommodate American callers' aural sensibilities, they must shorten their names, neutralize their accents, and become fluent in a host of experiences they have never had. These labor practices orient agents' consciousness away from India and toward America. Sarah Ahmed (2006) uses the concept of orientation to "rethink the phenomenality of space—that is, how space is dependent on bodily inhabitance" (6).[1] The body and the experiences one has as an embodied being become intelligible to the subject through a tangible relationship to the objects and the arrangement of objects that the body encounters, often without thinking. The body moves through space, touching objects—the body picks them up and sets them down, enters a building or leaves a room—in ways that orient the subject to and through the arrangement of objects within the immediate sphere of bodily inhabitance.

Yet as Ahmed (2006) argues, power intervenes.[2] The body becomes schematized within spatial arrangements deeply embedded in racialized, gendered, classed, and imperial relations of domination. "If the world is made white," Ahmed writes, "then the body at home is one that can inhabit whiteness" (111). World-making processes for call center agents are not primarily cast through visual displays of whiteness but rather through industry efforts to neutralize oral markers of difference vis-à-vis an unmarked American norm. As agents are trained to speak like Americans, they are engaged in processes of virtual assimilation in which they learn to inhabit whiteness. If the orienting function of Orientalism is a "world-facing" process that "gather[s] things around so they 'face' a certain direction" (118), so too is the world-facing project of call center labor. Call center labor provides agents with a sense of travel, movement, and proximity to America, even as agents remain physically bound in the Indian homeland.

Extending Ahmed's compelling insights about orientation, we consider the ways that call center labor reorients agents' bodily inhabitance by analyzing their vexed relationship to mobility. Call center labor both enables and constrains agents' "travel" between India and America. Perhaps captured most forcefully in the dreamy production of time and space as both accelerated and slowed in *John and Jane Toll-Free* (2005), call center labor generates compelling and deeply meaningful forms of virtual migration. It places agents into a visceral relationship with America that is both real and imagined. As we argue in the introduction, agents move toward America but never arrive. Call center labor enables a form of movement that is also not movement and travel that is also not travel, a virtual migration that enables all kinds of mobility (class, regional, national, global) that only becomes possible through the body's confinement to the homeland. Thus virtual migration is a function of U.S. American hegemony, which enables U.S. and multinational corporations to extract labor and resources from India while fortifying racial purity within the homeland.

Virtual migration is structured into call center labor, bringing agents near the American callers they serve while simultaneously keeping them far away. Call center agents extend the reach of the American caller by virtue of the agents' capacity to face America as they orient their knowledge frameworks, bodily expressions, and affective labor toward America. Attuning their attention to the mundane details of American life is a necessary component of their jobs; performances of Americanness enable agents to generate a kind of virtual proximity to the caller. The call center industry is a grid of power in which the agent's labor is mobilized as the prosthetic[3] body of the Western caller: the agent takes over the computers,[4] organizes the itineraries, and arranges flowers to be delivered to the loved ones of American customers. The experience of the call center agent gets reoriented to a host of experiences, knowledge forms, and daily events in American time-space. As Ganesh points out, while "eighty-five (out of eighty-seven) of them have never driven a car," agents become experts at speaking as if they had. Even as these reorientations turn their attention toward America, they also compel agents to turn away from a localized sense of bodily inhabitance.

The frameworks through which subjects experience the world are contingent on their orientation to the spaces they inhabit. Those spaces are in turn arranged within racial and imperial formations. When those spaces are reshuffled, they become unhomely.[5] As agents labor under emerging conditions of global capitalism and U.S. hegemony, their subjectivities are shaped by the intensive affective components of their labor.[6] Agents find they must repeatedly answer America's call to imaginatively experience the West. The subject of call center labor, then, is formed through a displacement as their inhabitance is both immediate and intentionally faraway. She is formed through the newly aligned conditions of her imagined and performed placement into a place that she will likely never go. Most agents have lived most of their lives oriented primarily toward India, so the reorientation that call center labor demands generates intensely new conditions for subject formation. Appadurai ([1996] 2000) has adeptly noted the ways in the emergence of technoscapes, financescapes, and in particular mediascapes have reconstituted—indeed reterritorialized—the global terrain of subject formation within India.[7] As we argue above, however, Appadurai does not account for the most recent shift in the ways these scapes converge to constitute a new landscape for subject formation for call center agents.[8] The interactive nature of call center labor—in which agents actively participate in and perform their encounter with mediated America—generates a new relationship among these forces of globalization.

The interactive relationship between faraway agents and callers enabled by telecommunications reconfigures the parameters of migration. Call center labor provides agents with the modernizing aspects of identity formation that Appadurai associates with physical migration, yet their access to such processes is mediated through virtual connectivities.[9] Attending to the intensity and affective dimensions of agents' experience of virtual migration deepens Aneesh's (2006) compelling insights into this new form of global (im)mobility. The mediated intimacies between agents and consumers give agents a sense of touching, interacting with, and being oriented toward America. Agents actively produce this sense of proximity to the American caller as they consume (internalize) and perform (externalize) American identities. These performances place the call center agent in an imagined relationship with customers in which she must both consume America and be consumed by America. She must proactively cultivate her performance of self in ways that are intelligible to Americans, assimilating as if she had migrated to the United States.

Agents must undergo tremendous psychic transformations in order to build a sense of sameness and in turn a sense of proximity to American customers. They must internalize American culture, images, modes of communication, and knowledge, then externalize those forms of expertise. This labor might be productively understood as biopolitical—as producing the call center agent as a modern subject through a dual process of negation (neutralization) and cultivation (discipline).[10] Foucault ([1976] 1990) argues that modern power is concerned not merely with impeding, controlling, or destroying life, but also with cultivating, optimizing, administrating, and organizing it. The production of biopower, however, is reconfigured within late capitalism's time-space accelerations. Our reading of interviews with call center workers reveals that the biopolitics of call center labor suppresses life (that of the Indian marked as such) in order to cultivate life (the call center agent as a neoliberal subject). Unlike the subject presumed within Foucault's work, who is imagined through particular normativities associated with Europeanness,[11] the call center subject is formed through the needs of nation and empire.

FORMING NEOLIBERAL SUBJECTS:
EXTENDING THE REACH OF WHITENESS

For Ong (2006), the project of neoliberalism is biopolitical as subjects are disciplined and cultivated to maximize their value within the global market. Yet subjects are differently located within and unevenly served by neoliberalism. Indeed, capitalism needs its inequities, just as outsourcing needs India's poverty to be viable. Ong captures this insidious paradox through the metaphor of the hinge, a moving part that opens neoliberal inclusion to some while necessarily closing it to others. This section examines this hinging function in the formation of the call center agent as a site of discipline, control, and value within a postmodern and information-based global economy. We consider the ways in which the call center agent becomes simultaneously included and excluded within neoliberalism's reach. Although Ong and others view neoliberalism as demarcating distinctions between those who are included or excluded by neoliberalism, the call center agent is simultaneously included and excluded. Rather, the call center agent is split through her labor. Call center labor actively cultivates Americanized subjects, which only becomes possible through the subordination of a prior subject—one marked in myriad ways by her Indianness.

The call center agent can certainly be counted among those whose stock is improved through their participation in the global economy. Yet this very inclusion is contingent on a host of exclusions. These exclusions occur through the negation, rejection, disavowal, suppression, or merely turning of one's attention away from those sites, belongings, and activities that formerly bound the call center agent to India in particular ways. Call center labor reorients its agents through the biopolitics of Orientalism's world-facing project, examined in the previous chapter. The agent is cultivated as a neoliberal subject through the double activity of disciplining the agents' speaking practices on the one hand, and of circumscribing aspects of the agent that fail to register within the exchange on the other. Yet agents resist these processes to carve out little and big ways of maintaining Indianness: taking time back, engaging in fleeting refusals, deploying strategies Winiecki (2007) describes as shadow boxing.[12]

For instance, call center agents are initiated into the industry by taking aliases or shortening their names. Such naming practices are framed as necessary to maximize the efficiency of the communication exchange between agents and customers. As Iqbal explains, using an alias "reduces the call length, which is a critical component, because we charge by the minute, you know." Iqbal is CEO of the company he and his brother have built and grown from venture capital they raised together in the United Kingdom. For Iqbal, the industry is based on logic and numbers, grounded in the value-added services it provides and the efficiencies of capital it creates. He explains that the practice of changing names "ensures the call time is not too long because the person is trying to comprehend a complex Indian name" (Infofloz, personal interview, 2004). The "complex Indian name" is one of many obstacles agents must overcome to create a sense of proximity to their American callers. The communication process centers on the Western consumer, who should not be burdened with the effort of trying to comprehend the complexity of the presumed foreignness of the agent's name. The capitalist imperative to reduce call lengths disciplines agents through such practices as taking pseudonyms, which is a naming practice that recasts one of agents' most formative senses of identity. Although agents' names must be excised as a condition of neoliberal inclusion, the act of renaming is also a form of exclusion. Agents may be included in this labor only by excluding this and other components of their Indian identities. The agent's mobility within neoliberalism is thus contingent on the agent's suppression of critical components of her Indian self.

Agents shed or shorten their Indian names to accommodate the (imagined) affective needs of the Western consumer. As Iqbal explains, "We don't really ask them to change their name to a John or a Jane. Other than [pause] basically if they have a longer name, to use some sort of abbreviation to that which they're comfortable with." The erasure of Indianness enables the maximum efficiency of the communication interaction. The industry frames these naming practices as necessary to manage difference in the virtual world of the telecommunication interaction. Agents produce a sense of identification, or sameness, designed to overcome the geographic distance between agents and callers. Iqbal continues, "And it's easier, because as it is, you can't see the lip movement." The suppression of the visual both enables the agent to overcome difference (as the caller cannot see the agent) and the condition necessitating the agent to recast her or his name in order to do so (the caller "can't see the lip movement"). Iqbal claims that agents prefer to change their names because "that way they're leading a separate life. That way they have a separate name and separate identity." Thus the call center subject is formed through a particular splitting of their subjectivities as agents are compelled to separate their identities. Iqbal downplays the toll of this loss of identity even as he locates a sense of agency in the agents who prefer to change their names.

Pseudonyms are one of many industry practices that function, like Ong's hinge metaphor, to demarcate lines of neoliberal inclusion and exclusion. Yet such practices enable agents' inclusion under the condition that they are also simultaneously excluded. As a technology of biopower, pseudonyms cultivate and manage agents' subjectivities; in turn, agents creatively take up and resist such naming practices. In the following excerpt, Raveena initially denies using an alias, then admits that, "in certain cases," she has used a "separate" name. She insists on narrating her negotiation with pseudonyms on her own terms. She describes the use of pseudonyms using the term "pseudo names," which aptly marks the simulated quality of call center naming practices:

SHEENA: Did you ever have to use an alias?

RAVEENA: No.

SHEENA: You have always gone with Raveena?

RAVEENA: Yes. Well, sometimes it would be tough for the costumer to get the name Raveena. So in certain cases, they would ask us to use pseudo names. And we were identified by pseudo names.

SHEENA: What is your pseudo name?

RAVEENA: Julia Blake.

SHEENA: What made you pick that?

RAVEENA: It was just a random pick. Julia I picked up from somewhere else and Blake also—it is the surname of one of my faculty, so I strung them together.

SHEENA: Where did you pick Julia from?

RAVEENA: I think Julia Roberts. (Raveena, BigBank, personal interview, 2004)

Raveena vacillates on the topic of the industry's pseudo naming practices, carving out a sense of agency as she recasts and resists their assimilating function as she frames her naming in both active and passive terms. Because it was "tough for the customer to get" her name, agents "were asked to use pseudo names," Raveena explains, positioning agents in the passive voice. Yet Raveena actively resists our line of questioning; her account shifts from passive to active terms as it moves from her individual story to the wider industry practice. Her use of the term "pseudo name" recasts the term *pseudonym*, a false or fictitious name, to *pseudo* (pretend, imitation) *name* (her designation). This neologism subtly shifts the power dynamics of the industry's naming practices. "Julia Blake" is not just a false or fictitious name, but rather a designation Raveena actively chooses to perform her Americanized identity. Her name is inspired by a personal contact (her mentor's last name) and a mediated relationship (Julia, she is reticent to admit, she takes from the American film star). The lived and mediated encounters Raveena has with these affective sites of Americanness converge seamlessly, yet with much ambivalence and resistance, in her name choice. This move returns us to Appadurai's ([1996] 2000) argument about mediascapes, technoscapes, and ethnoscapes, which here converge in the form of the pseudo name. Raveena negotiates a constellation of mediated and lived relationships that she in turn deploys in her virtual performance as a call center agent.

Although Raveena is reticent to admit to her use of a pseudo name, Ekaraj deploys naming practices as a strategy of resistance: "I used to call myself Elvis," he explains. "I thought this was the only way you could catch the customer off guard." Ekaraj appropriates the iconic quality of the infamous American pop star, Elvis Presley, for himself in ways that disrupt the power relations with his callers. Ekaraj is a worker by night and an aspiring photographer by day. He commutes on his scooter between the call center and his family home on the outskirts of town, where he lives in a multigenerational household with his parents, grandmother, and sister. Owning a car would never cross his mind. Ekaraj dresses casually in a kurta and jeans and smokes cigarettes on his breaks. His choice of the name Elvis is one of many strategies he engages to hold the strands of his identity together as the gap marked by his commute is symbolic of a much wider gap between his life in the call center and his home life. Whatever time of day or night he returns to his family home, he takes pictures of the plants in his small garden in various shades of light. He longs for time to stand still, if only for the fleeting click of his camera's shutter. The hours he works at the call center estrange him from his family and friends, which pains him. Occasionally he gets fed up with it all and quits, he tells us when the tape recorder is shut off. He knows that good agents are hard to come by; he'll get another job, then have an easy time of it for a few weeks of training. Resisting the power dynamics of pseudo naming practices, Ekaraj chooses a name not in order to make his difference invisible to callers, but rather to "catch the customer off guard." His choice of Elvis plays on an ironic articulation between his subordinated Indian identity and that of a white male star who epitomizes white American masculinity. Ekaraj continues:

> Okay, if you have a very complex name or typically your name is very difficult [pause] you know, what is hard to pronounce [pause]. You will have to shorten it. Something like, for example, Ekaraj, I don't think it would be very difficult for anyone to get. I mean if you call me "Ekaaaraaaj" or "Ekraj" that's fine with me. (Ekaraj, I2U, personal interview, 2005)

Ekaraj echoes Raveena and Iqbal's sense that "complex" names must be shortened, but he also chooses to use his given name sometimes, even if customers mispronounce it. This choice frees him to use his name, which, he explains, means not having to wear the mask that comes with the pseudonym. For Ekaraj, the corporate naming practice is an effacement of his Indian identity that he resists. His choice to retain his own name places the customer (as opposed to the agent) in the position to accommodate difference within the communication interaction. Ekaraj's elastic relationship to these pseudo naming practices allows him to navigate the splitting of the call center agents' subjectivity with options to resist and appropriate names in ways that suit him.

In addition to naming practices, call center agents' shifting class positions contribute to the splitting of their subjectivities. The changing class dynamics generated by call center labor create new lines of access and affinity that reorient agents' relationships to checkered geographies as well as to other, differently located Indians. In the Indian context, servants[13]

and homeowners, workers and employers have historically shared and
coinhabited social and personal space. Yet the kinds of interactions and
power relations previously structured through such class distinctions are
disrupted by call center labor. Call center agents and managers note that
agents find themselves in a new class category—one that supersedes that
of their parents and allows them access to spaces and purchasing power
from which they would have formerly been excluded. In this sense, call
center agents inhabit space and time differently—not only from other Indians of their own class background, but also from their families and former
selves. Iqbal explains:

> It's a very satisfying job, creating employment for people—giving them
> a standard of living where they can afford a much better quality of life
> for themselves and their children than what their parents were able to
> afford. It's not uncommon for our reps to . . . visit now the best nightclubs in
> Bombay. I often walk into them in the most expensive of places. That's had
> a very significant impact on the social side of things too. (Iqbal, Infofloz,
> personal interview, 2004)

Iqbal frames call center labor through a sense of (neo)liberal benevolence,
an enabling condition for upward mobility in which he, as CEO, is able to
"give" agents a "much better quality of life." He notes the "significant social
impact" of the encounter between employers and employees in "the most
expensive places"—sites previously demarcated through the strict management of lines of class privilege. In such mixed-class sites, individual
agents reorient class mobility even as the terrain of the social is reconfigured. Call center labor generates new kinds of affinities, encounters, and
connectivities that unsettle the previous order of things. Call center agents
are reconstituted as multiply classed subjects who might simultaneously
occupy varying class positions—living in a relatively humble home with
their parents, for example, while buying expensive cell phones and fre-
quenting upscale nightclubs. Iqbal's comment underscores the ways in
which call center labor, to use Ahmed's phrase, "extends the reach"—both
of the American caller and of agents who become the callers' prosthesis.[14]
This labor in turn extends agents' reach, enabling them to gain access to
privileged zones that might previously have been off limits to them.

What Iqbal does not describe are the interpersonal tensions that these
shifting class dynamics produce or the strain they place on intimate ties

among agents and their partners, families, and friends. Ganesh, a manager at TechNow, says of that strain,

> Many people are not able to cope up, especially those who have spouses who work in the mornings. There have been quite a few broken homes that I've seen in my tenure, because it requires a lot of adjustment. It requires both the spouses to be really—to understand how exactly it works. And in the end it's for the larger good. You want to have kids tomorrow, you want to give them a good education, you want to have a nice car [pause]. I mean I'll be honest [pause], when I was in hotels I had a Hero Honda motorcycle, and I drive a Honda Civic right now. All because I worked here, I made those sacrifices, went out to places to learn. So that's the way it kind of works. (Ganesh, TechNow, personal interview, 2007).

The call center agent emerges as a neoliberal subject through a vexed negotiation between the material and the affective: he gains the benefits of inclusion within global capitalism (here tangibly captured in the form of a Honda Civic) through the suppression of previously privileged affective ties (with spouses in this case). Ganesh uses "cope up" interchangeably with "keep up," which underscores the double gesture of this compromise. In order to keep up within the accelerated space-time of call center labor, agents must cope with a host of losses and sacrifices, as well as the suppression of former intimacies. This excerpt marks particular moments in the reorientation of call center agents, whose attention may have been previously directed at their immediate relations but who are now directed toward specific markers of class mobility. In Ganesh's case, the very orientation of his bodily inhabitance is reconfigured in the move from riding a Hero Honda motorcycle to driving a Honda Civic car. The Hero exposes one's body to others who coinhabit the roads (drivers, street venders, children, animals) to the elements, to smells and scents, to exhaust and to dust. The Civic, however, insulates the body from these forces and confines it within the security and isolation of individuated mobility.

Mobility and access serve as productive markers of a particular shift in class structure, social relations, and cultural identity. As Jaffer explains, "At the end of the day, money is what matters. Probably I can say that the money part has taken over the culture part. That is my personal opinion" (365-Call, focus group interview, 2006). Jaffer's account of the impact of call center labor marks the reorientation of the call center agent in starkly bifurcated terms: the orientation toward "money" displaces and replaces the orientation toward "culture." Here culture stands in for family and social relations, as well as a cultural orientation toward relationality rather than the materiality associated with Americanness. Jaffer's comment returns us to the biopolitical production and suppression of call center agents' subjectivities as a reorienting process. The micropractices and macroforces of the call center industry cultivate the subject, extending the reach of the call center agent through the suppression of or turning away from culture. This emptying process emulates American assimilation in which cultural difference is suppressed in favor of national inclusion. This form of assimilation compromises a sense of national and cultural belonging in favor of a sense of class mobility and global inclusion. Just as American assimilation is contingent upon approximating whiteness, so too does call center labor entail the neutralization of difference. Thus the biopolitical processes through which call center agents are cultivated as neoliberal subjects are also processes of exclusion, suppression, and erasure. This vexed relationship to global inclusion/exclusion historicizes biopower, locating theories and practices of governmentality within contemporary processes of transnationalism, postmodernization, and informatization. These excerpts help us to locate the industry's disciplinary technologies within the geopolitics of intersecting differences. In the case of call center agents, their communication practices become the primary site of discipline and control, even as these practices serve as the most potent vehicle for inclusion within neoliberalism.

COMMU(NICA)TING (TO) AMERICA: DISCIPLINING INDIAN SUBJECTIVITIES

The ensuing analysis of call center labor extends Grewal's (2005) work, which locates transnational connectivities within processes of consumption or informal familial ties to the West as call center labor extends the promise of inclusion in the American dream. Call center agents diligently hone their communication practices in an effort to seamlessly participate in the global economy. The disciplinary practices through which agents train are organized around a host of Americanizing cultural objects. These practices reconfigure the relationship between the Indian subject and what Grewal would call transnational America from a passive yet interactive consumption of America to an active performance of Americanness.

The global dispersion of Americanness might also productively be understood, following Ahmed's (2006) argument outlined above, as a world-facing process in which disparate global subjects become oriented toward America. Our reading of call center workers' stories helps us consider how such processes of orientation are interactive. Not only do agents participate in the American dream, as Grewal (2005) suggests, by consuming American consumer goods, images, ideas, styles, and values, but agents also engage in an active, outwardly expressed, and ongoing participation in America as call center labor requires a particular externalized expression of the qualities associated with Americanness. The call center industry has developed a host of disciplinary processes, designed to prepare call center agents to answer the call of the American customer. These processes are designed to orient agents' sensibilities, and particularly the outward expression or performance of those sensibilities, toward America. The industry's training programs provide a point of entry into mapping these emerging technologies of power.

Call center training is designed to discipline agents to speak to Americans by sounding like Americans. Not only are agents encouraged to speak with an accent and bear a name that will pass under the radar of the caller's aural sensibilities, but they must also cultivate an awareness of the details of the American way of life. Sunita describes the training process:

> It was about ten days, six hours a day. We went through the American culture. Basically, we were exposed to the American way of life, the society, their business ethics. For the voice and accent piece, there is a lot of role playing, a lot of pronunciation sessions, mock interviews where . . . they teach you how to pronounce words a certain way and then you . . . try to incorporate that into your speech. (Sunita, I2U, personal interview, 2004)

Such training practices are designed to govern agents' communication practices to accommodate an American imaginary of what an appropriate service person should sound like. This American desire for sameness is in turn reinforced through training activities. Such technologies of power make call center labor a critical site in the production of transnational America as the transnational connectivities between India agents and U.S. consumers are interactive, dynamic, and performative. Both the form (accent) and the content (the American way of life) of agents' speech are targeted within this training as sites to discipline call center agents' performance of self.

As we detail above, such practices point to the way call center labor instantiates a new moment in the Americanization of India. When thought through Appadurai's ([1996] 2000) theory, the mediascape connecting the two national imaginaries is no longer a one-way channel. Rather, the rigorous training, role-playing, and mock interviews serve as a crash course in assimilation, American style. As Pavitra puts it, speaking like they do on *Friends* models the right way for agents to speak:

> Yes, in fact we were advised to watch the series of *Friends*. . . . That's the way the customers would speak to us, and that's the right way of what we need to know. So they advise us to do that or watch movies and talk a lot of English. It was just one session about the cultural background of the people we are going to communicate with. (Pavitra, I2U, personal interview, 2005)

Pavitra's interaction with American pop culture moves beyond merely consuming its images and story lines to an imperative to model one's activities, sensibilities, and modes of communication after those performed within the real of the popular. The industry leverages American media (*Friends,* in this case) for pedagogic purposes. Pavitra watches *Friends* to learn how to appropriately perform ("the right way of what we need to know") within the virtual transnational American space generated within the phone conversation.

Call center training immerses agents in an America that is depicted through such popular shows as *Friends,* which reduces the complexities of America into consumable, mediated sections. This construction is distributed to the agent over a set course of time so that the agent might actively take up these discourses and in turn perform them for the American caller. Thus call center training moves agents from being passive consumers of transnational America (being "exposed to the American way of life") to becoming active, if virtual, participants in the formation of transnational America (the "voice and accent piece"). Training is a performance-oriented, communicative, and interactive process in which agents role-play, cultivate appropriate pronunciation, and participate in mock interviews in order to incorporate these particular communication practices into their speech. In this sense, communicating with Americans becomes a form of mediated travel in which agents virtually commute the globe.

Yet this virtual commute is also contingent upon their nonmovement: virtual migration enables agents to imaginatively, communicatively travel to America as their bodies remain in India. One aspect of this imaginative component of virtual migration is that agents become fluent in American culture. As they project their imaginations afar, they also depart from a localized sense of belonging. Thus virtual migration creates a disjuncture between agents' experience and consciousness—between embodied inhabitance and everyday performances of identity. Agents must constantly negotiate this splitting of their subjectivities through their psychic labor. As call center agent Lloyd explains, "We are not really experiencing America. . . . We have not lived the American way. Just because we talk American or think that watching *Friends* is American—that is not hybridization. I think that is confusion" (I2U, personal interview, 2005). Lloyd lives the contradictions of postcoloniality. At the call center, he works as a manager, but he'd probably prefer to be a philosopher or a postcolonial critic. In his thirties, Lloyd wears his hair long, and an ever-present pack of cigarettes creeps out of the pocket of his yellow button-down shirt. Lloyd's gestures and voice become animated when he shares stories about the mistreatments doled out by American callers. He refers to India as part of the "so-called" third world. With a keen awareness of American culture, the global world—and India's place in it—Lloyd epitomizes Fanon's (1967) ambivalent male colonial subject. On the one hand, Lloyd feels stuck and resentful about being bound within call center life, where he and his employees are subjected to the racism of his ignorant American callers. On the other hand, Lloyd sees himself as superior to the customers; their racism signals their lack of education. Lloyd's statements are laced with frustration as he reflects on these uneven encounters that he is consciously unlikely to transcend in the national or global arena. "Maintaining a false accent is very hard," he explains, "because, if you are living in America and talking to people you can see every day, your accent gets adjusted to that. That is a more natural thing." For Lloyd the lived experience of speaking like an American without physically being in America "is very hard." It feels "false," as opposed to the "more natural" experience of "living in America and talking to people you can see every day."

In the above quotation, Lloyd describes his psychic struggle as he navigates the space between embodied experience (or lack of experience) and the performance of an Americanized identity. His excerpts points to a sense of virtual assimilation that is enacted as agents demonstrate proficiency in culture. Lloyd underscores the slippage between the performance of Americanness and the lack of experience with America, pointing to the ways his subjectivity is stretched, mediated, and virtually produced through call center labor. He continues, "But here you are actually in no way relating to the person. There is no visual connection. You are doing this accent performance, because somebody decided that it is the right way to do it. And I think that is very hard to maintain" (I2U, personal interview, 2005). Lloyd reiterates the lack of "visual connection" between agents and callers to underscore the distinction between an "actual" relationship from the "performance" required by the oral/aural encounter. This lack marks, for Lloyd, the virtuality of the contact as unreal, with the visual serving as the marker of embodiment while orality stands in for the psychic demands of disembodiment. Lloyd attributes this disciplinary technology to a seemingly arbitrary force: agents must perform virtual assimilation "because somebody decided that it is the right way to do it," while the "hard" task of "maintaining" the fiction of proximity to America falls on agents. Thought of phenonenologically, call center labor decouples experience from agents' lived inhabitance as consciousness is redirected toward an imaginary site of difference. As Lloyd points out, experience and consciousness become decoupled as agents work to overcome distance by creating a sense of closeness to their American callers. The psychic demands of virtual migration form agents' subjectivity by dispersing it across the globe. This spacetime dispersion of experience and consciousness in turn generates a split in the conditions of subject formation that agents must continually suture through their psychic labor.

The communication practices of the call center industry, then, offer a critical site in which to explore how disciplinary power is exerted in the transnationalization of America. Team lead Anila describes a month-long session that focused on "phonetic, English comprehension, customer-service skills, and American culture. For the whole month we went through this training. We also had a sort of test in between. People get filtered in between" (I2U, personal interview, 2005). Anila's account resonates with Mirchandani's (2004) research, which found the use of progressive interviews to determine the inclusion and exclusion of agents. Mirchandani argues that this strategy was designed to generate desire and exclusivity for what is actually a repetitive, tedious job. As a broader neoliberal formation, practices of inclusion are contingent on a particular exclusion—not only of the trainees who fail the test, but also of those communication practices, those markers of Indianness that affix the trainee to his or her difference. The ability to fill dead air is a strategy agents learn to make American callers comfortable. This capacity requires agents to become proficient in both the form and content of American speech. One aspect of call center labor is to demonstrate expertise in various aspects of American content: history, culture, geography and regional differences, popular events and activities, catastrophes and weather patterns. Anila explains that training includes "learning about the U.S.: all the fifty states, the capital of each, what is each state famous for, and then going to certain terms which are used there, the usage of words" (I2U, personal interview, 2005). This training aims to attune agents to the regional differences among Americans, helping them to adapt their accents and their ears to connect with variously located American callers. Even as this cultural immersion strives to Americanize agents' communication practices, agents do not necessarily become any less Indian. Agents don't forego their Indian identities, but they must strive to suppress any traces of that Indianness that American callers might detect. On one hand, call center training and labor are evacuating activities: agents must empty themselves of various aspects of their immediate surroundings (accents and experiences, word usage and naming practices). On the other, call center labor and training are occupying activities: agents must fill their consciousness with details of American life.

This emptying and filling creates a push–pull dynamic that enables agents to overcome distance and difference. Lloyd describes the psychic labor entailed in this dynamic:

> The majority of people, for the early parts of the years working in this industry, tend to be very confused. Because my name is probably Jaikumar and I am saying, "I am Jerry," and I am trying to talk about places I have never been to, I have never seen, and my training tells me that *Friends* is the latest. (Lloyd, I2U, personal interview, 2005)

For Lloyd, those "early" encounters with the industry are most "confusing" because agents must consciously strive to internalize this push–pull dynamic. The "confusion," Lloyd explains, arises from a gap between lived experience and consciousness generated through such industry practices as watching *Friends* to taking on an American name to "talking about places

I've never been to, have never seen." His comments underscore what Ahmed would describe as the Orientalist phenomenology of call center labor. As a world-facing project, call center labor orients call center agents toward America. These processes also disorient agents, who inhabit time and space differently by virtue of their participation in this labor.[15]

Call center labor might be understood, in Grewal's (2005) terms, as a biopolitical force that participates in the transnationalization of America. This production elides the distinction between America and whiteness as agents neutralize their accents to mimic mostly white speech patterns. Call center labor participates, in Ahmed's (2006) formulation, in the whitening of the world, even as the bodies that are compelled to inhabit that whiteness do so uneasily. Call center labor strives to virtually whiten agents and simultaneously maintain the whiteness of America as their bodies remain brown and bounded within a visibly brown space. In the face of the tremendous force of these global and imperial formations, Lloyd underscores agents' agency as they learn to inhabit whiteness and in turn to temporarily uninhabit Indianness. He describes this negotiation through a neologism, pseudohybridization, that captures the ephemeral quality of virtual migration. Like Raveena's "pseudo names," which provide separate identities for call center workers as they move among different communication worlds, pseudohybridity captures a layer of in-betweenness in which agents might assert a modicum of power as they remain conscious of the virtuality—the pseudoness—of their labor. In this sense, agents might maintain a narrow gap between their identities and the whiteness to which they are submitted.

DISPLACING THE CORPOREAL SCHEMA:
CALL CENTER LABOR AND THE CATEGORY EXPERIENCE

In Fanon's (1967) well-known and deeply unsettling encounter with the white gaze, he finds himself utterly displaced by the fact of his blackness. As his account painfully conveys, his "corporeal schema crumbled, its place taken by a racial epidermal schema" (112). Fanon underscores the doubling and tripling of his subjectivity in the face of the white man: his body is assailed with a host of stereotypical images that he in turn takes on. These images reduce him to a "crushing objecthood" (109). Fanon's attention to the splitting of the colonial subject provides a compelling frame to approach questions of subject formation for call center agents. Like Ahmed (2006), Fanon's attention to the corporeal exchange between colonial subject and colonizer is phenomenological wherein the implicit knowledge of the body itself is reoriented.[16] The body's capacity to occupy space and time without prohibition decomposes and shatters as the colonial subject is constituted through a crushing objectification. The splitting of Fanon's subjectivity occurs as the immediacy of his "corporeal schema" becomes displaced by the "racial epidermal schema."

Fanon's schemas provide a productive point of entry into the conditions of subject formation for call center agents for whom the presumably natural relationship between the body and the space-time it inhabits is deeply altered, if not rendered impossible, by the crushing force of the virtual white gaze. As we detail above, call center agents project their consciousness around the globe to imagine a host of experiences they have not had in order to communicate with Americans, producing a slippage between agents' consciousness and experience. Whereas Fanon's account foregrounds the visuality of the colonial encounter, call center agents encounter whiteness within the virtuality of the phone call. This context resituates Fanon's schemas within an oral/aural register as agents' subjectivities are split through the continual subordination of the immediate in favor of the distant. The "naturalness" of the corporeal schema presumed by Fanon, in which the subject is composed as a "self" within "a body in the middle of a spatial and temporal world" (Fanon 1967, 110), is displaced from the get-go by the virtual quality of call center encounter. In other words, agents' capacity to inhabit their own "spatial and temporal world" is continually displaced through the necessity to project themselves as inhabiting another, imagined world: I've never driven a car, but I am asked to "speak like a pro" about cars; I've never been to a football game, but I must act as if I know what a Superbowl is; I've never lived through a tornado, but I must act as if I understand the tragedy of doing so.

An examination of agents' relationship to inhabitance calls into question the category of experience. For theorists of experience—from Mearleu-Ponty and Sarte to Fanon, from Joan Scott to Chandra Mohanty and Paula Moya—the category of experience presumes activity situated in real time and shared space.[17] That is, experience is presumed to occur simultaneously with bodily inhabitance as consciousness is said to arise from an interpretation, or meaning making, of experience. The corporeal schema for call center agents, however, is stretched across the time-space relations of call center labor: virtual migration is structured through a necessary slippage between the corporeal schema and the formation of consciousness, or sources of knowledge, toward which agents must orient themselves. Sanjana describes psychic consequences of this slippage as call center labor changes the "basic nature" of the agent:

> I am living a life where I feel so isolated, and that becomes to you—natural. Your basic nature changes because you are isolated for such a long time. It also changes the way you live the way you look at things, the way you take life. It's going to be so different from what you were before, you know? (Sanjana, I2U, personal interview, 2005)

As Sanjana narrates her experience, her pronouns shift from "I" to "you" in ways that both generalize her experience to other agents and also invite the interviewers to identify with her struggle. This subject of identification is marked by the melancholic, displaced, or affectively removed quality of her life: isolation becomes "natural," something changing "your basic nature," rendering the agent "different from what you were before." Sanjana describes isolation as an enduring quality of call center labor; it permeates "the way you take life" as distinct from a life prior to the call center ("what you were before"). Sanjana invites the interviewer to identify with this previous self through a shared collective pronoun, "what you were," and a final remark: "You know?" This gesture marks a relationality of her previous self and invites her interlocutors to be in relation with her. In this moment, Sanjana strives to build a sense of intimacy and empathy that might disrupt the crushing "isolation" of call center life. The isolation she describes is both a function of the hollowing out of experience (recall Lloyd's notions of pseudohybridization and confusion), coupled with a withdrawal from the daily interactions—the touches, smells, and sounds of the encounter with embodied others.

Avantika's account resonates with Sanjana's. Avantika has a slight build, wears a single neat braid, and dresses in professional Indian clothing that complements the earnest work ethic she brings to her job. She listens intently in the exchange in her focus group and is forthright and expressive about her own opinions. Avantika fears that India might be trading the "love and affection"—the "glue" that holds the family together—for a place in a globalized world. She feels she that as she loses "culture," the space it held becomes replaced by "mechanical work" of call center labor:

One thing is, we can't spend time with family because we work in a different field. When we meet our friends, who work in a day job, or my family, my parents, we feel that something we are missing: the love, affection. I mean, in this field we just come over here, there is mechanical work over here, and all only stuff about call center, BPO. Our own culture, knowing about our own culture, friction, parents—that we miss in this kind of job. It matters, our culture. (Avantika, 365-Call, focus group interview, 2006)

Although Avantika lives with her husband, she rarely sees him because he works a day shift. Their relationship has been reduced to a rote intimacy writ through quick meals grabbed between shifts in fast food stalls at a nearby mall. The burgers and french fries they share, she tells us, don't fill the gap of affection she craves. The losses are compounded as her own long working hours have strained her relationship with her parents. She misses the "friction" of the "relations" she reports are fading over time. Avantika builds strong ties and contributes to her job to recover some of these losses. She sees herself as a team player and takes pride in her ability to contribute to her family's future—aspects of her job she appreciates. The power temporalities of call center labor are lived conditions affectively felt by Avantika. These affective dimensions of bodily inhabitance—touch, "love, affection," and "knowing about our own culture" through daily habituation—characterize those experiences that call center agents forego and long for.

It is this longing, this absence of experience, that marks the whitening of call center agents' subjectivities. Ruth Frankenberg (1993, 4) has provocatively argued that "whiteness is the non-experience of (not) being slapped in the face." She characterizes the white experience within a racial corporeal schema through an ambivalent sense of experiential absence. Giorgio Agamben (1978) argues for the (universalized) "death of experience" within the age of colonial modernity. "Modern man makes his way home in the evening wearied by a jumble of events," he muses, "but however entertaining or tedious, unusual or commonplace, harrowing or pleasurable they are, none of them will have become experience" (14). These theorists suggest that the hollowing out of experience—the individuation, the suppression of affective experience, the numbing "jumble of events"—is a condition of the modern (white) subject. As call center agents become modern and whitened subjects, they become fluent in the jumble of events that make up American life. As they find themselves "missing" the "love and affection" within their corporeal encounters, agents undergo tremendous loss.

While agents forego the affect within the immediacy of embodiment, their fluency in the daily rhythms of American life enable a new host of virtual intimacies. To cultivate affective ties with American callers, agents must be aware of the mundane or catastrophic events that constitute life in the faraway place of America. Raja explains how he quickly came to discover the disjunctures between mediated and lived experience in the course of a phone call with an American consumer:

> If I speak to my friends about, let's say, anything to do with tornadoes, it'll be very, very exciting for them. They would say: "Wow, tornados, movies, twisters!" . . . But this is an experience I have had when I was talking to one of my customers over the phone. And that lady, she was a pretty old lady, said: "You know, I really keep worrying about tornados here, so I'm not interested in buying anything else." I was like, "Tornadoes, wow!" And she was like, "What is so 'wow' about it?" That made me realize that that is something that kills people, destroys houses. It's fun when you don't see it, but if you've got to relate to them, it's, "Oh tornadoes, sorry. Does that happen?" It's a different kind of reaction that you get back from them. It's just an example. That's why you need to know what's happening there. For your business. (Raja, 365-Call, focus group interview, 2006)

Over the course of his account, Raja shifts from the naive subject position of his friends, who inappropriately imagine tornadoes as "exciting," to his own vantage as a globally savvy agent. Through his encounter with the "old lady," Raja comes to realize that the lived experience of tornadoes involves destruction ("something that kills people, destroyes houses"). To effectively manage the affective labor entailed in his job ("if you've got to relate to them"), Raja must engage a "different kind of reaction" informed by the "need to know what's happening there." This need is framed as an imperative of call center labor: "For your business," Raja concludes.

Call center manager Ganesh provides an account of this imperative when he explains the importance of agents' awareness of American sports and holidays:

> Because at times you're there and a Super Bowl final would happen and the customer used to ask us, so, you know? We can't act like, "Okay, what Super

Bowl?" So there was [pause] we had a newsletter in which all the American sports were happening. In our training, they used to tell us what football is. What happens [pause] after Thanksgiving, I think there's this, you know, big game. So all those. So we were made aware of that. (Ganesh, TechNow, personal interview, 2007)

Ganesh's speech becomes slippery and uneven in this account, perhaps marking the moments in which his lived experience departs from the forms of expertise agents perform. Ganesh projects himself elsewhere ("at times you're there") as he performs a sense of having been there. He notes, "We can't act like, 'Okay, what Super Bowl?'" Rather, agents must "act like" they are familiar with those cultural events that are meaningful to Americans. Thanksgiving, a "big game," and "the Super Bowl final" are scheduled events that agents must be "made aware of." In this sense, agents attune their rhythms to a schedule half a world away.

Ganesh underscores the disjuncture between agents' lived experience and their oral performance of expertise in his earlier comment about how many agents have never driven cars, "But they talk about auto figures. And they talk like they're pros. And they do it really well" (Ganesh, TechNow, personal interview, 2007). Call center labor parses out lived experience, which is subordinated or forgone in favor of mastering imagined experience. Imagined experience is the basis for agents to perform knowledge in those details of American life "like they're pros." Like Fanon, the splitting of the agent's subjectivity is generated in the colonial encounter as a virtual racial schema displaces their corporeal schema. It is not, in these instances, stereotypes of backward Indianness that disrupt agents' bodily inhabitance. Rather, it is the continual need to perform Americanness—to avoid calling attention to the specificity of their Indianness—by demonstrating expertise garnered through an experience only imagined, but projected as lived. Agents' corporeal schema is displaced from the immediacy of the bodily inhabitance in favor of an imagined corporeal schema that becomes the invisible and yet privileged site of experience.

POWER TEMPORALITIES: TIME THEFT, REGULATION, AND REGIMENTATION OF CALL CENTER WORKERS

As we detail above, training and industry practices groom and manage agents, themes that permeate studies of time management in U.S., U.K., and Canadian call centers. Research on Western call centers demonstrates that agents undergo extensive electronic monitoring, resulting in high levels of turnover as agents navigate physical and emotional problems generated by the heavy management of time (Stevens and Lavin 2007, 41). Although workers are asked to account for every extra minute of break time they might take, management "steals" employees' time, expecting them to do extra work without pay (Stevens and Lavin 2007, 53). Further, call centers in the United States, Canada and the United Kingdom are organized through high levels of surveillance (Winiecki 2007), extreme regimentation of agents' speaking scripts (Cameron 2007), and the production of workers' subjectivities measured by statistical efficiencies (Winiecki 2007). Within a neoliberal context, time becomes a highly valuable and intensively managed commodity. Stevens and Lavin offer the concept of time theft to underscore the worker's relationship to capital: the corporation, not the worker, owns the worker's time (Stevens and Lavin 2007). Thus if the employee spends time in ways that disrupt or fail to meet measures of productivity, she is in effect "stealing time" and money from the employer (Stevens and Lavin 2007, 54).

Although these findings also describe elements of Indian call center labor, its Western basis does not fully account for the various layers that inflect its particular power temporalities. Pal and Buzzanell (2008) describe the sensibility in the Indian call center industry as pervaded by a paradoxical "sense of both casualness and urgency." "There seemed to be a degree of freedom for the employees insofar as they could take their own breaks when and how they wanted," they explain. "They were also eligible for perks that ranged from the 'employee of the week' award and weekly happy hours, to getting rides to and from their office. However, their work routines were dependent on time—number of calls completed in an hour, number of successful calls, amount of time to solve problems, and amount and type of purchases by clients—hence the sense of urgency" (38). Their account points to what Bauman (2000) describes as the postpanoptic quality of the Indian call center industry as labor, customers, and owners are spatially and temporally dispersed. These time-space dispersals place a tremendous burden on Indian call center workers to cover over, or render seamless, a host of displacements, disjunctures, and disparities. Particularly for agents working in Indian call centers, the arrangement of time (working the night shift, rotating work schedules) displaces them from their immediate surroundings. Their bodily habituation is shot through with a sense of displacement and exhaustion, as well as the need to continually recover themselves. As Samir explains, "I ask them [agents] what they do on weekends, and the most common answer is that they sleep" (U.S. Computers, personal interview, 2005). The demanding schedules and affective labor of call center labor restricts agents' time and energy, compelling them to use time off just to catch up on their sleep. This temporal structure in turn reconfigures agents' affective ties to local people and events in ways that mimic, even as they rewrite, the displacements that accompany physical migration. Agents' need for sleep during those hours when community activities are occurring displaces them from a daily mundane inhabitance or from corporeal and affective schemas. When asked during a focus group interview, "What are the ways in which you feel different from people who don't work in this industry?" Jaffer quips, "They see the daylight. They are lucky! [laughter]" (365-Call, focus group interview, 2006). Jaffer's sense of difference from those who don't work in the industry marks the temporal conditions of the agent's sense of displacement. Agents' difference is ironically posited against nonagents who are "lucky" enough to "see the daylight," as Jaffer distinguishes agents from nonagents through agents' unnatural relationship to time. Nature is condensed through corporeal tropes (daylight, seeing) that marks nonagents' privileged body clocks—awake in the day, they are able to "see the daylight." The group's laughter underscores the visceral humor captured in Jaffer's quip, revealing the vivid corporeality of agents' temporally inverted lives.

Samir fills out the picture of this sense of displacement referenced by Jaffer, underscoring the embodied and material dimensions of call center labor's power temporalities through the metaphor of a "shadow life":

> This whole shadow life comes to you. You wake up at different hours and drink at different hours and, you know, some people finish work at 10 or 11 A.M. and they finish drinking in the morning because it's the evening for them. It's, like, strange. You get some strange nightmares. But there are a lot of people [around] in the night. (Samir, U.S. Computers, personal interview, 2005)

Samir's "shadow life" plays with the metaphor of darkness as a sensibility and a material condition, inverting Jaffer's "daylight" metaphor. Both workers link agents' experience of temporal displacement to notions of light and dark, day and night. These references to natural markers of time underscore the "strangeness" of agents' bodily inhabitance, rendering it temporally out of sync. Samir captures this displacement through his description of the disruption of mundane corporeality: drinking, getting off of work, having nightmares. It is not these activities in and of themselves but rather the timing of these embodied activities (leaving work at 10 or 11 A.M., drinking in the morning, being around at night) that renders these mundane corporeal activities strange. Jaffer's "shadow life" marks agents' labor as a suspended mobility. Agents are suspended between night and day as they traverse local and global temporalities. His final reference to "strange nightmares" underscores the intensity of agents' psychic labor as they overcome global distances.

Although some agents, like Jaffer, consistently work the night shift, others work continually rotating shifts. Ekaraj describes revolving shifts as a "constant rotation": "Once in fifteen days. In fifteen days you sleep in the morning and then you wake up and then it's night. You have to come and work in the night" (I2U, personal interview, 2005). Ekaraj's account conveys an unsettling sense of surprise as he "wakes up" to find "it's night." He also underscores a coercive sense of time, noting "you have to" work the night shift. Sunita explains how this shifting schedule and the "long hours" she keeps are necessary to synchronize her work to the rhythms of the American workday:

> I come in about 11 in the morning, 11 or 1:00, and I am here until about 11 in the night. I work really long hours. Sometimes around 12:30 to 1:00. The reason being as part of the account manager role, I need to talk to clients every day, and our clients are both on the East Coast and West Coast, so my calls start anywhere between 7:30 in the evening until no specific time, usually about 12:30. So I work long hours. (Sunita, I2U, personal interview, 2004)

Sunita's account underscores the importance of the time arbitrage that generates real-time communication interactions with Americans. She must "work really long hours" to be present for her clients. Sunita's relationship to America is structured through the privileged coordinates of the East and West coasts of U.S. time-space. Her account vividly reveals the reconfiguration of biopower under late capitalism, particularly within the communication-based service industry. World-facing project workers such as Sunita are disciplined to align their bodily inhabitance to connect with those occurring halfway around the globe.

The costs of working the night shift, as Reena Patel (2010) notes, are intensified for women, for whom the time-space of the nightscape is inhospitable terrain. Patel notes that just as women are considered out of place in sacred sites during their menstrual cycles, so too are women considered out of time when they people the streets at night: "The profane space of the street, particularly at night, contaminates women's bodies just as the sacred space of the temple is contaminated by women's blood. This reflects how flows of the body (that is, moving about) and flows from the body (that is, menstruation) are spatialized in a variety of ways" (4). As we consider the displacements and multiple losses call center agents undergo by virtue of their inverted temporal lives, the gendered dynamics of these losses—and the dangers that accompany them—must also be underscored. Indeed, Radha Hegde (2011) argues that the rape case of a female call center agent reveals the ways in which "the body of the 'globalized' woman is constructed as sexually transgressive" and in need of discipline (180). The negotiations of power temporalities faced by female agents, then, are intensified by the spectacularization of their bodies as they dwell and roam outside of the temporal strictures of Indian tradition. As we argue in the previous chapter, women's bodies come to stand in for the vexed forces of modernization, globalization, and nation. Thus when Sunita describes the long hours she is required to work, she also signals a host of transgressions her mere presence in the nightscape represents.

As a result of the incentives associated with time arbitrage, call center labor gains its economic force through the alignment of disparate time-space zones. This alignment gets worked out on and through the bodily and affective inhabitance of call center workers. Iqbal describes the bodily reconfiguration agents undergo: "Initially, people find it difficult to adjust to it, so they may be, you know, vomiting or [pause] things like that happen. But eventually the body clock sort of shifts. And then they're fine with it. And then again, it varies from person to person, too. Some are more prone to it. Others adapt to it fairly easily" (Infofloz, personal interview, 2004). Iqbal differentiates among agents' uneven capacity to "adapt to it," downplaying the cost of bodily labor that exceeds the regimentation of call center labor. Even so, Iqbal acknowledges that the realignment of the agent's body clock entails a tremendous physical toll: the body purges and vomits, seeking to expunge or refuse the industry's world-facing disciplinary apparatus. Agent Ekaraj specifies the unhealthy "food switch" that accompany working the night or rotating shift:

When I work in the night, another problem is your food switch[es]. You don't have your three meals. You don't get to have a breakfast, lunch, and dinner. It's always [pause] you get to have your dinner and the next thing you know, it's morning and you are going to have breakfast at home. Of course, you can eat in between, at work, but you cannot compare it to your ideal lunch. Many times when you go home in the morning, you are too tired to have your breakfast. So when you skip your breakfast, it's always very unhealthy. (Ekaraj, I2U, personal interview, 2005)

Ekaraj attempts to maintain an eating schedule that follows a local temporal schema (that is, to eat breakfast in the morning) against the force of his work schedule, which is oriented toward an American temporality (that is, going to work during his night). The collision, he reports, is "unhealthy."

In spite of the substantial upheaval and affective displacement agents describe, agents navigate power temporalities with tremendous resilience. They craft practices and carve out time through which to salvage a sense of well-being and resistance. For instance, Ekaraj explains his emerging passion for the art of photography. "I am more interested in photography," he says, so

whenever I come back, whether it's at 1 at night, I make sure I spend some time. I have a small digital camera and I at least go to my small garden and start picturing insects, even if it's 1:30 in the night, just to make sure that I have done something that I like. (Ekaraj, I2U, personal interview, 2005)

Ekaraj's practice allows him to assert a modicum of power over his relationship to time and space: he goes into his "small garden" no matter what time of night; he attends to the minute movement of life by "picturing insects." The photograph is a metaphor for Ekaraj's resistance to the industry's power temporalities. The practice empowers Ekaraj to capture an image, freeze a moment, slow time. Photography enables Ekaraj to suspend the rapid pace of his rotating schedule and defer the continual demands of his oral performance. In his garden, it is Ekaraj, not the American consumer or a manager or CEO, who controls the gaze of the camera, who carves out a certain stillness and consolidates a particular corporeal connection, even to a small piece of the natural world.

Samir underscores the revitalizing power of stolen moments, allowing him to regain a sense of control of his time: "I kind of enjoy it sometimes. ... After 4 and 5, it's like great and lovely. I love that time of morning. I get to see a lot of sunrises, which is great, and I love breakfast early. I still have moments for myself" (U.S. Computers, personal interview, 2005). As Samir dwells in those fleeting moments of morning, he gains tremendous pleasure from a sensual contact with nature. He carves out crucial "moments for [himself]"—seeing "a lot of sunrises" and attending to his body's needs on his own time clock ("I love breakfast early"). Ekaraj and Samir find ways of slowing down, suspending, or expanding time, reconnecting to the natural world and forging a sense of empowerment in their capacity to own their time ("I still have moments for myself").

Affective Labor: Time for Intimacies

If the temporalities of call center labor displace agents from the immediacy of local intimacies, they also create conditions for agents to build virtual intimacies with American consumers. Indeed, the latter is a condition or effect of the former. Call center time reorients agents' affective labor away from those with whom they coinhabit space but not time. These power temporalities in turn redirect agents' affective labor toward those with whom they share time but not space. This time-space reorientation invites us to rethink the structures of intimacy through which affective labor is organized. We do so here at two levels. First, we consider how agents redirect affect from their local community to a faraway American customer. Second, we attend to the communication-based, interactive, and virtual quality of call center work as constitutive of a particular postmodern, postpanoptic form of affective labor.

Our reading provides new insights to current theorization of affective labor. We problematize Hardt's (2003) argument that affective labor inverts certain biopolitical processes or mobilizes biopower for transformative possibilities. As we detail above, agents creatively resist the industry's biopolitical imperatives. Yet the compulsory labor of generating positive affects,[18] coupled with the radical restructuring of time, space, and community for call center agents, reveals the oppressive nature of the industry's demands for affective labor. Although agents gain some pleasure from their capacity to effectively produce positive affects in American callers, the labor entailed in order to do so is tremendously taxing. Call center labor, then, is contingent on a host of concessions, suppressions, and reconfigurations of agents' daily inhabitance. These activities are designed to accommodate the perceived needs and sensibilities of Western callers. For theories of affective labor to account for virtual migration, they must interrogate underlying assumptions of a shared space-time between consumer and laborer. We must consider not only the affective relations agents develop with customers, but also the displacement and loss of their local affective ties. We argue for the importance of expanding the frame of affect to account not only for the production but also for the reproduction of labor. Expanding the purview of affective labor enables us to account for agents' affective losses accrued through the reorientation of their affective labor.

As we explore above, power temporalities configure agents' bodily relationship to those resources that enable them to reproduce their labor, such as food and sleep. Temporal inversions also recast agents' affective ties to their communities, friendships, and families. Because time and space constrain their capacity to maintain relationships in home communities, agents often opt to build ties with one another. For example, call center agent Avantika explains,

> Every month here the time changes. The time you sleep this month, eight hours, the next month you might sleep in a different time. So the living— the health, me, my personal health—all change. I am mingling with people here. Here the way you mingle with people, outside you can't. (Avantika, 365-Call, focus group interview, 2006)

For Avantika, the boundary between corporeality and relationality collapse within a context of intense change: the continual "time changes," rotating sleep patterns, "personal health," and "mingling with people." She explains that time with intimate relations outside the industry is "very rare. I can't spend time with my own husband because he works in a day shift! That is what matters. So we miss our own things over here" (365-Call, focus group interview, 2006). Avantika shares space, but not time, with her husband. Agents like Avantika may cohabitate with their most immediate and intimate relations, but they are temporally displaced from building and maintaining those ties. Time is arranged in ways that suspend their intimate relational lives and encourage agents to build ties with other agents with whom they share space and time. Many agents—as we explore in a later chapter and which is evidenced in Avantika's narration—develop intimate ties with other agents.

Such affective ties constitute call center agents as a hybridized transnational sociality. This sociality emerges, in many ways, as distinct from traditional Indian culture and modes of belonging. It is a community formed not so much through shared *spatial*/global migration as through shared *temporal*/global migration. As agents forgo time with local friends and family (as with Avantika's frustration over not being able to see her husband), they find creative ways to redirect their affect to align with the new temporal structures of their lives.

Even as power temporalities hinder agents' capacity to maintain local ties, workers are invited—indeed, compelled—to direct their affective investments toward American callers. For many agents, the affective component of their encounters with American callers is the most rewarding part of their work. Joel describes his encounter with a "sweet old man":

> I spoke to him for about thirty minutes. And I had to take care of my time, like my handling time, but then I had to be like, "OK, you are a very sweet man." I just kept on talking. I had taken enough calls. And OK, it wasn't very busy day [pause] so I just talked to him. At the end of the whole thing, he says, "You've been such a sweet person." A typical elderly person like, you know, he spoke very softly with a deep voice. Very respectful. He knew I was a young guy, he knew I was a young boy. But then, like, he would be like, "Yes, sir." He was pretty cool. You get some customers who call and are very sweet. (Joel, U.S. Computers, personal interview, 2003)

As an agent, Joel is attentive and observant, particularly to the relations in the industry. He speaks thoughtfully, sometimes fondly, and with a kind of reverse paternalism toward those customers in the United States who remark on his Indianness. He describes the romances that often develop between his coworkers in the call center; he is engaged to a woman who does not work in the industry. Though the long hours he works at the call center do not allow him much family time, Joel likes his job. He is content with the stable and respectable income, higher than his own parents made, and he seems to relish sharing his story with us. Like Ekaraj and Samir, who carve out time from the highly regulated time of call center labor to interact with nature, Joel also carves out time to dwell in an interaction that he perceives as "sweet." Joel resists the industry imperative to closely manage time, taking the time it takes to produce positive affects in his callers under the rigid constraints of "tak[ing] enough calls."

Agents often describe the schedules and the cultural shifts that accompany call center labor as troubling their relationships with their parents. In this account, Joel finds an intergenerational connection with his elderly customer, redirecting his affect from Indian parents or grandparents to American callers of the same generation. Likewise, Ekaraj describes a memorable encounter with an older woman:

> Yes, in fact, there was, I would say, three calls which I remember a lot. One was a seventy-two-year-old lady who called me with a question, and I had to walk her through the removal of the motherboard that's the heart of the system. . . . So we talked for an hour and we got to know each other. Now I don't find time to e-mail them or keep in touch with them—maybe once or in five months or asking how she is. That is a very memorable call. (Ekaraj, I2U, personal interview, 2005)

In this account, Ekaraj conducts two forms of labor. He extends the reach of this caller by "walk[ing] her through the removal of the motherboard," and he produces and in turn receives a positive affective encounter with the caller. Ekaraj's account invites us to consider the affective labor of call center work within a broader sociocultural, familial, temporal, and spatial milieu. These forces and practices span the global and the local. If we expand the lens through which we theorize affective labor beyond the moment of the "sweet" encounter between worker and customer, we gain a more complex view of the multiple affective investments, withdrawals, and realignments at work.

Conclusion: The Conundrum of Postpanoptic Experience

In this chapter, we rethink the dispersed and disparate machinations of globalization from the perspective of the Indian call center industry and its workers. We argue for a more nuanced and complex sensibility about the role of power in the affective relations that people such processes. Thinking power in this way invites us to attend to several related movements of power by placing current theories of (post)modern power in conversation, both with each other and with the accounts of call center workers. Several points worth noting emerge from this constellation. First, we situate the biopolitical production of the call center worker as neoliberal subject within a framework informed by phenomenology that underscores the world-facing project of Orientalism. This framework enables us to attend to the embodied and affective orienting functions of virtual migration. The virtuality of call center labor also invites us to think biopower as a postpanoptic formulation in which nation, transnation, and belonging are produced through a mediated communication interaction. To theorize this historic moment in turn compels us to attend to the power temporalities entailed by the dispersion of postmodern biopower. The affective contours of call center labor are incurred not only in interactions with customers, but also through the withdrawal from interactions with other previously held affective ties. This affective reorientation invites us to rethink the scope of what counts as affective labor beyond the immediacy of the worker/consumer encounter to consider the multiple sites in which affect is (re)directed through globalization.

To situate biopower within a neoliberal, postcolonial, or postpanoptic frame is to think the role of the sovereign beyond the work of the nation-state. Our analysis points to the importance of attending to the multiple and disparate sites in which power is exerted, orchestrated, and mobilized across time and space. Indian call center agents are temporally and spatially separated from the callers they serve. It falls on workers to make up time, overcome space, and restructure their affective and bodily inhabitance in order to meet the customer in real time and virtual space. Agents do so with tremendous dexterity: the caller situated in the West may ask the agent where she or he is, but will not likely ask when she or he is. To the extent that agents produce a seamless encounter with the American caller, they overcome distance through two related processes: the suppression of time and the mobilization of affective labor. When imperial power reaches out to those who are far, inviting them to extend the reach of the West, those subjects must undergo a radical host of transformations in order to answer the call. Agents undergo these shifts not only as a set of disciplinary structures, but also through the recalibration of a range of life events. They change their names and immerse themselves in American accents and culture; they perform within the "as if" of American experience to bridge distance and difference; they adjust their schedules to accommodate the rhythms of America; they withdraw their intimacies from those who are near and to (re)direct them toward those who are far.

Thus to theorize the experiential dimension of postpanoptic power relations is to attend to the ways in which the category of experience itself becomes destabilized. Experience becomes stretched to its limit and reconstituted by the sheer force of the time-space compression. On the other side of such compressions, experience appears as a vexed relationship to consciousness and agency. The newly mediated intimacies enabled by the telecommunication of call center labor compel workers to continually place themselves in relation to/with American customers and in turn to displace themselves from the immediacy of their embodied inhabitance. This labor of stretching oneself affectively, ideologically, relationally, and temporally enables agents to touch those who are, spatially and in terms of global power, out of reach. This labor is often elided by either homogenizing accounts of biopower or generalized theories of globalization.

Closely attending to the accounts of call center workers suggests that agents undergo a continual process of displacement. They communicatively display a fluency in a whole host of experiences they have never had, even as they forego much of the immediacy of their daily lives. Such displacements entail a radical corporeal and affective reorientation. As agents direct their affective labor toward America, they simultaneously lose touch with the intimacies of India. The interrelated moments that constitute what we have come to think of as experience thus become reconfigured through power temporalities. Shifting relations of affect and embodiment and the continual effort to project one's consciousness elsewhere remake agents' subjectivities. A slippage arises among experience, consciousness, and agency as these aspects of embodied being become stretched and are made strange to these global workers, who must, in ways both metaphorical and material, carry the freight of the time-space compression on their backs.

3 "I Interact with People from All Over the World"

The Politics of Virtual Citizenship

The most [satisfying part of my job] is the fact I get to interact with people from all over the world.

—PAVITRA, personal interview, I2U, 2004

It's a natural evolution. People in North America will, as a result of this [call center industry], move into doing more value-added kind of jobs.

—IQBAL, Infofloz, personal interview, 2004

Contemporary citizenship is caught somewhere between the national and the transnational. A host of forces have rewritten conventional notions of citizenship: the emergence of transnational economies, global flows, outsourcing, and the internationalization of human rights.[1] As free market systems become increasingly transnational, the sources through which individuals imagine themselves as part of a collectivity become dispersed, as do the resources through which they gain the benefits of citizenship. Such processes, in some cases, undermine the capacity of the nation-state to protect and provide for its citizens. Multinational corporations are mobilized not by traditional notions of national belonging but through the pursuit of ever-expanding profits and cost-saving modes of production. As a result, the elements that are traditionally associated with citizenship (rights, entitlements, a bounded geographical space) are often generated for citizen-subjects under neoliberalism not by nations, but by market forces.

Neoliberal market processes animate this shifting terrain across multiple, and often competing, notions of and claims to the benefits associated with citizenship. Nineteenth-century notions of citizenship were rooted in a sense of national belonging in which the nation is imagined as a bounded and unified territory; the surrender of the will of the individual to the sovereign nation-state is exchanged for the protection of the public good.[2] These ideals are increasingly unsettled by free market capitalism.[3] Contemporary citizenship is deterritorialized from national landmasses and reterritorialized within capitalism's uneven developmental processes.[4] No longer bound in any necessary relationship to national territory, citizenship is scattered across the globe, propelled by capital's relentless search for cheap labor markets and expanding consumer bases. Further, recalling our argument above, the "network geography" of late capitalism emphasizes the convergence between physical and virtual space to reconfigure territory and social relations (Abramson 2002, 198). As a result of these upheavals, neoliberal citizenship provides benefits to many of those formerly excluded from the privileges of global belonging. Yet neoliberal citizenship also rescinds entitlements from those who have formerly imagined themselves as normative subjects of national inclusion.

This increasingly unsettled negotiation over the territory and entitlements of (trans)national inclusion is not without its contestations. The terrain of neoliberal citizenship is fraught. It is animated, on one hand, by dreams of inclusion and belonging, especially for those previously marginalized subjects of what Chandra Mohanty would call the "Two-Thirds World" (2003, 228). On the other hand, those formerly privileged subjects of the "One-Third World," who fear they might find themselves pushed to the margins of global economic inclusion, lash back at new forms of inclusion that exceed and often compromise the traditional power of the nation-state. These contestations over the relationship between neoliberal and national modes of sovereignty often remain overlooked within contemporary theorizations of citizenship.[5] As with undifferentiated notions of the time-space compression, such theorizations often circulate through a universalizing set of assumptions. Such a frame offers little insight into the concrete, daily, and intimate sensibilities through which differently located global subjects experience and negotiate such contestations. Further, there is very little scholarship that provides a comparative analysis of competing and converging articulations of national and transnational citizenship.

This chapter deepens contemporary theorizations of citizenship by attending to the competing investments at stake in global and national notions of belonging. The previous chapter illustrated the ways in which call center industry workers evacuate markers of cultural identity (names, accents), locally driven rhythms, and relational ties to mobilize their labor, and indeed their subject positions, in the service of neoliberalism. This chapter contextualizes the ways in which such processes are mediated through contested sensibilities about national and global citizenship. The virtual intimacies generated by call center labor places Indian call center agents and American consumers in ongoing interpersonal exchanges. Such mediated encounters provide a rich site to examine a host of tensions that constitute the terrain of contemporary citizenship. As the opening excerpts suggest, the call center encounter serves as a condensed communicative site in which macro political, economic, social, and (trans)national antagonisms that constitute global and national belongings get played out. The call center exchange is a metonymic locale in which contestations over neoliberal, Indian, and (transnational) American forms of citizenship are formulated within the context of mundane, daily telecommunications.

These contestations arise as neoliberalism recasts the terms of citizenship unevenly vis-à-vis national inclusion. Consider the uneven rise and fall of India and the United States. While globalization dilutes the claims many U.S. citizen-subjects make on America, Indian national identity begins to "shine"[6] under free market practices.[7] Its national imaginary has shifted from a discourse of India as a third world and developing nation to one that envisions India as an emerging global superpower (Bhandare 2007; Bhagwati and Calomiris 2008). India's double-digit economic growth and its billion-plus consumers are mobilized to manifest this new vision. India has increasingly asserted its military presence on a global stage, downplaying such endeavors as merely serving national security purposes. For instance, India defied U.S. and international pressures in 1998 to conduct nuclear fusion tests.[8] India is also gaining visibility on the silver screen through the distribution of popular Hindu films or Western productions set in India, including *The Best Exotic Marigold Hotel* (2011), *Slumdog Millionaire* (2008), *Water* (2005), and *Monsoon Wedding* (2001). These multiple registers of global recognition have generated an emerging sense of national pride in India, especially among the rising middle class. Local and national newspapers proudly display the success of such films as *Slumdog Millionaire* as evidence of India's rising status on the global stage. These representations suggest that India imagines and values itself through its success at endeavors associated with the West and the Western recognition such successes create. In this sense, the formation of Indian national identity is undergoing a shift in the politics of recognition through which the nation imagines itself.[9] This outward-looking gaze in turn shapes how call center agents value their labor vis-à-vis the nation and the West. Just as India increasingly imagines itself through the gaze of the West, so too do agents make sense of their own subjectivities through the approval or rejection of their American callers.

Even as global tensions and (trans)national disparities unravel previous articulations of citizenship, new components come together. Tracking call center agents' experiences reveals new lines of affinity and antagonism generated under transnationalism, particularly between the United States and India. Neoliberalism places U.S. and Indian national projects in tense relation, both to one another and to globalization. Those on the receiving end of neoliberalism's realignments include Indian business owners, managers, and workers whose standing is improved by transnationalism and U.S. American business owners whose profits are increased by outsourcing: Outsourcing and call center labor ideologically and affectively align these disparately located groups. The rising Indian citizen-subject, however, presents a tremendous threat to the aspiring American whose labor value continues to decline in the global market. Even as transnational affinities are intensified in the post-9/11 context, in which geopolitical allies are mobilized to ensure global and national security, global antagonisms are also intensified as old U.S. American racisms get reanimated against a new brown invasion.[10] For the American citizen-subject, who perceives himself or herself at risk under globalization, the Indian call center agent represents a political, cultural, and economic threat.

As we argue above, the American dream becomes increasingly transnationalized through the exportation of American products, media, and jobs; through the global migration of people between here and there; and through the increasing telecommunications that mediate new intimacies among disparately located subjects.[11] This transnationalization of America means those who feel they might have a claim on its promise become increasingly diverse. If the American dream is no longer the exclusive prerogative of U.S. citizens, its imagined unifying vision and material practices begin to unravel. Indeed, as previous chapters suggest, the very notion of what and where America is and who Americans are may no longer be taken for granted as outsourcing generates a new terrain of citizenship, territory, and migration.[12]

These contestations and their attendant affective investments and resentments[13] animate the micro, interpersonal terrain in which the daily interactions between Indian call center agents and American callers unfold. For

Indian call center agents, the American dream of global leadership, visibility, and recognition comes within their grasp. As Pavitra puts it, "I get to interact with people from all over the world." For agents, managers, and CEOs, free market logics shape the imaginary of the call center industry as a natural evolution, which, they argue, should mitigate American resentment of job losses. Against the force of this logic, however, agents find themselves the brunt of a host of American resentments: "You people. You've taken our jobs!" Jaffer exclaims. Call center labor circulates through an unprecedented point of virtual contact in which the performance of Americanness is both a condition of agents' inclusion in the global market and a potential threat to American callers. Thus it provides both a crucial site of intercultural communication through which older forms of xenophobic racism and new transnational affinities get played out.

This chapter attends to some of the tensions and convergences through which contemporary global citizenship is negotiated within call center workers' accounts of their interactions with American customers. We find that as agents talk to faraway others, they gain a sense of global, national, and local empowerment. This emerging sense of neoliberal citizenship does not make them feel less Indian, but rather empowers them as dynamic Indian and global citizens. Agents map their sense of empowerment through tropes of Americanness, such as American business practices and codes of civility, providing agents with a tangible sense of actively participating in transnational America. Although agents often find this enculturation pleasurable, many of their American clients reject their Indian interlocutors, who demand to speak to an American. Such callers remain entrenched in traditional notions of Americanness as spatially bounded and ethnically pure against America's deterritorialization. Such callers mobilize their Americanness and their positionalities within capitalism as customers to wield power over what we call the virtual borders of America. Call center workers, in turn, mobilize their increased power as neoliberal subjects. Echoing CEOs such as Iqbal, they leverage the logics of capitalism to resist racism, recasting American racists as uneducated and as failing to cooperate with capitalism's inevitable progress.

"I CAN TALK TO ANYONE IN THE WORLD": GLOBAL CITIZENSHIP, INDIAN CITIZENSHIP

Contemporary Indian national identity circulates through a vexed relationship to its expansive population, simultaneously cast as the nation's greatest weakness and its greatest potential strength. After all, the story goes, one of the world's largest populations, if given the right circumstances, can be retooled as one of the world's largest consumer markets. India transformed in the post-1991 era from socialism to capitalism. The nation's capacity to reinscribe the contentious specter of its massive population is contingent upon its ability to transform its citizens into consumers, particularly its growing middle class, now one hundred million strong (Bhandare 2007; Kamdar 2007; Sharma 2009). Books like Edward Luce's *In Spite of the Gods: The Rise of Modern India* (2007), citing a national GDP in the double digits, note the competing and converging forces that go into India's miracle: the extremes of poverty and wealth that coexist in India; the clashes between tradition and modernity; the ways in which its particular colonial history and culturally mixed society create a sense of possibility as India emerges a technological leader in the modern world.[14] These writers cast India's future as "hers for the taking," referring to the fact that India is increasingly produced on the global stage as "the country to watch." As one of the world's largest emerging economies, India leverages its seemingly unending supply of English-speaking engineers and technology workers for national and transnational economic growth. For instance, many of India's leading companies (Wipro, Infosys, Tata Motors) have gone public and are traded on the Nasdaq and other U.S. stock exchanges.

The question at stake in India's miracle, then, is not how many Indians the nation houses, but what kind of Indians. This question signals both the pressures and possibilities through which contemporary Indian citizenship is galvanized: to step up to globalization's demands and lay claim to its entitlements. Under such pressures, Indian citizen-subjects are valued according to their capacity to participate in the global market; to be a global subject is to be a good Indian. Likewise, the call center agent is empowered to imagine himself or herself simultaneously as a national and global subject; agents gain traction as a viable Indian citizen-subject by virtue of their capacity to perform within the global communication channels availed by their labor. This paradoxical feeling of belonging, to nation via globalization, is an effect of agents' capacity to pick up the call:

It's easy to just pick up the call. You don't know this person, and the person is depending on you, asking you for help, and you are there. You can give it to them and that feeling is great and that is very nice and positive working at the call center. (Pavitra, I2U, personal interview, 2004)

For Pavitra, the world "easily" falls within her grasp as she is repeatedly hailed by faraway others over the course of her workday to "just pick up the call." She has repeated opportunities to establish her capacity to fulfill the needs of her callers; to have something to "give them" gives Pavitra a "great feeling." This feeling is structured through the sense of global utility her labor provides, producing an ongoing process in which she is repeatedly called by a distant consumer, then is successfully able to fulfill that caller's needs. This repetition produces her subject position through a global hailing that simultaneously extends beyond the nation-state, even as it constitutes her viability within it.[15]

Pavitra underscores the sense of empowerment she derives from her capacity to serve this globally distant other, who is drawn near through her labor ("the person is depending on you [. . .] and you are there"). This bridging is also captured in her continual use of the conjunction *and*, which frames her encounter with "people from all over the world" as a series of interrelated moments. She uses the universal subject, *you*, to describe her own subject position and that of a generic call center agent, who is empowered through the dynamism of the interaction and especially by her capacity to fulfill that other's need: the "person [who] is depending on you." Pavitra imagines and values her subject position through the mediated intimacy of the exchange: she gains a sense of power from her capacity to attend to the callers' needs and to meet the callers' demands. The thrill she derives from the interaction, then, is inspired both by the power derived from meeting her customers' needs and from doing so for a particular unknown audience. The global distance through which she constitutes the source of the call marks the globality of the call center agents' subject constitution. Pavitra's sense of self in relation to others is not constituted primarily in relation to nearby, Indian, others. Rather, she makes sense of herself in relation to distant, global others whom she has the power to bring close. The ongoing labor of repeatedly answering this global other's call generates a new component of Indian subject formation that is structured through the recognition of a distant other.

Even as the promise of American citizenship becomes diluted under transnationalism, certain kinds of Indian citizenship become fortified. The contemporary formation of Indian citizenship, especially for those subjects whose status is improved under neoliberalism, is enabled by globalization. The following excerpts suggest that call center agents experience an empowering sense of national belonging that is mediated through their daily communicative encounters with globally distant others. As agents' subjectivities are reshaped by their labor, a sense of global interconnectivity transforms their senses of themselves. Agents such as Avantika underscore the importance of such communication contacts in cultivating an empowered subject position. She explains how she gains a sense of power through speaking and feeling connected to faraway others. Responding to the question, "What has changed most for you since you began working in this industry?," Avantika replies without hesitation:

> Interaction. That you now will just be so bold in interacting. Now you've got used to go[ing] out and [you] don't fear. Wherever you go, you don't fear: you'd be bold and interactive. If we were not here, we would not have all those skills. Coming into this industry we have all those skills. (Avantika, 365-Call, focus group interview, 2006)

With her prompt reply, Avantika performs the "bold in interacting" subject position that she describes. In her account, Avantika frames her empowerment through the metaphors of travel, mobility, and covering distance: "going out" without "fear," "wherever you go, you don't fear." Call center labor locates her body somewhere particular ("If we were not here, we would not have all those skills")—a placement that in turn provides psychic and communicative modes of travel that enable Avantika to feel confident "wherever you go."

Avantika's comment underscores the critical role that global communication interactions generate in enabling her to feel a sense of global belonging. She acquires not only a new set of skills, but also a new relationship to others she encounters in her daily travels. The circuit of the empowerment she describes flows from the global interaction to those she encounters in local settings and then to a ubiquitous placelessness. That is, Avantika first becomes "bold in interacting" with global customers at work, then feels she can "go out and don't fear." She then maps this fearless sensibility onto both a generalized place ("wherever you go") and a universal subjectivity (here she shifts to the pronoun *you*). The movement in this passage suggests an expansive experience of subject formation—grounded in virtual communication processes—that allows Avantika to imagine her subject position as both local/Indian and global/universal. Or rather, her capacity to imagine herself as a global subject empowers her to feel more fully, or legitimately, like an Indian citizen-subject.

Roshan calls herself an introvert, but call center labor has "opened up" her "small world." She wears Western clothes: she is dressed in a neatly ironed blouse and a straight black skirt. She wears her hair neatly pulled back, revealing her determined expression. Her work places her in the global public sphere, allowing her to imagine and experience new friends and a sense of global belonging. She reiterates Avantika's sense that call center labor has helped her develop "more confidence." "I have changed a lot," she explains. "I'm a very shy person, no, reserved [pause]. I don't know. You could call me an introvert. I'm not an outgoing type of a person. I have changed. I have more confidence. More friends. [My] otherwise small world has now opened up" (BigBank, personal interview, 2004). As with Avantika's account, call center labor recasts Roshan's sense of self, both affectively and spatially. Her self-account moves from an interior subject (she describes herself as a "shy person" and an "introvert") to a relationally oriented subject (she has both "more confidence," and, it follows, "more friends"). She then casts this relational unfolding onto an expansive spatial register, concluding that her "small world has now opened up."

Avantika and Roshan's comments provide insights into the gendered aspects of call center labor. Patel argues that while women's participation in call center labor provides new forms of independence as they gain access to previously inaccessible night spaces, their mobility is also hampered by the need for a male escort to ensure physical safety and to ameliorate the perception that such women are "too bold." While Avantika and Roshan use the same language to describe their growth as call center workers, their sense of being bold has a positive valence: their labor has empowered them by making them "bold in interacting." Patel (2010) acknowledges that the gendered dynamics of call center labor are vexed. She notes that while "call center employment is associated with *modernization,* it also intersects with a woman's worth in ways that conflict with and degrade their bodily value in spaces deemed *traditional,* such as arranged marriage" (12). This tension seems to play out for Avantika and Roshan. On one hand, they describe how their capacity to speak with global others provides a sense of virtual mobility that emboldens them both in local spaces and interpersonal relations. Yet Avantika consistently complains, as we saw in the previous chapter, that call center labor undermines her relationship with her husband and family members. So while the global sense of mobility might give female agents an affirming sense of increased boldness, it also places them in a vexed relationship to tradition. For instance, Patel sees women's presence in the nightscape is the primary source of the disruption of tradition, while Avantika attributes such disruptions to working long hours. In either case, women's empowerment in the workplace is structured through the virtual migration that generates a sense of proximity between agents and callers that in turn emboldens them interpersonally within local settings. These dynamics also inform the gendered production of modernity that is central to the narrative of Indian national identity. In these passages we see that a host of global and local forces become condensed in call center labor that mimic, even as they produce, the broader dynamics of Indian national identity. As the nation gains confidence through its increasing recognition as a global player, so too do female agents become emboldened through the microcommunication practices of call center labor. This global recognition in turn empowers female agents to confidently interact wherever they are. Thus somewhere in particular gives way to everywhere, anywhere, and nowhere as female agents feel their worlds open up onto the expansive terrain of globality.

Virtual migration reconstitutes the intra- and interpersonal lives of agents, a transformation that is recognized by agents' superiors. The following excerpt, taken from a focus group interview at accounting agency, Premier Accounting, provides a sense of how managers and owners view call center agents vis-à-vis other Indians. Armaan, an American Indian living in India and working as a manager at Premier Accounting, initiates this turn in the conversation. Armaan notes the characteristics through which he identifies call center agents as a group:

> One is accent. Two is certain words that they use. And three, that they're very comfortable dealing with different nationalities, you know? They're not hesitant. Sometimes, very traditional people, they'll almost defer to you. These guys, they'll not necessarily defer to you, they'll treat you like colleagues, you know? (Armaan, Premier Accounting, focus group interview, 2005)

For Armaan, the call center agent emerges in distinction to "very traditional people," the difference marked by their communication practices associated with cosmopolitanism and travel. Agents not only communicate with different accents and words, but they also exude a certain confidence that defies more traditional interpersonal displays of "deference" to managers' higher position. Agents communicate with a sense of their own power, which levels their differential positionalities: "they'll treat you like colleagues." This leveling is significant given Armaan's American identity. It suggests that virtual migration gives agents a sense of being modern and global in ways that someone like Armaan would recognize.

Wynona, a white American manager, stands out in India with her full head of blonde hair, fair skin, and high heels, which add height to her already tall frame. She exudes a professional image, dressed in a beige pencil skirt and formal blouse. Unlike many of her Indian colleagues, Wynona speaks favorably of agents' Westernization. Wynona is in India because that's where the industry is happening—at least for now. The corporate bottom line and efficiencies are her highest priorities. She joins in the conversation in support of Armaan's comment, and a conversation with a call center chief operating officer, Laveena, follows:

> WYNONA: Yeah, they'll come and talk to me—like at a grocery store. They'll see that I'm struggling with something, and they'll have the confidence to come over and have a conversation with me.
> LAVEENA: You mean you don't scare them off? [laughter] (Premier Accounting, focus group interview, 2005)

The group laughter consolidates a cosmopolitan identity among the three conversants that is established through their collective relationship to agents, whose confidence the group finds appealing. Agents are positively evaluated according to their ability to communicate in ways that erase power differentials, as if such imbalances were easily transgressed and also foolishly upheld by traditional Indians. This latter group is distinguished by their fear of the power and difference associated with Wynona's white American femininity, whereas agents are praised for their capacity to bridge distance and difference to converse with Armaan and Wynona. Agents stand in for globality, established through their difference from traditional India, here cast as a provincial locale and traditional cultural site.

"You Speak Well": (Tele)Commu(nica)ting in Transnational America

The previous section explores the ways in which a global sense of belonging empowers Indian call center agents to feel more at home in global, local, and national contexts. This section considers the ways in which this very sense of globality is mediated through transnational America. Indian citizenship becomes permeated with and inseparable from transnational American citizenship as the American dream comes to saturate call center agents' sense of empowerment and belonging. Virtual migration becomes particularly associated with America as Americans stand in for the faraway global customer. Agents express a tremendous affinity for working with Americans. This desire is articulated through the global logics of neoliberalism and yet articulated to a nationalized imaginary of becoming American. This is not to suggest that agents imagine themselves as becoming American; becoming Americanized is perhaps a better way to put it. Agents express a tremendous desire for America, which comes to mean American business practices, codes of interpersonal civility, and virtual forms of assimilation. As agents immerse themselves in the dailiness of working with and for American customers, they pleasurably come to see themselves both as internalizing these American qualities and as being recognized by Americans as demonstrating such qualities. "America was so important to so many across the world," Inderpal Grewal (2005, 2) writes, "because its power enabled the American nation-state to disseminate the promise of democratic citizenship and belonging through consumer practices as well as disciplinary technologies." America becomes transnationalized in Indian call centers through ongoing, interactive communication processes. The industry generates possibilities for class mobility and consumerist sensibilities that also resonate with the American dream. The call center industry becomes a dense and interactive site in which Indian citizenship is mediated through both global and transnational American citizenship.

Contemporary citizenship processes are increasingly mediated by new transnational affinities. Agents' accounts display a host of "transnational connectivities"[16] that are experienced as simultaneously interpersonal, national, and transnational. America signifies a universal promise of neoliberal inclusion. Agents constitute themselves as aligned with these sensibilities to render their own subject positions intelligible—indeed, valuable—through neoliberal logics. Their communication interactions with Americans are imagined as the psychic and interpersonal ground for their own becoming as savvy, business-minded global/American(ized) subjects. Contemporary practices of citizenship get recast within call center labor—not primarily or only along (trans)national lines of affinity and belonging, but also along lines of converging economic and affective desires and needs.

This articulation is palpable among most call center agents, who offer glowing accounts of working with and for Americans. This affect provides a sense of how virtual migration shapes their subjectivities. In their accounts, Americanness and neoliberalism become sutured through agents' emerging sense of self as mediated through and responsive to American sensibilities. Call center account manager Sunita explains:

> The best part I like about my job is because I interact with Americans on a daily basis. The whole way they approach their business, the way they run their business, their expectations of people who work on their things— I like that. (Sunita, I2U, personal interview, 2004)

While the previous section argues that call center agents are empowered by their ability to "talk to anyone in the world," Sunita's response emphasizes the importance of talking to Americans in particular. She underscores "how they approach their business" as a particular site of American identification. Her remark illustrates the slippage between "talking to anyone" and talking to someone in particular. The iconic American, as a quintessential American "approach to business," stands in for globality. In this sense, America mediates the agent's relationship to the globe and, as we argue above, to the local and the national.

The affective experience of America is grounded in what agents perceive of as American business practices. Grewal underscores the fact that the transnationalization of America circulates through a host of consumer practices and desires. This dynamic certainly resonates with Indian call center agents' experiences, but they also find a sense of particularly Indian agency in the production practices associated with transnational America. Sunita continues:

> Well, I love working with American clients. I think I really love the whole business structure [pause]. I love the whole concept about, you know, actually working with someone who is twelve hours away, being able to bring a lot of that work over here to India to do things out of India. (Sunita, I2U, personal interview, 2004)

Sunita recasts power temporalities through a positive affect here. She finds the labor entailed in overcoming distance—of "working with someone twelve hours away"—to be one of the most fulfilling aspects of her job. We might understand this affective investment as one she gains from her capacity to overcome geographic distance as she virtually migrates to

America— or between India and America, as the passage also suggest a simultaneous investment in America and India, and the particular inter-face between the two that call center labor enables. Sunita situates her labor within larger transnational and nation-building projects in which "Ameri-can clients" and "business structure" are productively engaged in India. She underscores the national importance of call center labor industry's capacity to "bring a lot of that work over here to India."

The exchange with Americans that agents speak of is often grounded in a positive affect that makes America feel accessible, not hostile, to agents. Yet these encounters establish a clear power relation between agent and consumer, India and America. "I really find certain people of the U.S are very polite. Very, very polite and usually [they] don't easily lose their tem-per," Pavitra explains (I2U, personal interview, 2005). She underscores her encounter with "very, very polite" Americans who display control of neg-ative emotions, such as anger. Agent Tushar feels a sense of connection to his callers because doing this work allows him to imagine a global sense of belonging. When his customers tell him he speaks good English, he is pleased. Tushar describes the affirming affect that circulates in his exchanges with some American customers: "But at the same time, few customers are very pleased. When they ask you, 'Where are you from?' and you say, 'India,' they say, 'You're doing a great job. You speak very well.' They compliment" (365-Call, focus group interview, 2006). Although Pavitra and Tushar describe their interactions with Americans in positive terms, their excerpts situate their own subject positions as subordinate to the callers. For Tushar, the compliment the Americans offer of his speech unwittingly recenters English language and American accent as norma-tive. This privileging in turn places the agent in an always already inferior position of otherness and lack. The agent is infantilized in both of these accounts as agents derive pleasure from the callers' benevolent withhold-ing of anger and the recognition of their capacity to "speak very well"— that is, like an American. So the transnationalization of America in the vir-tual borderlands of call center labor generates a host of positive affects. But it does so by positioning agents in a subordinate relationship to American callers. This positionality (re)positions India as subordinate to America, thus containing some of the threatening dynamics the industry represents to American callers.

These efforts to maintain current geopolitical power relations might productively be understood within a larger context: economic shifts under contemporary globalization continually unsettle such relations. Placed in a global context, agents are charged with an untenable interpersonal task: to ameliorate American anxieties over the decline of the American dream, even as they secure personal and even national power by their own capacity to see themselves as participating in that dream. Now we turn our attention more fully to the ways in which agents negotiate the shifting terrain of (trans)national inclusion and exclusion.

"ARE YOU AN INDIAN?":
POLICING THE VIRTUAL BORDERS OF THE U.S. NATION

U.S. citizenship has historically been articulated through a vexed relationship to migration. American exceptionalism is built on an investment in individualism that presumes new immigrants, like other disenfranchised groups, should pick themselves up by their bootstraps. Thus rugged individualism is the basis of the national narrative of America as a nation of immigrants. Although it is true that the nation has been built through the undervalued labor of third world migrants, American identity is also formed through a desire for whiteness, a dynamic that positions the third world immigrant as both an object of desire and repulsion. This dynamic has shifted over the last two centuries in response to economic conditions and the mobilization of racialized, gendered, and heterosexed xenophobia. Although U.S. immigration was encouraged from 1864 to 1868, both the Chinese Exclusion Act (1882) and the Immigration Act (1924) mark a shift to a more bounded production of national identity. The *bracero* program replaced the Chinese Exclusion Act in 1943 to allow Mexican farm workers in to do seasonal, contracted labor. H-IB visas were granted from the 1990s through to the present to import temporary high-tech labor, often from India and China. America's relationship to Asia is organized through a similar set of contradictions, often animated by a push–pull relationship to maintaining territorial coherence while meeting shifting economic demands. "Historically and materially, Chinese, Japanese, Korean, Asian Indian and Filipino immigrants have played absolutely crucial roles in building and sustaining of America" and have served as a "simulacrum of inclusiveness," Lisa Lowe (1996, 5) writes. Yet "the project of imagining the nation as homogenous requires the orientalist construction of cultures and geographies from which Asian immigrants come as fundamentally 'foreign' origins antipathetic to the modern America society that 'discovers,' 'welcomes,' and 'domesticates' them" (5).

U.S. American citizenship in the 1980s and 1990s was constructed against the figure of the illegal alien, who challenged the purity of the nation's whiteness. The criminal alien was positioned as actively penetrating the U.S.–Mexico border, constructing the nation a passive victim to an aggressive external invasion. The figure of the migrant worker was constructed against the well-being of the nation. He was racialized, sexed, and nationalized in the 1990s through such metaphors as the penetration of the border, the criminal migrant who harmed good citizens, or the illegal alien who threatened to outbreed white Americans and drain the welfare state (Ono and Sloop 2002; Carrillo Rowe 2004; Shome 2006). Kent Ono and John Sloop (2002) note the particularly egregious example in the rhetoric of California's Proposition 187, which "shatters the cultural assumption that the United States is a 'post-racist' society, that mass, public racism cannot happen today, and that the United States is an open land of opportunity for all those who want to improve their family's lot" (3). Such measures and the discourses through which they circulate reinscribe a traditional sense of the line of demarcation between self and other as indelibly territorial: the U.S.–Mexico border.

The stakes of the nation's perseveration were indelibly altered in the wake of the events of September 11, 2001. At this historical juncture, a previous set of national anxieties were reanimated even as the terrain of the nation was unsettled by the 9/11 attacks on iconic U.S. national sites (the World Trade Towers, the Pentagon). The events of September 11 coalesced "a new identity category that groups together persons who appear 'Middle Eastern, Arab, or Muslim,'" Leti Volpp (in Puar 2007, 38) notes, "wherein members of this group are identified as terrorists and are dis-identified as citizens." In the wake of September 11, 2001, South Asian bodies, previously constituted through discourses of model minority status, were refigured as a potential threat to national security as South Asian and Middle Eastern racial and sexual codes were conflated.[17] The visibility of South Asian bodies were codified through racialized tropes such as dress (men wearing turbans, women wearing *salwar kameez*, or veils) to the non-whiteness of their skin. These codes of visibility were mobilized to produce an increased surveillance of foreign (potentially terrorist) bodies. The media and the U.S. government generated ambivalent rhetoric to reinforce suspicion (for example, Bush's security doctrine) and to produce tolerance (educating Americans on the differences among South Asian groups and the long-standing presence of these populations in the United States).[18]

Contemporary U.S. national identity is vexed by a host of global and national forces. The transnationalization of America, processes of virtual migration, and the threat of flexible citizens both within and beyond the geographic bounds of the U.S. nation generate a new set of concerns over how to define and control America's borders.[19] Outsourcing and offshore production in particular come under scrutiny as foreign bodies, even those safely contained in their own national territories, are framed as a new threat to the nation. Although outsourcing answers America's previous concern over criminal aliens penetrating its borders, it also extends the reach of Americanness to foreign places. This outward reach in turn Americanizes those places and the workers who engage in outsourced labor. As a result, America becomes paradoxically unbounded via an ever-expanding set of values, market practices, and communicative sensibilities, even as it increasingly invests in policing its boundaries, shoring up its territorial ranks, and often brutally excising those whom it excludes. America is simultaneously everywhere and somewhere in particular. At the interstices of this (extra)territorial tension, it becomes increasingly difficult to manage (im)migration, the boundaries of national inclusion, and the borders of the national territory.

The Indian call center industry is situated among these ambivalent interstices. On one hand, they generate a set of economic advantages for Americans: cost-effectiveness that increases profits for corporations, reduced prices on goods and services for consumers, relief from mundane forms of labor. Yet they are also part of a broader wave of outsourced labor and neoliberal mobilizations that increasingly threaten middle-class American jobs. Outsourcing intersects with a host of neoliberal structures that disadvantage the economic security of middle- and working-class U.S. citizens: the rollback of the welfare state, the pressure on the individual to gain status in the global market, the high costs of living and production in the United States and its attendant reverse brain drain,[20] labor arbitrage,[21] global recession, national debt, ballooning military spending. Free markets hold no necessary allegiance to U.S. citizens. Rather, neoliberalism's benefits and entitlements are unevenly distributed to and withdrawn from differently located workers. Transnational capitalism is animated not by national allegiance, but by economic imperatives. This global dynamic in turn gets played out in the interpersonal exchanges between agents and American callers. Consider Jaffer's account:

I spoke to a lady whose son was into a call center. When I asked for her son, she was like, "Are you an Indian?" I said, "Yeah." Then she started crying, "My son is unemployed just because of you. You people. You've taken our jobs!" Kind of puts you off for some time. But then again, you get back saying, "It's our job. What can we do?" (Jaffer, 365 Call, focus group interview, 2006)

The figure of the victimized American man[22] haunts Jaffer's account. It circulates as a vexed and highly activated figure of sympathy and hysteria, a trope for a wider set of American anxieties about what might be described as a "virtual invasion."[23] Outsourcing benefits American consumers through low-cost labor, and it presumably protects America's borders by maintaining its labor pool outside the geographical boundaries of the United States. Yet it still poses a tremendous threat to nation, here marked through the angst associated with labor arbitage.

The anxiety generated by these forces becomes distilled in the figure of the white male worker, who symbolizes America's promise that a college degree in science guarantee a "means to masculine economic and social success" (Ong 2006, 159). U.S. outsourcing of high-tech jobs undermines this promise. In Jaffer's encounter with the displaced worker's mother, antagonisms over (trans)national inclusion get played out in the virtual borderlands. While American anxieties that have historically been localized onto the spatial frontier of the geographical border continue, virtual migration expands and dislocates the reach of such antagonisms. Jaffer's caller mobilizes a traditional xenophobic rhetorics ("You people. You've taken our jobs!") to reclaim the national purity of America's virtual border. Although such callers may view the virtual borderlands as a site of national control, they are organized through free market systems. In the absence of state-sponsored monitoring, agents become vulnerable to American callers' vigilante attacks. Jaffer describes the "few calls where the customer would ask you, 'What's your nationality?' And when you say you're an Indian, then we've got responses like, you know, 'Even if you're the last person on this planet, I don't want to talk to you!'" (365 Call, focus group interview, 2006). The fact of Jaffer's Indianness is the basis of the rejection as the caller reasserts distance and difference by positioning Indianness of the agent beneath "the last person on this planet." Raja's account echoes Jaffer's: "Nowadays you get callers who just say, 'Indian? I don't want to speak to an Indian. Get out! Get me an American on my line.' I wonder how they

[Americans] would be able to serve you better?" (365 Call, focus group interview, 2006). American callers reject the agents through a nation-based form of racism, which, as in Raja's account, strives to (re)secure the border. The caller demands that Raja "get out!" and insists that the agent "get me an American on my line." The caller's rhetoric asserts a sense of ownership over the virtual territory ("my line"). The phone call becomes remapped as a bounded space that he or she seeks to police against the threat of an Indian invasion.

"Do You Come to Work on an Elephant?": Recalibrating Registers of Virtual Racism

As the previous section suggests, call center labor represents a contentious component of outsourcing and of contested inclusion and exclusion in global and national forms of belonging. These contestations might productively be situated within a broader historical context in which citizenship itself is becoming radically redefined. Transnationalism works through a host of new global alignments and antagonisms that exceed nation-based loyalty. In this context, free market and nation-state modes of citizenship tug at one another, positioning the call center exchange as a volatile site of (trans)national belonging. This resurgence of American supremacy is situated within a longer history of "remasculinzing the nation" (Jeffords and Rabinovitz 1994). The remasculinization of America emerged in the wake of the emasculating Vietnam war and gained spectacular visibility in the 1980s through the circulation of hard-bodied masculine figures such as President Ronald Regan, Rambo, and Arnold Schwarzenegger (Jeffords 1994).

This earlier remasculinzing impulse historically converged with, or perhaps set the stage for, contemporary neoliberalism[24]: the rollback of the welfare state and the denigration of the black female welfare recipient; the emergence of the white male victim and the dismantling of civil rights advances. These incipient neoliberal processes gained tremendous momentum under the Bush–Reagan regimes. In the case of call center labor, remasculinization is paradoxically bound up with the feminization of labor. On one hand, call center agents' pink-collar, service-oriented labor is situated within a larger trend of feminized global labor. But its association with the appropriation of American jobs, and by extension the American dream, masculinizes their labor vis-à-vis the emasculated American male breadwinner. The deterritorialization of the American dream "separates traits associated with middle-class American masculinity, while reterritorializing such features in skilled actors located elsewhere" (Ong 2006, 158).

The picture we sketch in this section attends to the resurgence of U.S. remasculinizing and nativist rhetorics in the context of virtual migration. Virtual migration amplifies a host of anxieties surrounding the declining American middle class under globalization. Such sentiments get mobilized as a new form of oral/aural racism within the particular site of Indian call center labor. U.S. racial formation has often been tied to embodied features associated with stereotyped racialization (see Omi and Wynat 1994). Alternatively, call center labor reconfigures "a regime of visuality to aurality where the racism occurs through a control of language, voice, and accent all carried out under the label of 'cultural neutralization'" (Shome 2006, 108). The phone call serves as a virtual contact zone in which vexed power relations get played out, providing a site where agents gain power through imagined participation in the American dream. Yet for some Americans, for whom the Indian call center agent symbolizes the decline of America and its promise, the phone call becomes a site in which to reassert the power of older gendered, racialized, and xenophobic rhetoric. Team leader Anila describes this dynamic as "the worst stress" of her work: "You would either get abused, or maybe you get scolded, and you can't do anything about it [. . .]. There are consumers who, if they know that you are not an American or not in the U.S., may become racist" (I2U personal interview, 2005). Anila's account underscores the extent to which the virtual borderlands become a pervasive site of racialization in which macro contestations over global and American inclusion and exclusion get played out within the micro context of the interpersonal exchange. This dynamic suggests that the complexities of the deterritorialization of citizenship are in turn animated by the resurgence of investments in reterritorialization of U.S. citizenship.

The American dream seems to be moving beyond the reach of many of its territorial citizens. Callers, such as those whose accounts we engage in this section, do not sit idly by. Rather, they violently grasp at older rhetorical forms in an effort to retain its promise. For these citizen-subjects in decline—as for the Indian call center workers who find this dream suddenly within their reach—America is on the line. Between such antagonisms, America is simultaneously constituted as a metaphor of promise and belonging, and as a site of bitter betrayal. This contestation gets played out in the mediated encounter of the phone call. For example, call center agent Sanjana shares a story in which "this consumer said, 'Are you from India?' [. . .] So I said, 'Yeah, I am an intern. I am here doing calls. I am talking from Bangalore.' She is like, 'I don't like to talk to Indians'" (I2U, personal interview, 2005). For Sanjana, working in the call center as an intern is an opportunity to participate in the global economy, and by extension in a particular form of the American dream. She sincerely sees herself as equal to anyone in the world and operates an assumption of a color-blind global society. Her face registers genuine shock as she describes the racism she encounters on some of her calls. Sanjana repeatedly questions us about American racism, confused by the contradiction of racial hierarchies: if Indians welcome Americans in India, why should Indians experience an "unwanting" there?

Alternatively, for the caller, the Indian agent represents a suspect whose presence must be detected ("Are you from India?") and rejected ("I don't like to talk to Indians"). The account reveals some of the nuances of the new racism that plays out in the virtual borderlands. The oral/aural quality of the encounter departs from the visuality that underscores traditional racism. Virtuality challenges the caller's ability to categorize the agent as Indian as the caller demands to know Sanjana's location. Sanjana offers a long explanation to the caller's yes-or-no question as she strives to downplay her power and subordinate herself to the caller. She explains that she is an intern who is merely "doing calls," a form of labor that agents presume to be unworthy of Americans. In spite of Sanjana's efforts, the caller rejects the agent because she is Indian. Her rejection iterates, even as it relies upon, a presumed normativity of territorial Americanness. This move reasserts a narrowing of the boundaries of the U.S. nation by excising Sanjana's foreign body from the proximity generated within virtual space.

As Sanjana continues her narrative, she maneuvers among a series of affective responses to the caller's racism: "That was very probably—for that one day I was feeling very bad because, I mean, what is the difference as long as you can help? So any more I don't think that you should be Indian or an American. It really doesn't matter. But then, you know, I guess there are that kind of people" (I2U, personal interview, 2005). Sanjana moves from the hurt she experiences at the caller's rejection to a power-evasive critique of the caller's marking of difference. Sanjana at last reverses the caller's racial exclusion by lumping him or her among "that kind of people." Sanjana uses the remainder of the interview to try to develop an account of the caller's subordination of her Indianness: she wants to square this experience with her idealized notions of America. By the end of Sanjana's long interview, she begins to turn the tables in the interview process, asserting her own set of inquiries:

> I want to ask you ask a question. Why is that when we Indians are prob- ably open, and the people out here would never fear an American, we would always welcome the other, not deny them. But why [pause] do you feel that kind of unwanting there? They never let Indians feel comfortable anymore. "Okay, you are an Indian. Please stay out!" You know? I've heard from—well, I don't know if this is really true, but I've heard from people that in the U.S., Indians are not like "inside." I think that is totally discour- aging when you say, "We are democratic. We are number one, but you stay where you are. You stay where you are!" (Sanjana, I2U, personal inter- view, 2005)

Sanjana here asserts her agency as a subject who seeks information and an explanation. She demands what Gloria Anzaldúa (1987) would call an accounting for the painful racist exclusion she experienced in her encoun- ter with the caller. Sanjana leverages her incisive reading of this encounter to lodge a damning critique of American exceptionalism against an ideal- ized sense of Indian inclusiveness. Her critique constructs an ambiguous relationship to geographical space. She moves between accounts of the virtual policing of America she encounters with the caller and the stories she's heard from Indians living in the United States: "But why . . . do you feel that kind of unwanting there?" is the question she poses directly at the close of the interview. The "there" in which this unwanting takes place is both "there" (within America's geographical boundaries) and "there" (within the virtual borderlands of the phone call). The thereness of Amer- ica thus doubles as Sanjana recognizes the reterritorialization of America through the network geography created by call center labor. For instance, Sanjana draws on transgeographical evidence as she makes sense of the caller's racism. She has heard that Indians living in the United States are outsiders (they are "not like 'inside'"); and she has experienced this un- wanting that so palpably permeates the "there" right there in India. Or, perhaps better said, this rejection occurs in the virtual borderlands in which she encounters America every day.

Sanjana inverts the power dynamics of the interview to get answers to her own questions about America. In the process, she incorporates her interviewer, Sheena, as a diasporic ally. Sanjana positions Sheena as more knowledgeable about American racism as a result of the interviewer's position as an Indian living in the United States. Sanjana positions herself as a new arrival of sorts as her awareness vacillates between innocence and a fall from the grace of the American dream. This theme resonates with transnational feminist accounts of the displacement and politicization that women experience upon arrival to the United States. M. Jacqui Alexander and Chandra Mohanty, in their introduction to *Feminist Genealogies, Colonial Legacies, Democratic Futures* (1997), write:

> We both moved to the United States of North America over fifteen years ago. None of the racial, religious, or class/caste fractures we had previously experienced could have prepared us for the painful racial terrain we encountered here. We were not born women of color, we learned the particular brand of U.S. North American racism and its constricted boundaries of race. (xiv)

The racialization to which Alexander and Mohanty are subjected upon arrival resonate with those Sanjana undergoes in her encounter with the American caller. Yet because her body remains bound within the Indian context, her location does not give her access to the identity of a woman of color that Alexander and Mohanty, and other U.S. women of color, have forged to resist American racism. Whereas Alexander and Mohanty become politicized as women of color through the radical writings and movements of U.S. women of color,[25] Sanjana does not have access to these communities, movements, or writings. Yet the palpable displacement she experiences, coupled with the rumors of U.S. racism she hears from Indians living abroad, generate an incipient woman-of-color consciousness. Sanjana reterritorializes a form of U.S. third world feminism as she redirects the terms of the interview to position Sheena as proxy for and ally within women of color feminism.

This exchange underscores how the racialization to which the caller subjects Sanjana fails to register within the Indian context. As opposed to the direct force of the caller's racism, racializing discourses in India often circulate in contradictory and implicit ways. Especially in the context of globalization, race represents an uncanny and often unnamed anxiety around recolonization. Thus race is foreign and imposed from the outside. Yet skin color politics pervade popular culture and advertising, even as othering discourses are explicitly attached to axes of caste, religion, region, and class. The politics of race in India are contested and elided. For instance, the Indian government refused to acknowledge the convergences between race and caste when the U.N. held its World Conference Against Racism, Racial Discrimination, Xenophobia, and Related Intolerance (WCAR) in 2001. Dalit activists protested the government's refusal.[26] Within such a context, race is both affirmed and disavowed, prompting Sanjana to incorporate her interviewer as a translator of racial difference. Her account circulates race as a meaningful, ambivalent, and imported category in India. Although caste, religion, and region might be recognizable categories of difference, race is a less familiar category of difference. Especially finding herself on the receiving end of racism, the exchange catches Sanjana unaware. Although race and caste might function in similar ways (both are processes of othering and exclusion), Sanjana's confusion over the American racialization to which callers subject her suggests that race and caste are incommensurate categories. Sanjana's confusion also suggests her virtual migration subverts the power relations through which she imagines her positionality. Agents may often be previously caste-privileged subjects who are then subordinated under the weight of an imported racial, imperial script.[27]

Like Sanjana, Ekaraj tries to make sense of American racism to which agents are subjected. Ekaraj recasts these virtual racializing processes from an oral/aural to a perhaps more recognizable visual register. Callers, he explains, are "typically looking at your accent in the way you speak." Even as Ekaraj explicitly locates agents' accents as the oral/aural source of callers' rejection, he also evokes a visual register: callers are "*looking* at your accent." As Ekaraj continues, a visual register continues to permeate his account: "Maybe it is just a white skin–black skin factor. Whether you really don't know it, they [Americans] consider us black skin." (I2U, personal interview, 2005). Ekaraj maps the orality of callers' racism onto the visual register of white and black bodies, reinscribing British subordination of Indian bodies as U.S. imperialism. Ekaraj evokes the category of blackness, which is a politicized Indian–U.K. identity, perhaps as a point of resistance to map virtual racism onto previous South Asian struggles. Yet like Sanjana, Ekaraj hedges in his reading of the interaction, seemingly uncertain about American racialization. Even so, his speculations adeptly mark the racialized negations through which whiteness is produced over and against the rejection of blackness. As he puts it, blackness is "not in part with which" whiteness/Americanness defines itself. Whereas U.S. race is constructed along black–white axis, in India, difference is organized along multiple sites of difference (Bharucha 2004). This distinction suggests that the pressures of India–U.S. migration—or in the case of the call center agent, virtual migration—are structured through shifting notions of difference. Indians in an Indian context do not necessarily see themselves as black (other) but as Indian (self). In his experience of virtual migration, Ekaraj recasts the terms of the virtual (from the oral/aural to the visual) and his own subjectivity from Indian self to American other.

Ganesh's account also maps the oral/aural rejection of Indianness onto a visual landscape of stereotyped Indian backwardness. He attributes callers' racism to "the level of ignorance there at times." Mocking their ignorance, Ganesh continues: "'Are you in India? Oh, do you come to work on an elephant? Okay, so tell me how is it? You have tigers roaming around?'" As with Ekaraj's incisive reading, which recasts the aural onto a visual register of American racism, Ganesh maps the callers' racist rejections onto the visual terrain of stereotypical tropes of India. Ganesh derides the "ignorant" caller through his own retort in which he paints India through images that echo the cartoon images featured in the *30 Days* "Outsourcing" episode we examine in chapter 1. As he speaks to the American caller, Ganesh reverses the direction of rejection as he subordinates the caller through a caste-based reference to a lack of education.[28] As Ganesh puts it, "It's an amazing amount of ignorance. It's not funny how ignorant some of the people in the U.S. are! Many of them now, probably, get to know that India is getting advanced. But some of the ignorance levels are high!" (TechNow, personal interview, 2007). Here Ganesh articulates resistance through national registers: "ignorant" Americans are those who don't realize how "advanced" "India is getting." National identity is assessed through a neoliberal calculation based on a global politics of recognition. As India "gets advanced," a sector of Americans remains "ignorant" to India's new global status. Their failure to recognize India's progress is also a failure to recognize the natural progress of neoliberalism; this failure is leveraged as evidence of their ignorance.

Echoing Ganesh's account, Lloyd describes a subset of Americans who send "abuse e-mails with all the foul epithets." These customers insist on "telling me I am brown. I like it, I don't have to go burn in the sun to get the tan. I had people getting very few e-mails like that." As with the excerpts above, Lloyd calibrates American racism through the visual politics of skin color and reclaims his brownness as a quality he "likes." "But looking at the language in the e-mail," Lloyd continues, "I think it's the uneducated lot. I haven't seen any good articulated person writing so far. It is typically people who can't put two words together properly in a sentence who would be doing that" (I2U, personal interview, 2005). Lloyd's account moves from an antiracist reclamation of brownness to a reassertion of his own superiority as he condemns his perpetrators as "uneducated." The movement of his story suggests that neoliberalism's emphasis on an individual's fitness for global inclusion becomes a more potent antidote to racism than brown pride. These two counternarratives, however, might coexist or mutually reinforce one another.

Ganesh's account provides a layered sense of the formation of responses such as Lloyd's. He explains:

> Because we have clear reference, we have people say, "You took our jobs away" and all that. We say, "That's a global company. That's something that we are not responsible for." Yes, so we just go with the standard line. We say, "We're a global company. We have offices in all parts of the world, including [the] U.S." (Ganesh, TechNow, personal interview, 2007)

While American callers respond negatively through a nationalistic register of possession ("You took our jobs away"), the company's "standard line" undercuts the national through the transnational ("we're a global company"). The response reappropriates and supersedes the legitimacy of the United States as a national territory ("We have offices in all parts of the world, including [the] U.S."). Accounts such as these suggest that neoliberalism's antagonisms are getting played out between the national and the transnational, between a territorial investment in the American dream and its neoliberal deterritorialization. As each of these excerpts suggests, agents cultivate critical reading practices through which to map American racism within its deterritorialized site of reception. They also deploy these critical reading practices as strategies of resistance. In the following section, we detail more fully the multiple strategies call center workers deploy to resist the racism that permeates Indian call center labor. This theme signals the global tensions at work in the call center exchange as micro and macro forces converge within the condensed site of virtual migration.

"We're a Global Company":
Strategies of Resistance and Incorporation

The strategies of resistance that workers mobilize are situated within the prevalent discourses and disciplinary practices through which the industry imagines itself. The Indian call center industry is steeped in logics of neoliberalism. The project heavily invests in capitalism's promise of upward mobility to interpellate call center workers at virtually every level of the industry. For instance, popular news coverage and scholarly research suggests that organizing Indian call center workers is very difficult. "Call centre agents' identity of being professional complicated the process of unionization," Premilla D'Cruz (2006) finds in her phenomenological study of fifty-nine call center agents. D'Cruz concludes that "the identity of 'being professional' among Indian call center agents not only posed serious challenges to unionising but also dictated the strategy and the course that initial union organizing took." Srabani Maitra and Jasjit Sangha (2005) report that call center agents' resistance to trade unions' efforts to organize its workers might be based in the gap between union issues, such as salary and job security, and the mobility of call center labor. "None of our interviewees in India had any knowledge about trade union activities in Indian call centers," they conclude, "nor were they very enthusiastic about the presence of trade unions at their work place" (42).

This lack of interest in traditional modes of engaging labor politics signals the extent to which call center labor is organized and imagined through the logic of neoliberalism. The industry is structured through a liberalizing free market system. It features "more employment flexibility, greater decentralization in bargaining structures (especially in public enterprises) and hence less government intervention in the bargaining process, fewer strikes, and a possible halt to the fragmentation of the union movement" (Bhattacherjee 1999, 27). This context suggests that older forms of politicizing labor fail to mobilize call center workers, even as a new host of disciplinary, discursive, sociocultural, and economic benefits do. In this chapter's final section, we consider the ways in which call center workers mobilize resistance to American racism from within the neoliberal terrain of call center cultural life. We build on the previous section's argument that agents resist and recast racist encounters by mobilizing an incipient antiracist countercritique. This section attends to the ways in which workers leverage their own privileged status over American callers through neoliberal calculations. Agents marshal neoliberalism against U.S. racism.

As we argue above, the power of the American dream interpellates a wide range of neoliberal subjects as America's territorial boundaries become increasingly diffused. Under late capitalism, transnational America's ideological, material, and affective reach supersedes its geographical terrain. The Indian call center industry is located within these expansive neoliberal processes. The thrust of this expansion becomes universalized and naturalized for call center workers through Darwinian narrative of upward mobility. This logic permeates the ideological formation and affective investments of Indian call center workers, especially among managers and owners. As CEO Iqbal observes, the call center industry is

a natural evolution. People in North America will, as a result of this, move into doing more value added kind of jobs. It's really the bottom-most kind of work that's coming to India and people in India are quite happy doing that right now, you know? (Iqbal, Infofloz, personal interview, 2004)

Iqbal's narrative echoes the logic of Ronald Reagan's catchphrase that "the rising tide lifts all boats,"[29] which assumes capitalism circulates as a "natural evolution" that benefits workers at different stages of development. He explains that "people in India are quite happy doing that right now," temporally locating the Indian worker behind the North American worker, who should "as a result of this, move into doing more value-added kinds of jobs." His discourse echoes that of the reality documentaries examined in chapter 1, which naturalize capitalism's capacity to circulate predictably, inevitably, in upwardly mobile cycles.

As a CEO, Iqbal's account provides an official industry story. The narrative resonates with broader global discourses of neoliberalism initially envisioned by Ronald Reagan and Margaret Thatcher in the 1980s. Following Marx, Stuart Hall (1996) provides an account for the ways in which such themes such as "'Freedom,' 'Equality,' 'Property' and 'Bentham' (that is, individualism)" become naturalized as standing in for the market's democratizing function under neoliberalism. Such ruling ideological principles of the bourgeois lexicon, he continues, "which in our time, have made a powerful and compelling return to the ideological stage under the auspices of Mrs. Thatcher and neoliberalism" inform "our own practical commonsense thinking about the market economy" (34). While categories seem to transparently capture the market's progressive operations, they "conceal" another set of relations: those "which do *not* appear

on the surface but are concealed in the 'hidden abode' of production"
(35). The hidden aspects of the market include the reproduction of labor,
the unevenness of its developmental apparatuses, the consolidation of
wealth at the expense of workers, and, particularly under globalization,
the unbalanced costs of labor and production that motivate multinational
corporations to outsource to developing countries.

These hidden aspects remain below the radar in Iqbal's account. Yet it
is this set of relations that becomes the most contentious force animating the exchanges between call center agents and American callers. From
the positionality of the call center managers and owners, this aspect is one
that must be disavowed in favor of the logic of capitalism's rising tides. As
operations manager Lloyd explains:

> I think the American public and probably the American polity need to tell
> the people that it is good for so-called third world countries to get this job.
> And it is good for them because they move further up the value chain. They
> should, ideally, move further up the value chain, because I think that is what
> has always driven any kind of valuation. I think that is very macroscopic.
> (Lloyd, I2U, personal interview, 2005)

Lloyd offers a macroscopic approach to outsourcing—one he wishes
Americans would take. His account presumes a mutual benefit of market
forces to "so-called third world countries" and to "the American public."
As Indians "get this [call center] job," Americans are in turn freed from
low-end jobs to "move further up the value chain." Lloyd wavers at this
moment. Although he asserts this progression of capitalism "has always
driven any kind of valuation," his iteration is peppered with uncertainty:
"I think," he says twice, and "ideally" Americans "should" gain better
employment.

Lloyd's equivocation marks the fissures in the neoliberal logic that animates call center workers relationships with Americans in decline. A close
reading of Iqbal's account also reveals such fissures: "Really, I mean, this is
a stage of evolution, you know?" he explains. Iqbal asserts the inevitability
of outsourcing as a "stage of evolution," even as he solicits the interviewer's
agreement. Providing evidence for capitalism's evolution, he offers:

> It's like how manufacturing jobs moved out of the U.S. to lower cost coun-
> tries [...] This is another thing [pause] another side effect of globalization

you've got to be prepared for. You can't fight it. You got to join in and make the most of it [pause] because eventually your competitors are going to do it. And they're going to provide a far better quality of service at a much lower cost to their customers [pause], which will result in you losing yours. (Iqbal, Infofloz, personal interview, 2004)

Iqbal's usually seamless word flow ruptures in this account. His speech is filled with pauses as he nonverbally struggles over the contradictions in his narrative, even as his argument of capitalism's inevitable evolution gains momentum. His commentary culminates in a universal *you,* which may be read as a veiled threat directed at those Americans and American companies who might seek to "fight" globalization's imperatives: it "will result in you losing yours," or read as a justification for Indian companies making "the most of it" because if they don't, "eventually [their] competitors are going to do it." The fissures within neoliberalism's simultaneous investments in individualism and democratization erupt within the subtext of Lloyd and Iqbal's commentary. These contradictions manifest as nonverbal expressions of uncertainty and antagonism.

Lloyd and Iqbal leverage a neoliberal logic to resist American racism. Within the logic of pure capital, American racism is senseless. Racist backlash is a form of false consciousness: Americans fail to see that Indian call center labor actually benefits them. Call center workers at various levels of the industry leverage power from within neoliberal ideology to combat American racism, but also to sidestep a more liberatory potential of decolonial or antiracist modes of resistance. This is not to suggest that this sense of antagonism permeates call center worker's imaginary or interactions with Americans, but it does signal a fissure within the deep investments in workers' America. The articulation between America and neoliberal inclusion is violated, for instance, in Iqbal's account by the American who refuses to act in concert with the inevitable tide of capitalism's most recent development. Such callers defy Iqbal's own investment in both America and neoliberalism—and the seamless articulation between the two. A struggling, underemployed, or poor American is virtually impossible to imagine.

Conclusion: Virtual Citizenship

This chapter interrogates the emerging forms of belonging and exclusion that get played out within Indian call center labor. Our readings of call center workers' stories suggest that while neoliberalism is certainly recast-ing the conditions of citizenship, the nation-state form is both resurgent and recalcitrant. The investment in the nation-state form and sites of national belonging are mobilized from both ends of the line animating the call center exchange. Indian call center agents recast their subjectivities through their newfound power as global players and as active partici-pants in transnational America. Yet they also retain a sense of localness and Indianness. Indeed, they mobilize their empowered global subjectivities to recast their own positionalities as emboldened speaking subjects within local and Indian contexts. From the other side of the call center exchange, some American callers praise agents for their capacity to assimilate to American codes of speech and civility, while others reject agents' presence in the virtual borderlands. In either case, subjects struggle to retain the coherence of the U.S. national form as America is posited in contradictory ways. America emerges as a site of multicultural and global inclusion capa-ble of absorbing distant others; alternatively, America is reasserted as a site of territorial exclusion that must be protected by vigilant callers.

The tensions between emergent neoliberal citizenship and more tradi-tional national forms get played out in a virtual borderlands. Inside this contested network/geography, the Indian call center workers' subjectivities are produced from within these very contradictions. Call center agents, especially women, encounter a new sense of empowerment as they partic-ipate in India's emerging status as a global player. They proudly participate in this national project as agents increasingly forge their subjectivities through the recognition of the faraway other. Thus the Indian national form converges with the virtual conditions of the call center agent's sub-ject formation. The needs of globalization converge with those of the Indian nation-state: agents contribute to India's nation-building project through their successful communication with global others. Neoliberal citizenship is often posed in contradistinction to the nation-state form or to evidence its decline (Appadurai [1996] 2002). Yet for call center work-ers the two processes actually prop each other up. Agents' neoliberal inclu-sion within an increasingly global circuit of exchange converges with their capacity to participate in transnational America.

These convergences, however, generate a sense of national decline for those citizens invested in previous (territory-based) forms of the U.S. nation-state. Agents present accounts of such callers as seeking to banish Indian workers from the virtual borderlands of the call center exchange. In moments such as these, the borders of the U.S. nation-state are mobilized within a virtual contact zone as if those lines were territorial. American callers play out anxieties over territorial invasion and national decline, even though the territory of the call is a virtual one. This affective force suggests the extent to which network geographies recast the social, cultural, political, and national terrain of identity formation. It also suggests that call center workers and the American callers experience neoliberal and nation-state modes of citizenship in divergent ways. These competing relationships to neoliberal and national citizenship signal the complex and hybrid positionalities that global subjects take up within this historical moment. They further suggest that our current understandings of neoliberalism, so often animated through rhetorics of national decline, unwittingly privilege U.S. or Western standpoints. The insurgence of neoliberal citizenship might signal the hallowing out of the nation-state form for those scholars and citizen-subjects located within the U.S. academy. Yet neoliberal inclusions seem to fortify both the Indian nation-state and the call center workers' capacity to imagine herself as contributing to it. These affective investments of callers and agents point to the social force of virtual migration to recalibrate notions of citizenship. The fact of this movement's virtuality should not be seen as undermining its capacity to recast the terrain of global, local, and national modes of belonging. Rather, they underscore the extent to which the virtual and the affects enabled by new communication technologies generate new contexts in which the politics of citizenship get played out.

Diverging U.S. and Indian positionalities constituted through neoliberal citizenship suggest that virtual migration generates new global antagonisms. These contested notions of belonging get played out within the virtual borderlands of call center labor. The production of these borderlands signals the extent to which the boundaries of America occupy a complex relationship to territoriality. The virtual borderlands emerge at the nexus of a host of contradictions that animate U.S. national identity production under neoliberalism. Neoliberalism fortifies an integrated and privileged U.S. national project. Outsourcing provides American consumers with lower costs on goods and services enabled by cheap labor, resources, and production expenses—and it does so while keeping foreign, particularly South Asian, bodies outside of its territorial borders. Yet the processes that enable this aspect of U.S. economic growth, such as outsourcing, body shopping, and virtual migration, also relocate increasingly desirable jobs outside of the United States and often in India. Perhaps these processes of exchange, in which the Indian worker services the needs of the American consumer, have worked too well. Particularly in the post-9/11 historical context, the South Asian body emerges as a double threat. It is forged within the nexus of the terrorist body on the one hand, and its value within the global exchange of labor on the other.

Although this body remains physically distant from the American caller, the mediated intimacies that animate the call center exchange generate a sense of proximity. As we argue in the previous chapter, agents are charged with the task of overcoming geographical and temporal distance by producing a sense of affective proximity between themselves and their callers. Here we discover that their capacity to do so in turn generates a host of anxieties for American callers. The virtual borderlands are marked by their territorial ambiguity. Agents and callers alike seem to constitute this space through tropes of Americanness. Agents leverage their disciplined codes of speech, civility, and business savvy to assert their belonging and to counter callers' xenophobic border policing. Thus the telephonic space of the call center exchange emerges as a virtual American borderlands through the communication practices that give that space meaning. These communication practices are contested sites in which the politics of citizenship are negotiated.

Within this virtual border space, the category of race gets played out in ways that are unprecedented, even as they recirculate older iterations of U.S. and British imperial racial formations. The coding of the racialized body within the call center exchange occurs within an oral/aural register (Shome 2006), even as call center workers recast these racializing processes within a visual register. The stereotyped visual tropes that call center workers evoke in their accounts of American racism suggest an incipient, if virtual, immersion into U.S. racial formation. Agents depict such encounters through an abject visual alterity. They deploy tropes such as blackness and exotic landscapes to account for the ways they find themselves affixed by the white U.S. gaze, even though the call center exchange is oral and aural. This rearticulation underscores the social force of virtual migration. Transnational feminists living in the United States find themselves immersed in racializing processes upon arrival, whereas call center agents are racialized within a virtual borderlands, even as their bodies remain bound within the homeland. Theirs is a virtual racialization. It suggests that while call center workers remain in India, their subjectivities are formed through a hybrid convergence of Indian, American, and global forces of inclusion and exclusion.

From this hybrid location, agents mobilize various forms of resistance. They often assert resistive power from a privileged vantage, marking their insider status within logics of neoliberal inclusion. American callers seek to subject agents to nation-based forms of exclusion. Yet agents resist this exclusion by asserting their inclusion within neoliberal citizenship over and against American's outdated sense of national citizenship. The terms of this antagonism—both American's efforts to put Indians in their place through national exclusion and agents' assertion of neoliberal privilege—provide a sense of the complex contours of contemporary citizenship. They point to the competing and converging forces constitutive of global, local, and national forms of belonging: privilege and access, rights and entitlements, and the power to circumscribe the terms of inclusion and exclusion through which self and other are negotiated.

4 "I'm Going to Sing It the Way Eminem Sings It"

India's Network Geography

If you like the music you listen to it. You listen to try to understand what they are trying to say. If you like the music you listen to it. If you like it you'll repeat it. When you repeat it you get the hang of it. I mean, I love Eminem, I love all the songs. So when I sing it, and I sing an Eminem song, I'm going to sing it the way Eminem sings it. I wouldn't sing it the way an Indian sings it. There's a lot of cultural exchange that happens.

—KAPIL, BIGBANK, personal interview, 2004

This chapter explores how network geographies reterritorialize the material spaces and practices of call center agents. Virtual migration animates agents' subjectivities beyond the telecommunication spaces of their work lives. They live out these transnationalized subject positions in their daily lives as well. As we argue in previous chapters, their labor reconstitutes class boundaries, spatial, and temporal relations. It generates new conditions of possibility for call center agents to virtually migrate across class, national, and temporal boundaries. But this virtual production is also coconstitutive of a host of material and affective adjustments, shifts, and anxieties. As agent Kapil asserts, "So when I sing it, and I sing an Eminem song, I'm going to sing it the way Eminen sings it. I wouldn't sing it the way an Indian sings it" (Kapil, BigBank, personal interview, January 22, 2004). Kapil is a recent college graduate who feels comfortable with the ways call center life has Westernized him. He likes to work out, and he dresses his fit body in casual Western attire: blue jeans, a T-shirt, and sneakers. Kapil identifies with the West. He favors rap music and blockbuster films. We can glimpse Kapil's self-presentation in his account: he demarcates his performance of American icon, Eminem, as distinct from "the way an Indian sings it."

135

In such moments as the one narrated by Kapil, the Americanization produced through call center labor is not easily contained within the virtual confines of call center spaces. Agents' performances of Americanness reach beyond the particular bounds of the phone call. Such identity performances are often seen as excessive, even as they bind agents to one another through the emergence of a shared sense of belonging, time, and culture. The Americanization of call center agents generates ruptures that mark out new modes in the production of identity and difference, belonging and nonbelonging. The edges of Indian national identity become frayed. Agents perform a highly contested rupture in which India is produced through an anxious temporality: social actors must continually mobilize a series of disciplinary technologies to suture its present to its past and to its future.

Such identity performances—and the Americanization of India they represent—are highly contested, not only between management and agents, but also among agents. Lloyd, a call center operations manager, projects his uneasiness around the cultural shifts entailed by call center life onto others. He scarcely veils his disdain for the "patently false" American accents that inflect the speech of his workers. "But they think it's American," he muses, and what's worse is the public display of agents performing this false accent "outside," on the "streets of Bangalore." "Don't leave reality," he offers as a warning. It's the question of morality that concerns Ganesh, a TechNow manager: the ear piercings; how the agents say, "Hey, dude"; the internalization of a hip-hop sex and drug culture. Similar is H.R. coordinator Harish's concern that young couples are "actually living together," earning more money than their fathers did at retirement. He worries about the future of Indian culture and society where none of the traditional rules seem to apply. Agents' class mobility converges uneasily with their uncanny Americanization.

Sunita has been watching American television since she was young. Hearing and seeing American life on the screen is a persistent feature of her life, but she always recognized that "it's just TV." Since she's been working in the call center, something has changed. She finds herself "constantly interacting" with Americans; she learns to "think" like them. Not only does this persistent verbal interaction with Americans remake her, but so too does the "economic freedom" that allows her to "implement whatever it is" she is internalizing through these encounters. The money she earns allows her to buy into the lifestyle she has only formerly viewed as a spectator. Now she herself enters the action of a scripted American lifestyle, whether it is through a performance of an American sense of professionalism or a consuming lifestyle. These bodily markers and cultural practices differentiate agents' performance of identity from those of their parents' generation. They also signify a precarious temporal rupture of rapid development that threatens to sever India's future from its past. We call this acceleration—a function of virtual migration spilling out into material relations—network temporality. Building on Abramson's (2002) notion of network geography, which underscores the layer of networked spaces atop physical places, network temporality attends to the layering of different and disparate temporal registers. Because virtual migration reconsitutes both space and time, this chapter attends to these temporal shifts.

The narratives of call center agents provide a compelling point of entry into theorizing the discursive and material formation of these new boundaries. Their stories are constituted within the cultural imaginaries through which call center agents make sense of their rapidly changing subjectivities. It has been convincingly argued that Indian cultural life is undergoing a tremendous economic shift after liberalization.[1] Such shifts are not easily contained within previous imaginaries of Indian national identity. Agents' class mobility, for instance, reverberates with previous forms of Indian upward mobility—with a twist. As we argue above, call center agents' class mobility is structured through global and local, national and transnational, senses of belonging. Thus their mobility also resonates with those living in the Indian diaspora; agents experience a sense of nostalgia, longing, loss, and displacement. However, the virtual quality of their migration does not entirely map onto either formation. Agents are upwardly mobile, like those of India's rising middle class; agents are Americanized, like those living in or returning from the Indian–U.S. diaspora. This pseudohybridity,[2] or virtual in-between-ness, becomes the source of tremendous anxiety over what the formation of call center subjectivities means for India's future.

Our previous chapters attend to the shifting terrain of class and of national and transnational identities in India. These transformations are reterritorializing more than India's physical geographies.[3] Rather, the terrain that is being reterritorialized is simultaneously material and virtual, in ways that Abramson's (2002) concept of network geographies describe. India is increasingly interpenetrated by Western zones carved out of its landscapes—a checkered geography. Likewise, call center agents are continually immersed in the virtual borderlands between India and America.

We cannot account for these extensive shifts through one-dimensional explorations of social space. Rather, network geographies are layered, creating a dynamic interplay between virtual and physical spaces. These emerging relations of space, time, and virtuality generate a more radical reconfiguring of space than we have seen in previous explorations of critical geography. Network geography, in turn, animates contemporary notions of Indianness that reconfigure conditions of class mobility and migration. Fernandes's (2006) important study of India's rising middle class explores the reconfiguration of geographic landscapes, such as gated communities, shopping malls, and theaters.[4] These spatial transformations are also interanimated by those virtual reconfigurations we've tracked above as virtual migration converges with agents' class mobility to create new conditions for middle-class formations.

In this chapter, we attend to the ways virtual migration spills over into the material spaces of India. We argue that virtual migration reterritorializes and retemporalizes the material conditions of agents' lived experiences. Virtual migration generates India's network geography. The inverted temporalities through which call center labor is structured also generate network temporalities. The first section marks moments in agents' accounts that demarcate the possible futures associated with the call center industry from the past associated with Indian tradition. Next we consider the temporality of credit, which yokes agents to consumer-endebted futures. This temporality of credit departs from more traditional Indian modes of consumption: those based in real time. Finally we consider the stakes in the new affective relations that call center labor generates and the threatening futures they pose.

"We're Being Bangalored!": A Time of Diaspora

The narratives of agents, managers, and CEOs tell a story of the loss of Indian culture, which is magnified in the call centers by agents' Americanized performance of identity. These accounts resonate with popular discourses that bemoan the Westernization of Indian culture that circulate in the press, in political debates, and on talk shows. For example, the Bharatiya Janata Party (BJP), one of the India's major political parties, gained popularity and majority control in Parliament in the late 1990s, running on a platform that valorized Hindu rule and that often conflated Westernization and colonization, or that blamed Westernization for a loss of Indian culture. Perhaps more worrisome to call center workers is the extent

to which agents internalize, and in turn come to embody, American culture. Although agents often register this concern, they never express such
worries about their own loss of culture or identity; it is always some other
agent who is at risk of losing touch with India. Their accounts underscore
the rapid acceleration and modernization of Indian culture, encapsulated
in call center culture. Many fear that call center culture is developing so
quickly that it will cause workers to lose touch with Indian tradition.
Others express nostalgia for Indian traditions and a sense of cultural purity
untainted by the speed of call center labor and consumerism of American
culture. Several accounts express a fear that Indian tradition will be lost
to a future that is embodied in the youth of the call center agent. In such
accounts, the agent becomes a placeholder for a temporal rupture that
threatens to render Indian futurity unintelligible from its traditional pasts.
Agents, the story goes, are going too far and losing touch with India. As
Harish exclaims, they "actually are living together!" Call center agents are
out of sync with other Indians: they are out of time (working the night
shift) and virtually, but not really, modernized, Westernized, and Americanized. Harish's anxieties signal a broader fear of a future in which children of call center agents have no anchor in India's past.[5]

Part of the problem is that the cultural performance of Americanized
identities is not contained to call centers and night shifts. These performances leak outside the boundaries of the call center to permeate all aspects
of agents' hybridized identities. In such daily contexts, agents are marked
as a distinct subculture: they are a "club"; they are "immediately recognizable." Call center CEOs and managers describe call center agents as "easily
distinguishable" from the rest of the Indian population, noting agents'
Western accents, their interpersonal openness, and the air of "confidence"
they exude. Such accounts, shared by members of the Indian diaspora,
speak to the blurring of the boundaries between the diaspora and the
Americanization of agents at home—between migration and virtual migration. Agents' virtual migration not only reconfigures their interior landscapes, but also permeates their communication practices and consumer
habits in ways that mark them as culturally distinct from other Indians. It
is their Americanization that demarcates them. As Kapil underscores, he
would "sing it like Eminem" and "not like an Indian."

The category of diaspora foregrounds the cultural transformations generated by the movement of populations across national territories. The
concept serves as a useful frame to examine the new Indian identities

emerging in the call center industry. However, the notion of a diaspora often presumes a point of arrival geographically distinct from the subjects' point of departure. For agents, some kind of diasporic movement—a virtual migration, one lacking a point of arrival—animates cultural sensibilities, anxieties, and hybridities. Their identities are not remade by a physical global migration, but they are forged through the formation of what Brian Keith Axel describes as a "diasporic imaginary"[6] that narratively produces the Indian homeland as a pure site of nostalgia and longing. So if call center agents virtually migrate, what kind of diaspora might they form? What might their virtual migration mean for how we conceptualize a diaspora?

One theme that marks the discourse of call center employees, particularly managers and CEOs, is that the call center agent internalizes and performs an Americanized identity. A conversation we held with a group of BPO executives turned to the controversial figure of the call center agent, whom they described as follows:

ARMAAN: It's interesting, but I meet people in my interviewing or I meet them outside. I can tell who's from a call center. I can tell by speaking to them—
HARISH:—looking at them—
ARMAAN:—immediately. You are working or have worked at a call center. You have accent training, you have this. It's almost a definitive group now. Right? They're all kind of clubbed. The call center club thing going on. [laughter]. (Armaan and Harish, Premier Accounting, focus group interview, 2005)

Armaan "can tell by speaking to them," while Harish recognizes the call center agent just by "looking at them." These executives insist that their ability to recognize agents is "immediate" and that the "group" they form is "definitive," a "club." The formation of a "call center club thing" marks the cultural shifts of virtual migration, which spill beyond the walls of the call center, to animate agents' embodied identity performance. These accounts also underscore the anxiety the managerial class experiences at the sight or sound of the call center agent. Managers' insistence on their "immediate" recognition of agents signals their investment in not being fooled by agents' inauthentic performances of American culture.

Call center agents gain intelligibility as a distinct group through certain cultural codes that are identified by outsiders. These meanings are constructed in the moment of sense making by demarcating distinction. They define the parameters for determining who is and who is not Indian. As the conversation continues, Armaan identifies himself as a second-generation Indian living in the United States. He personalizes the contestations over what it means to be Indian, admitting that his own "confusion" is similar to that of the call center agent:

> I'm an Indian who's never been to India before. I came for the first time last year. I grew up in New York and, many people would say, I'm an "American Born Confused Desi." You know, jokingly, I was never confused about being an Indian until I came to India. Now that I've come, now I'm confused! (Armaan, Premier Accounting, focus group interview, 2005)

Armaan draws a comparison between the "confusion" he experiences as an "American Born Confused Desi" (ABCD)[7] and the "confusion" of call center agent. An ABCD is a well-known descriptor of second-generation Indians born abroad, who are marked through their cultural impurity and confusion. This defining sense of confusion defines both groups, blurring the distinction between real and virtual migrants. Armaan explains that before his trip to India, he could easily distinguish between Indians and Americans: "people belonged to certain pockets" and he was able to categorize them "very easily." His encounter with call center agents has destabilized his capacity to categorize people.

Faced with this blurring of boundaries, Armaan and the Indian CEOs and managers seek to distinguish their group from the "call center club." Agents are often depicted as "confused," but they also create "confusion" in others. In spite of (or because of) the similarity Armaan sees between his own ABCD identity and agents' hybrid identities, agents emerge as other in the conversation. They identify call center agents as members of a "club," for instance, which doesn't recognize the group as a legitimate subculture or cultural group. This club identity is distinct from the real diasporic and cosmopolitan group that has actually lived in the United States. Agents are recognized as somehow neither traditionally Indian nor fully diasporic. This account recalls Raveena's account that agents are not "really" cultural hybrids but are "pseudohybridized." This formation naturalizes India as the unspoken subtext against which the call center club is figured as a new and different—and indeed unsettling—social formation.

Virtual migration invites us to rethink the boundaries of the category of diaspora. As Appadurai ([1996] 2000) observes, "Many people find themselves exiles without really having moved very far" (171). His insight suggests that although cultural workers tend to imagine processes of exile, global movement, and migration as occurring across national boundaries, we might also consider how such processes occur within the nation-state. Call center agents are subjects who migrate across increasingly checkered first world and third world spaces, even as they virtually migrate through time. These new forms of migration unsettle the temporal, spatial, and (trans)national categories traditional notions of diaspora assume. These categories are themselves effects of a broader rhetorical production in which different social subjects and fields of inquiry invest. Agents denaturalize formations of time, space, and nation that are often taken for granted in cultural studies and feminist knowledge production. Virtual migration then denaturalizes the categories culture workers deploy to understand and intervene in global power relations.[8] For instance, as Axel (2001) argues, most accounts of diaspora within the field of diaspora studies "conceptualize the homeland as a place or origin and site of departure that constitutes a certain people as a diaspora" (425–26). Yet the notion that a diaspora is "community of people who live outside their county of origin" assumes clear distinctions between here and there, the now and then—all of which are unsettled by virtual migration. Returning to Armaan's account that agents are a "clearly identifiable group" that is marked through certain "diasporic" qualities, we might consider the ways in which this diaspora is formed virtually. Virtual migration is not a physical departure from a homeland; nor is it marked by an arrival to a country outside the country of origin. Rather, it is the movement through network geography and temporality.

Agents experience their lives as the movement through network geography. As Raja puts it, "America exists in India" and "India is getting into America." As agents virtually migrate, they also gain access to modernized, Americanized, and first world zones. These mobilities produce a sense of spatial and temporal convergence between India and America. Raja explains:

We have the U.S. getting into India. Considering the kind of life they live there, and the kind of life we have here [pause]. Bangalore is getting in the U.S., I should say. Isn't it? We're talking about being Bangalored! So in that way, the U.S. is right here. Other than definitely Las Vegas and Niagara Falls, I think you get everything that you want, what you want. Maybe the infrastructure, it's a little behind. But it's not too far until we get there. (Raja, 365-Call, personal interview, 2006)

The boundaries between the United States and India are simulteneoulsy blurred and reified in Raja's account. Extending the telos-driven narrative like those featured in the reality programming explored in chapter 1, Raja's account positions America as India's future and, in turn, India as America's future. For instance, he states not only that America is in India, but also that Bangalore is "getting into America." This interpenetration signals a present and gestures toward a future in which the spatial boundaries between national zones recede. National identity is imagined through the cultivation of a certain lifestyle ("the kind of life they live there, and the kind of life we have here"). Bangalore is framed as a verb in Raja's account, giving the global, high-tech city an agentic force that compels the reconstitution of the social subjects it forms ("We're talking about being Bangalored!"). He refers to a collectivity (the "we" of "we're talking") to underscore a shared process of subjectification (not just his own personal experience). This sense of a collective identity gains coherence within an imagined community of call center agents as future-oriented, transnational subjects. The reference, "being Bangalored," emerged during World War II as Bangalore was developed as a powerful weapon-producing British army town. Raja draws on contemporary outsourcing rhetoric[9] to rearticualte the phrase to account for contemporary cultural politics. Being Banglalored marks a historical shift from the ambivalence of military occupation to the negotiation of neoliberal economic relations. To be Banglored in the current historical moment invokes the movement of jobs to Bangalore through an imagery that replays its previous military trace. This trace maintains the force, vitality, and potential of empire, even as the two-way movement of cultural influence in his account envisions a leveling of power.

So on one hand, Raja defines India's difference from the United States through temporal and spatial markers: Las Vegas and Niagra Falls remain spatially removed, while India's infrasturture is a "little behind" that of America. On the other hand, he asserts India's agency through the nation's compression and acceleration of time ("But it's not too far until we get there"). In popular discourse, America is positioned as the telos toward which India is moving. Yet this "toward" is complicated by Raja's nationalistic ambivalence, which distinguishes an "away" from America that is vital to the formation of an Indian imaginary. As Raja continues, he specifies some of the markers of India's time-space movement:

> It is so true. We are definitely getting Westernized. There is a lot of things that prove that, right? Again, the brands. There used to be times when, if I meet my good friends, I would talk in the regional language. Now I won't. I don't know. It's not because I am consciously doing it. It is just happening. If you do not know English these days, you are not anything. Of course, it is just catching up. I am definitely not saying that our own culture is going off. That will still remain, no matter what I do. If I become a parent tomorrow, I would still want certain values, certain things to be the way I have learned from my parents. Definitely getting Westernized, but not to a bad extent. (Raja, 365-Call, personal interview, 2006)

Raja frames Westernized India through a crosscut temporality. India's Westernization encounters its limit as Raja envisions himself as a parent, which grounds his identity within a more traditional Indian nation-building future.[10] Raja imagines he would instill "certain values" in his child that he has "learned from his parents." In spite of his insistence on India's rapid and intimate Westernization, Raja's narrative retains a sense of temporal continuity. Gestures such as these signal the rhetorical and psychic work he exerts to suture India's future to its past.

The Americanized identities and space-time migrations of call center agents represent an unsettling temporal rupture between India's past and its potential futures. Just as the labor of overcoming space-time compressions fall on the backs of call center agents, so too does the labor of suturing India's past and future. For instance, Raja asserts his agency to bridge these disparate temporalities when he asserts he will carry on tradition and extend his parents' values to his children. On the other side of tradition is the compelling force of keeping up with the demands of globalization. Raja goes so far as to suggest that the mastery of Americanized English is necessary to becoming a modern subject, without which one risks annihilation: "If you do not know English these days, you are not anything." He frames this imperative through a developmentalist frame: "Of course, it is just catching up." India emerges as temporally behind the unacknowledged referent of America. The nation's uneven development is marked through India's temporal lag as the nation must "catch up" to America's "infrastructure," "brands," and mastery of (American) "English." The passage marks the conditions of subjectification through which Raja imagines himself to emerge as a viable (modern) subject. For Raja, the Indian subject must be both fluent in America's linguistic and consumer forms through which he imagines India's increasingly Westernized future. Yet India's past, marked through Raja's reference to his parents, is also framed as a longed-for future in which he simultaneosly invests. Raja's navigation of multiple time-space realities stitches together India's network geographies and temporalities.

Whereas Raja's account sutures disparate time, space, and national identifications, I2U owner Laveena describes an anxious relationship to these tensions. The agent in Laveena's account is defined through her psychic, economic, and material departure from home and, by extension, tradition:

> You have youngsters of twenty-one and twenty-two working night shifts. Many of them are away from home because they end up getting in a situation where they are unable work in their hometowns. They live in town and come in [to the centers]. They are away from their parents, away from a traditional environment. They suddenly have newfound feelings, a lot of money and, as a result, there is that breakdown in terms of the environment they grew up in. (Laveena, I2U, personal interview, 2005)

Laveena depicts call center life through shifting markers of time and space: agents work night shifts, live away from home, and gain economic mobility. These new relations mark a time-space rupture from the forces through which this subject was previously been defined. As Laveena puts it, they create a "breakdown" in the social environment through which the subject knows herself.

Call center owners, managers, and CEOs like Laveena frame relationships between themselves and agents as intergenerational. Laveena refers to call center agents as "kids," which underscores agents' youth as both a marker of their vulnerability (the call center agent emerges as an impressionable, flexible subject) and of futurity (the youth of today is the future of India tomorrow). Intergenerational references also position call center leadership in a parental role in relation to agents and the call center as a family. As Ronit puts it, "As the H.R. head I was head of the family." The family metaphor positions management to assume responsibility for the impressionable youth they oversee, compounding their anxieties over agents becoming too Westernized. Thought of as a network temporality, agents are at risk of drifting too far from their parents and hence from traditional environment. Laveena and Ronit's parental positionalities emerge through an alignment with—and in many ways as an extension or replacement of—agents' parents. This positionality and the affective labor that management exerts to mentor young workers also contributes to the larger project of suturing India.

Returning to the concept of diaspora, call centers illustrate another way that virtual assimilation displaces the presumption of arrival within diaspora. For instance, although agents often view America as a site of desire and becoming, it is often rejected, deferred, or disavowed as a point of arrival. Agents may virtually migrate, but they do not necessarily want to physically migrate. Ekaraj describes the desire to go to America as a "craze" that agents negotiate:

> [The pull to go to the United States] was there initially, but now it has calmed down. People tell me it was very hard living. There was a lot of demand. Now it has calmed down, but then it goes up. But personally now I think that that craze is gone. In a way everyone wanted to go into the U.S. and now it's more like [pause] what can they do there and come back? But I don't want to go there. (Ekaraj, I2U, personal interview, 2005)

Physical migration, which marks a would-be telos for those living in the diaspora, remains an unsettled issue for agents. The desire to move to the United States seems to ebb and flow for Ekaraj and others he describes. The "pull to go" has "calmed down," tempered by the accounts of those presumably diasporic subjects who return with stories of the "very hard living." Ekaraj's relationship to physical migration is deferred and ultimately disavowed: "I don't want to go there," he concludes. So although call center agents virtually assimilate, they seem to have a different relationship to India and America than diasporic Indians. At least for Ekaraj, virtual migration entails no geographic point of arrival. Rather, it relies on agents becoming consumer-savvy, Americanized workers. For call center workers, the boundaries between India's rising middle class and Indians living in the United States are not entirely distinct.

VIRTUAL ASSIMILATION IN NETWORK GEOGRAPHY AND TEMPORALITY ACROSS REGIONAL BOUNDARIES

Globalization theorists have argued that the checkering of national space is a defining feature of late capitalism.[11] Yet little attention has been paid to what this spatial arrangement means for those who cross those regional, classed, and indeed national borders. Alternatively, transnational feminist scholars have argued for new concepts of citizenship to account for the nation's incommensurate relationship with traditional nation-state boundaries.[12] Grewal (2005) evokes the compelling figure of an H-IB visa-holding Indian to capture these shifts. Grewal defines this figure as seeking

a future in which the desire for consumption, for liberal citizenship, and for work came together to produce a specific subject of migration. Although this H-IB visa holder may not have called himself an American, he certainly participated in the discourse of the American dream while simultaneously seeing himself as an Indian national. Was his participation in the dream any different from that of people who entered the United States as immigrants or who became citizens? (5)

Grewal's H-IB visa holder blurs the relationship between national territory and imagined national or transnational belonging. While the migrant's desire is directed toward a longed-for future that aligns with Western narratives of modernity, he or she is simultaneously aware of himself or herself as an Indian national. Grewal's example suggests American assimilation may begin before the diasporic subject's arrival to the United States. This blip in time decouples the relationship between the formation of the Americanized subject and the territory of the U.S. nation-state. Alternatively, the H-IB visa holder already imagines the conditions of his or her subject formation through tropes of Americanness through an affective investment in those practices and promises associated with America: consumption and liberal citizenship. When, then, might assimilation be said to begin? The time-space slippage at work in Grewal's account suggests that assimilation bears no necessary relationship to territorial location. Rather, such processes might be mapped onto a different spatial arrangement from those assumed within traditional notions of migration and diaspora.

Our analysis seeks to recast the relationship between the time-space processes through which the diasporic subject is produced. This section rethinks the category diaspora through the slippage between material and virtual migration. For instance, call center agents' lives are accelerated not through physical migration, but through virtual migration. This observation contextualizes Grewal's insights about the H-IB visa holder's spatially dispersed participation in the American dream. The checkered and network geographies through which agents move enable them to imaginatively and materially travel across national boundaries within the bounds of India. This section considers agents' movement through checkered and network geographies in relation to the category of diaspora to expand the concept of arrival presumed within diaspora studies. For agents, arrival is deferred and disavowed; most have no desire to ever leave India for the United States. Yet as Raja's account suggests, America comes to India. The processes of subjectification that circulate within the accounts of these call center employees points to an accelerated or condensed time-space, creating psychic ruptures that agents must navigate as they suture their disparately located identities.

For instance, transregional migration becomes a form of global migration: agents who migrate across regional boundaries often narrate their movement as a transnational migration—as a movement to(ward) America. Recall Raja's account of building friendships not in regional dialects but through American English. His account suggests that the structures of feeling through which he and his friends create belonging are performed not through regional or even Indian national inflections. Instead, it marks Raja's communication practices and performance of identity signal a psychic and interpersonal movement toward Americanness that has no necessary relationship to a physical movement to the United States. It suggests that agents' assimilation is not contained to their conversations with American callers, but rather that their Americanized performance of identity spills out into their daily lives and animates their intimate encounters. Likewise, call center agent Taiba experiences regional migration as an accelerated and transformative experience. Taiba is from Manipur, in the northeast part of India, a rural, lush region that is distinct from Bangalore's urban sprawl. His life was oriented around the changing seasons and local community, but now he concerns himself with corporate targets and regimented workdays. For him, regional migration has reconstituted his "way of life" as an "entirely different thing":

> For me it has been a great learning process, coming to this industry. I come from an entirely different background culture: I am from the northeast. In

fact, he [pointing to one of the other focus group participants] was the one who rectruited me there, in Manipur. [He addresses the recruiter.] Maybe you don't know me. I still remember you! [laughs] Last year, January. It has been a good learning process. I have been here for the past one and a half years. So every day, like I said, it's an entirely different thing. All the northeast life is very different. After coming to Bangalore, joining a call center as a whole, every day you have to achieve certain targets. That way, it affects my way of thinking, attitude, and way of life. After learning every day, it has been a good learning process, as far as I am concerned. (Taiba, 365-Call, focus group interview, 2006)

Taiba marks his transformation through metaphors of acceleration. He moved from Manipur to Bangalore just a year and a half ago, yet he has entered an "entirely different" life process. This difference is marked through the daily activities of call center labor: "every day it's an entirely different thing," "every day you have to achieve certain targets," "after learning every day." This dailiness underscores the repetition of a particular cultural performance that renders his subject position unrecognizable: Taiba thinks that the very recruiter who brought him to Bangalore might not even recognize him ("Maybe you don't know me. I still remember you!"). Whereas CEOs and managers such as Laveena, Armaan, and Harish claim that agents are immediately recognizable, Taiba imagines his identity as unrecognizable. The question he poses to his recruiter invites external confirmation of the psychic transformations he has experienced. His question conveys a sense of being unrecognizable to his former self and perhaps even to those left back home. It charts the accelerated psychic distance he feels he has traveled in his transregional migration from Manipur to Bangalore.

Taiba's relationship to his recruiter marks a complex network temporality. He encounters the recruiter in the present (in the focus group), but the recruiter is a person from his past who, at the time of their previous encounter, anticipated the transformed self whom Taiba now finds himself to be. Yet Taiba implores the recruiter to recognize this previous self within his present self. Taiba turns the tables, recruiting the recruiter to suture his past, present, and future selves. This exchange signals the ways in which virtual migration animates the material conditions that generate Taiba's accelerated transformation. His immersion in the virtual borderlands entails a performance that he cannot merely leave at the door of the call center. Rather, Taiba feels he may have changed beyond recognition: he frames the accelerated conditions of his subject formation as "an entirely different thing." Taiba seeks the recognition of his recruiter in an effort to suture this expansive difference to contain the accelerating forces that threaten to rupture his past and previous senses of self.

Like Taiba, Pavitra imagines her transregional migration as a form of transnational movement. For instance, she distinguishes the "opportunities" available to her in which Bangalore over and against her hometown of Goa:

> I am basically from Goa [pause] and came here after I've done my BA and my law studies. I did not come here with the intention of really working in a call center. I just wanted to get out of Goa because, as far as career option is concerned, it's lacking in Goa, and Bangalore is considered as [a] really good place for career options. I came to Bangalore not knowing so much. Every move I make I am worried about. Is it something that is going to develop me and my life, and all of the others around me? (Pavitra, I2U, personal interview, 2005)

Pavitra signifies Goa through its lack. She pauses as she names her place of origin, and she goes on to frame Goa as subordinate to Bangalore. Against Bangalore's potential, Goa is figured as a site of professional stagnation. In spite of her advanced legal training (she was a practicing lawyer in Goa), the sleepy beach town cannot provide Pavitra with the resources to "develop" herself that Bangalore can. Goa is a tourist destination that caters to middle-class Indians who take holidays there and to European and American tourists, who see it as an affordable destination desired for its tradition and relaxed culture that retains its 1960s reputation as a popular hippie destination. Regional space emerges within Pavitra's narrative as unevenly gendered: Goa is feminized through a slippage between home, lack, and ambivalent point of departure, against which Bangalore is constituted through the phallic power that Pavitra seizes there. Bangalore allows her to "develop" herself and "others around" her; she associates the city with an accelerated sense of time. Pavitra's migration across regional space means that time passes differently as she places herself within a temporal trajectory marked by its development. The psychic process Pavitra's regional migration entails is not limited to her own subject formation (relocated to Bangalore). Rather, Pavitra imagines her development will, in turn, develop "all the others around" her. Over the course of the conversation, we learn that those around her include the family members she left behind in Goa. This collective sense of development enables Pavitra to suture time and overcome the difference and distance that might otherwise estrange her from her previous life and the family that stayed behind. Her affective labor sutures the stretched generation gap and geographic distance that call center labor often creates between agents and their parents that have become scrambled by her regional migration.

For call center agents, regional identity is a formative site of difference. Call center labor and its attendant class, linguistic, and cultural shifts assimilate regional difference in ways that mimic global migration and assimilation to another culture. For Sunita, this difference is marked through accent: "I think it [accent] is more region based. Like people from the south obviously have the thick accents. People from, like, AP [Andhra Pradesh] [and] Chennai have a certain way they pronounce words. But for the most part of it, I wouldn't say it's class dependent; it's more region based. And again, it depends on where you studied" (Sunita, I2U, personal interview, 2004). Sunita distinguishes regional accents, which, she claims, overcome class difference. She underscores differences among agents as a function of their class mobility and the kinds of shifts in culture and national identity they undergo in the industry. The "thick accent" she attributes to those from the south is a greater detriment to upward mobility than class background. Yet Sunita underscores the importance of "where you studied" as a vehicle upward mobility. Thus class mobility is simultaneously regionally constrained and unmoored from the class-based marginality. Upward mobility is enabled and constrained through the subject's participation in the pedagogies of Americanization of call center labor.

Virtual assimilation is organized through accent neutralization, which is increasingly institutionalized within the educational system. As Raja explains, "Many [schools] now include English as a major part of the course. Before they did not focus on English. But in the I.T. industry now it's important how you speak. H.R. is going to ask you; and now there are schools that produce really good English speakers and concentrate on that" (Raja, 365-Call, focus group interview, 2006). Raja connects agents' empowerment as neoliberal and national citizen-subjects to their fluency in American English. The fact that schools inccreasingly feature this emphasis suggests the extent to which India is investing in neoliberal pedagogies that produce a form of America assimilation that may either begin before phsyical migration or may enable virtual migration. This pedagogy signals the extent to which class mobility is bound up in American-style assimilation.[13] It suggests that as we consider the role of the rising Indian middle class, we must also consider the forms of virtual migration and assimilation that enable class mobilty. It signals the extent to which network geographies are remade through outsourcing as the formation of virtual and telephonic space reshapes material and cultural conditions.

Raja's account underscores the importance of cultivating an American accent as a resource for agents' class mobility. Investment in a consumerist lifestyle is also considered a point of entry for the call center agent to identify with the American consumer. TechNow manager Ganesh explains of the importance of agents' recognition of status markers in American culture:

> They [call center trainers] tell about credit cards and those kinds of things [...]. So how important is a car for an American? How important is a credit card for an American? Because a lot of the outsourcing work that came into India, at least in my knowledge, in the beginning was a lot of financial work—a lot of credit cards, you know, credit card customer service, taking payments over the phone, doing collections. Those were the kinds of business that we got in the beginning. So there's a whole cultural module that was developed. And our company during that time was a pioneer in that. (Ganesh, TechNow, personal interview, 2007)

Virtual assimilation in is enabled by a fluency in American consumer practices in Ganesh's account, resulting in the creation of "a whole cultural module." These early training practices set the stage for call center labor and training practices that feature a consumer values and practices that still pervade the industry today. American values are framed through consumer practices, so agents are trained to become fluent in discourses and practices of consumerism. The industry's early equation between America and consumerism remains formative of agents' class mobility, which is inseparable from their internalization of America. In Ganesh's account, for instance, Americans are defined as car owners and credit card users. Because these consumer habits structure agents' interactions with the customer ("taking payments over the phone" and "doing collections"), Americanness becomes equated with consumption. Agents' capacity to perform their job is contingent on their internalization of the culture (that is, consumer practices) of the American customer. Training practices such as those Ganesh describes provide a pedagogical site in which agents are assimilated (Americanized) through cultural modules. They are one of multiple sites through which virtual migration is enabled as network geographies reshape the material conditions of industry practices. Although these forms of cultural training are designed to align agents' lived experience with consumerist discourses, they also extend to agents' consumer practices beyond the bounds of the call center. As Ganesh's account unfolds, he describes a series of shifts in key markers of identity, such as class mobility, talking to Americans, and naming practices:

> And then, of course, when you get that extra money at a young age and you're interacting with the Americans, then you start thinking like them as well. It's not a bad thing, to be honest. Everybody has their own way to live. But [pause] some of the guys really became Yankees, cool. Most of them had nicks, you know, nicknames. My name is Ganesh. They started calling me Gary. Because Ganesh is so, you know, old [pause]. So they used to call me Gary at that time. I was okay. I didn't have any [pause]. So, you know, we, each and every one of them, had, you know, an alias. We never used to call it alias at that time. We called it [a] business nickname. (Ganesh, TechNow, personal interview, 2007)

Ganesh's speech excerpt is filled with pauses, suggesting his ambivalence toward the industry's assimilationist pedagogies and practices. As we explored in chapter 2, the naming practices of the call center industry are a critical component of agents' performance of Americanized identities. Ganesh extends this insight when he notes that call center labor begins with the phone call ("interacting with the Americans") but spills out into agents' daily psychic lives ("thinking like them"). Ganesh points to the ways in which the cultivation of call center agents as an "immediately identifiable group" (recall Armaan's experience) was orchestrated by the industry "in the early years." It suggests the extent to which network geographies work in multiple directions: the virtual remakes the material, even as material conditions enable virtual inclusion. Further, returning to Armaan's comment, we can see how locally based industry training techniques are routed through the virtual, then return home to revamp localized and daily performances of group identity.

One theme Ganesh's account reveals is the hybridized sensibilities that inform industry practices. For instance, the use of nicknames is a common practice in India as a sign of intimacy; family members often give children affectionate nicknames such as *baba* or *guddi*.[14] In call centers, the use of nicknames recasts this tradition as a strategy of virtual assimilation. Pseudonyms enable agents to overcome difference and distance with their American callers, but they also offer agents an insider status within call center subculture. Ganesh's narrative moves from a universal *you* to his own subject position as he apprehensively discloses his negotiations with virtual assimilation. He concludes that "everybody has their own way to live," downplaying the industry's responsibility for cultural shifts by locating them within individuals. But as Ganesh's tone shifts (note the conjunction *but*), he returns to a collective and differentiating pronoun *(they)*. These shifting pronouns marks Ganesh's ambivalent relationship to virtual assimilation, particularly as he describes the ways in which these practices reshape agents' identities beyond the confines of the call center exchange. "Some guys really became Yankees, cool," he notes. The term *Yankees* suggests an association with true Americana that the call center subculture has taken on in Ganesh's account.

Ganesh's account also signals the network temporalities through which call center labor reworks and layers time. Like Raveena's account in chapter 2, Ganesh resists owning his use of a pseudonym, framing his account in passive terms: "They used to call me Gary," which was "okay" because "Ganesh is so, you know, old." Ganesh then pauses and loses his words ("I didn't have any"). He recovers his fluency as he reverts to the language of business processing: "We called it [a] business nickname," he concludes. This rich narrative moment is marked by the ambivalence surrounding network temporalities: the name Ganesh is "old," so his pseudonym, Gary, becomes the name by which he is called—not only, it seems, for the purposes of the phone call. His account thus suggests that virtual migration is animated through the reworking of network geography as Ganesh becomes Gary within the community, but also of time: Ganesh is old world, and Gary is presumably modern.

"You Do Get into That Mode of Thinking Eventually": Worker/Consumer, Indian/American

In this section we explore the institutional production of virtual assimilation. This process is organized through agents' cultivation as what Carla Freeman (2000) calls worker/consumers. Freeman's rich ethnographic study of Barbadian women working in the outsourced informatics industry examines the production of the worker/consumer. Building on her work, we consider the ways in which the call center agent is produced simultaneously as a worker and consumer. We extend Freeman's insights on the globalization of gendered labor to tease out the national and transnational components of this subjectification process.[15] The stories of call center agents suggest that the formation of their identities as workers is inseparable from their formation as consumers. Further, agents frame their cultivation as worker/consumers as a form of virtual assimilation. Sunita describes the dailiness of call center labor, coupled with the economic lifestyle that labor enables in her daily life, Americanizes her:

> Over here [in call centers] . . . when you are constantly interacting with them and interacting along their wavelength, you do get into that mode of thinking eventually. And also, again, I said, the economic freedom we have now is much more. So before you could only watch, and now you have the money to implement whatever it is. (Sunita, I2U, personal interview, 2004)

Sunita underscores that her performance of an Americanized identity in turn provides the material means by which agents can locally perform their Americanized identities as consumers. Her relatively high wages provide her with the economic freedom to participate in the forms of consumerism in which she is immersed in the call center. This buying power extends the fluency in consumerism that is necessary for her job into her daily life, empowering her to implement whatever it is as a set of material practices. This move marks Sunita's cultivation as a worker/consumer: call center labor initially invites agents to internalize American culture, then to perform American identities on the phone. Finally, they are enabled to extend those Americanized identities into their lives outside of the call center.

One way call center agents are formed as worker/consumers is through the use of credit cards. They describe the credit card as a tool to recruit and retain call center labor. For instance, many agents say that they were given cards when they were hired. Credit cards symbolize agents' virtual migration: it enables agents' performance of consumer identities, even as it binds them to their relatively high-paying call center jobs in order to manage their debt. Further, credit cards shift the relationship between money and time, embedding agents in a temporality of credit in which immediate gain is secured through future debt. Anila suggests that the credit card is a marker of entrance into the call center industry, which interpellates agents into an unsustainable lifestyle:

> SHEENA: What about issues of debt? Are you finding people getting things on loans or credit cards?
> ANILA: Yes, credit cards, I guess, are much more common, more than loans. Credit card, I think almost everyone got it when they started earning, once they entered the industry.
> SHEENA: Are they using it, like, almost beyond what they should?
> ANILA: They use for the mobile bill. This I know from my friends, because they cannot afford to pay the mobile bill. (I2U, personal interview, 2005)

For Anila, the credit card becomes part of "earning" for agents who "entered the industry." The economic freedom it extends to agents enables their consumerist power beyond the capacity of their "earning," tipping them into spending practices they "cannot afford." The "mobile bill," for instance, becomes a marker of this overextension. The cell phone is both a means of communication (it is a device that allows agents to speak to one another) and a marker of class status (as Ganesh points out, call center workers all want to have the latest cell phones). Agents' identities as consumers are expressed through their communication practices, mediated through their late model mobiles.

So while technological devices such as the cell phone become tropes of class status, they also recalibrate agents' sense of money and time to align with temporality of credit. Mobiles are secured in the present as agents wager their future to maintain the device and the interpersonal communication and cultural capital it enables. Markers of class status that define the present are enabled through a future constrained by a promise to pay—and in turn a commitment to the kind of labor that will enable the agent to continue to do so. As Harish, a manager, observes:

> They want to have the latest cell phones, which have the latest features. Most of them don't want to use the three-K or four-K rupee cell phone. They want the twenty-K rupee type, which can do one hundred things. It can do everything, apart from talking, you know? [laughter] People have [pause] peer pressure is so much. Everyone is showing off their latest cell phones that they have. (Harish, Premier Accounting, personal interview, 2005)

Harish is part of the group of call center leadership who claims that agents are an "immediately identifiable group." He offers the cell phone as a sort of trope for agents' class-striving identities. Harish undercores the peer pressure that compels agents to become consuming subjects; agents perform status and secure peer acceptance through consumption patterns, signified through the metonymic mobile.

Raja also underscores the active role of the call center industry in reconstituting the worker as consumer by providing them with credit cards:

> Let me tell you my own experience. Of course, when I started working in this industry about four to five years back, and started to get a good amount of money, I started swiping cards. Credit cards, when they first came to Bangalore, it was all about getting cards—gold, platinum. What you don't realize is that credit cards are not what you have. It is what you don't have and what you're going to have to pay for—you don't really know that. It's a status thing in the beginning. We also had that kick about getting credit cards when we started working. Obviously, these guys used to come around and give out credit cards. I had eight credit cards, which I got for no reason but to flaunt it. Then I realized the negative things about it, and slowly had to reduce it. I ended up having two. (Raja, 365 Call, focus group interview, 2006)

Raja notes that the credit card craze was a formative part of his call center agent identity: "It was all about getting credit cards—gold, platinum." His framing marks the arrival of the cards in Bangalore as a specific historical moment in the formation of the call center industry as a network geography and temporality. He also underscores how the cards shift agents' relationship to time and money; possession is reconfigured through a present that is now indebted to the future. For Raja, possession is paradoxically reconstituted as dispossession. Echoing Harish's account, the object of possession is the source of the agents' status. But the conditions under which agents acquire the object also slips to one of dispossession: what you "have" becomes what you "don't have" and "what you're going to have to pay for." This ambivalent metaphor marks Raja's subjectification as a move from innocence (he lacks knowledge about credit) to that of savvy consumer who manages credit by cultivating restraint ("I ended up having two").

Raja's relationship to time and money, possession and dispossession, is recast through his immersion in the call center industry. Samir underscores the role of the call center industry in cultivating the agents' relationship to credit as a function of labor relations. Samir explains:

> But then is the fact that most companies have like an agreement in the campus to offer a credit card. Like a U.S. Computers card. I have a U.S. Computers card account for services they will give you there. But then underneath there is a problem. You are going to have people who are going into credit debt. Yeah, that comes for everybody, no matter what sort of job you do. But then you have to work it off. (Samir, U.S. Computers, personal interview, 2005).

The credit card, for Samir, emulates the "campus" life in the high-tech industry in the United States as cards offer agents an opportunity to gain a "service," but they also present a lurking "problem." As with Raja's account, the problem for Samir is hidden—it's "underneath." The problem is framed through a temporality of credit: a future debt may not be detected in the present. The future he evokes is one that binds the worker to his or her labor: "But then you have to work it off." As with Raja's account, Samir carves out a limited form of agency within the economic freedoms and constraints entailed by call center labor. The industry cultivates worker/consumers to retain its leverage over its mobile workforce: the credit card indebts the worker to a future in ways that actually limit the range of choices available to them in the present.

These passages suggest that the use of credit—and the kinds of devices it enables agents to purchase—inform agents' lived experiences in ways that cultivate their identities as worker/consumers. This experience may better equip agents to identify with their American customers. In this sense, the practice of giving agents a credit card upon hire at some call centers is an aspect of network geography and temporality. The credit card is one layer of the converging network and material forces that constitute virtual migration as agents' cultivation as consumers within localized settings comes back to inform their labor. It further signals the ways that industry practices are designed to maintain the virtuality of agents' migration as agents become bound to the industry by their need to sustain their debt.

Freeman (2000) argues that the Barbadian informatics industry engages "flexible management strategies": cultivating professional-looking work spaces and workers; offering bonuses and rewards, including trips to San Juan, Miami, and New York; sending thank-you cards. These strategies, she argues, are designed to cultivate informatics laborers as worker/consumers within a global economy. For instance, the informatics industry offers the experience of global travel as a reward for high-performing workers to motivate good work habits. In the case of the call center industry, dispersing credit cards is one such flexible management tactic. Another tactic, similar to those Freeman identifies in her study, is the social events the call center industry hosts. The industry provides a host of practices that converge to cultivate agents' sensibilities as Americanized worker/consumers. Jaffer's account suggests the extent to which agents internalize these industry activities in the production of their own identities. Jaffer sees agents' presence in "high-end" restaurants as evidence of their "increasing standard of living." "Yes, standard of living is increasing," Jaffer explains. "Five years back, I used to go to a lower range of restaurants. Now, you'll find me in high-end, star restaurants. So you'll find the age group of eighteen to thirty years making an average of fifteen thousand per month" (365-Call, focus group interview, 2006). Echoing the notion that network geography remakes material space, Jaffer marks his class mobility in terms of increased mobility and access as he notes that he can be "found" in "high-end, star restaurants." He frames this activity through an omniscient *you* who witnesses his newfound mobility, suggesting the importance that his presence there is recognized by others. This recognition constitutes how he experiences his subjectivity in relation to a broader group of call center agents, who are also recognizable through particular markers of age and class. The scene of recognition is a space of consumption (the high-end restaurant), which, recalling Ganesh's account, is also the site call center managers extend to agents to cultivate them as worker/consumers.

The worker/consumer identity that Freeman (2000) identifies provides informatics workers with a sense of themselves as "modern" working women (33). Likewise, the worker/consumer identity cultivated in the Indian call center industry is bound up in the rapid modernization of agents. This modern(ized) subject is also bound up in struggles over national and transnational identities. The call center agent is caught between multiple and often competing interpellations: American, Indian, and global; traditional and modern; present, past, and future. Saurabh is an agent in a small call center who takes his work seriously, which often creates a sense of distance and difference from other agents. While many agents embrace the worker/consumer identity, Saurabh sees it as a threat to Indian identity. He worries about a "loss of control" that agents experience when they get money and a sense of freedom. Saurabh is concerned about intergenerational conflict and a loss of Indian identity. He worries because agents have become so Westernized that they have begun to disrespect their parents.

> They spend whatever they want. They go out. You can say that the economy is booming, but [pause] there is no control, and in the sense, typically, you have guys who are twenty-one, twenty-two, staying away from home and earning fifteen grand, which is a lot of money, you know? And you have no control. The parents are not here, and you lose control. So I guess that is what is happening more than the fact that we are losing our identity because of speaking with [U.S.] customers. (Saurabh, I2U, personal interview, 2004)

Although Saurabh is himself an agent, he depicts the agent in his story as other, referring to agents as "they" and as gendered as male. The agent/other is marked through an accelerated relationship to space and time that is bound up in his newfound economic mobility. He moves through space with "no control" ("they go out," "staying away from home"), generating space-time distance from the previous generation ("the parents are not here"). An anxious space-time rupture animates Saurabh's account as the acceleration of class mobility is ultimately a fear over "losing our identity." For Saurabh, a collective Indian identity is at risk, not only because agents are immersed in what we've called a virtual borderlands as workers, but also because agents are excessive consumers. This collective identity, framed through his repeated reference to agents' lack of control, is laid in precarious balance between a familiar Indian past and an unknown future.

Saurabh continues to make the point that agents have been thoroughly cultivated as consumers when asked what agents do with their money:

> Shopping, buying, clubbing, clubbing, clubbing. And that's fine, I guess. They are spending money and having fun. But a lot of guys do not have focus on what they are doing. So they don't—they see it as easy money, but I don't know how many of them are actually taking it as a very serious career, or even thinking in the long term, of what they will do. (Saurabh, I2U, personal interview, 2004).

In a formulation that extends Freeman's argument, Saurabh goes so far as to suggest agents forego their identities as workers (they earn "easy money" but don't take "it as a very serious career, or even thinking in the long term") in favor of their identities as consumers ("shopping, buying, clubbing, clubbing, clubbing"). Alternatively, agents like Saurabh cultivate their worker identities against those of the worker/consumers in ways that suture India's past and future. Many agents describe their participation in the call center industry as worker/consumers, whereas Saurabh underscores the importance of rejecting consumption to counteract the rapid force of Americanization.

Like Saurabh, Sunita imagines a future of increased Western consumerism, which she experiences as an anxious sense of acceleration:

> I think the impact is going to be tremendous. There is a lot more demand for a lot of the Western consumer goods—whether it is the clothes, or [pause] electronic goods. It's just a faster way of life. It's—everyone wants to be up with the latest and most current. So I think the demand for Western-based consumer goods is definitely going to go up. There is no doubt about that. (Sunita, I2U, personal interview, 2004)

Sunita anticipates the call center industry as having a "tremendous impact" as Indian agents increasingly internalize Western consumer practices. While her account evokes a sense of cultural imperialism, its force is not externally imposed. Rather it is the agents' "demand for a lot of the Western consumer goods" that animates the "faster way of life." Sunita's concerns resonate with Saurabh's sense that agents' mobility and misdirected consumer power pose a risk to India's future. Sunita searches for her words as she identifies a set of risky consumer items. The breathless affect that permeates her account captures a sense of acceleration with which she herself cannot keep pace—a "faster way of life" and an imperative to "be up with the latest and most current." Sunita's affect animates agents' accelerated identity formation as worker/consumers as they strive to suture continually sliding network temporalities.

Laveena depicts a cultural transition within the call center industry that is organized through the trope of the national holiday:

> There is the issue of Indian holidays and then Christmas time. In some cases that is a big time, and then Thanksgiving was a very low time [in terms of call center demand] for the U.S. So I think there is that, you know, in some areas resentment where they think, "Hey, why do we have to celebrate U.S

holidays and take them off and not Indian holidays?" (Laveena, I2U, personal interview, 2005)

For Laveena, the timing of holidays becomes a contested temporality through which India and America get played out. The industry's recognition of American, not Indian, holidays organizes agents' time. They get days off for American holidays, but Indian holidays go unrecognized. Like the night shift, this temporal arrangement contributes to agents' sense of virtual migration, or their migration through time. Scheduling holidays is a power temporality; America's time clock supersedes India's, which Laveena describes as a source of "resentment" for agents. They receive time off for Thanksgiving, but they often cannot get a holiday on Diwali, even though it is a significant Hindu festival of lights and the start of a new year, similar in importance to Christmas and New Year's Eve in the West. The observance of religious holidays marks a temporal struggle in which religious and capitalist temporal arrangements commingle within modernity: "Religious festivals like Christmas, Passover, and Ramadan are important moments in the calendar even where religious observance has been largely replaced by a secular society. Thus earlier senses of time related to the natural world and religion coexist in the time of modernity" (Baldwin et al. 1998, 185). Such temporal arrangements place agents out of time. The struggle over scheduling holidays is metonymic of the temporal struggle over national identity, neoliberalism, and American belonging. India and America emerge through the production of contested temporalities affixed to Christian, Hindu, and global time. Under neoliberalism, power is secured through the economics of a temporal struggle in ways that unsettle the cultural specificity of locality and nation. Just as religious festivals like Thanksgiving and Christmas dominate the lives of agents, so too do the affective ties they develop within these temporal constraints. Belongings are constricted by the rhythms of call center life and so morph to accomodate the temporal demands of the industry.

"Romances, Breakups, and Makeups": Affecting Time

This section attends to the ways in which network geography and temporality reshape agents' relational lives. As we argue in chapter 3, power temporalities constrain agents' capacity to build and maintain affective ties with family and friends outside of the industry. Alternatively, we argue here, agents tend to bond with each other. This section extends our previous discussion of affective labor to consider the horizontal distributions of immaterial labor[16] that animate call center life. We extend Hardt's (2003) observation by considering the horizontal forms of affective labor that bind agents to one another as a function of network temporality. The affective labor occurring within the workplace converges with the temporal, spatial, and affective relations shaped by the industry's temporal inversions. For instance, Saurabh finds community with other agents with whom he shares time:

> My friends have always been the guys with whom I worked. Guys whom I am working with. Or guys whom I have worked with and transferred to other companies. So it has been pretty much the same. They also are in call centers, they have long shifts, so they understand. (Saurabh, I2U, personal interview, 2004)

These friendships endure a certain spatial distance as Saurabh forges ties not only with "guys whom [he is] working with," but also with those who have "transferred to other companies." The shared temporality of call center life extends beyond a mere convenience for agents to get together. Perhaps more profoundly, agents bond over a shared experience of time: "They also are in call centers, they have long shifts, so they understand." The temporal inversion that structures agents' lives animates their material and affective lives beyond the space-time of call center labor. It also shapes their daily lived intimacies. In this sense, the shared experience of virtual migration spills out beyond the contained space-time of the phone call to shape agents' lived experiences and relational choices.

As the virtual and the material conditions of call center life interanimate one another, time and space are reconfigured. This interanimation creates what we have been calling a network geography: virtual connectivities reconstitute material space. However, network geography in this case is enabled through agents' shared experience of time. The potency of the industry's network geography, then, is its reconfiguration of affective ties, generated through a shared sense of time, or network temporalities. Network temporalities not only reconfigure agents' relationships with other agents, but also animate how they build ties with those outside of the industry. For instance, Dev explains:

Working in the call center affects the people in my neighborhood, affects my
friends and my family. They think it is some different concept. The impact
would be the effect on them. Being the first graduate, I should be at the call
center. Because I have a lot of a software experience. This thing has given
me some knowledge and some position. If I go anywhere, I can get any job
maybe. (Dev, I2U, personal interview, 2004)

Dev is proud to be a call center agent and the first in his working-class
family to go to college. He is trained in software and believes this background will help him get a job anywhere. Dev sees the effects of call center
labor as widespread, sharing thoughtful reflections about the reach of
the changes the industry is creating—not only for agents and their families, but also their neighborhoods and beyond. He marks his difference in
relation to his former community (the "people in [his] neighborhood")
through metaphors of proximity and distance. The "impact" of his call
center labor is experienced through its "effect on them." These relations
are affected by his absence and his presence in a very "different" world.
While Dev frames his former community through a metaphor of spatial
proximity (neighbors), he marks the unfolding distance that defines their
relationships through tropes of class mobility as difference. Dev's virtual
migration thus extends beyond the intimacies that he builds with other
agents to reconfigure his relational life with those outside the industry.

Raja's account turns our attention to the romantic ties agents build with
one another. He notes that the temporal constraints that call center labor
places on agents' intimate relations reconfigure his sense of the Indian
family:

The kind of livelihood that you live, because of the timings, that you go
back and sleep during the day when the rest of the world is around, and
you actually don't get the time to meet with another circle of people outside.
So where do you go? For a date? [laughter] That's how people do end up
dating each other here. I'm not too sure if those really end up in serious
marriages, because quite a lot of them have, but not most of them. (Raja,
365 Call, focus group interview, 2006)

In this focus group conversation, Raja's reference to call center agents' "dating
each other" evokes laughter. The group's inside joke signals a giddy awareness of interagent intimacies. Raja equivocates over the outcomes of these

relationships: he is "not too sure if they end up in serious marriages, because quite a lot of them have, but not most of them." Raja's account signifies a widespread anxiety shared by agents, managers, and owners. As agents form intimate heterosexual ties that even end up in agents marrying one another and having children, the boundaries of the traditional Indian family are threatened. Whereas above we explore the ways the future these children represent as threatening to the nation, here we seek to underscore the importance of horizontal forms of affect that are generated by network temporalities. Indeed, Raja attributes the formation of these romantic ties to agents' capacity to share time, linking call center romances to virtual migration.

Likewise, Jaffer describes the pressures through which agents assess each others' gender performances through their capacity to "adapt" to the faster pace of call center intimacies. "The changes that have come now in our culture with call centers. Earlier, when you used to date, you were an outcast; and now if you don't date, you are an outcast! That's how it is, that's how we've adapted" (365 Call, focus group interview, 2006). In Jaffer's account, heterosexual coupling becomes a relational imperative within call center culture to which agents must learn to "adapt." Joel concurs that the call center industry is known for its "romances" and underscores Jaffer's sense that even the pace of dating has accelerated. He says:

> [laughing] Oh yes! A lot of it. Actually, that's one of the most happening things in a call center. I should have mentioned it long time back. A lot of it. I see a lot of romances and a lot of people breakups and makeups. You know? Suddenly a guy will be with a girl and the next day, he will be with someone else. You know, a typical English movie kind of thing. (Joel, U.S. Computers, personal interview, 2004)

Joel describes call center romance with a pervasive sense of acceleration, instability, and rapid relational change: people break up, make up, and "suddenly" shift partners. He shares this account with the thrill of being on the inside of the rapid pace of call center dating, which he describes as "one of the most happening things in the call center." The figure of Joel's narrative is gendered male and heterosexual, marked through his "English" relational orientation. That Joel's imagination of call center romance is informed by the figure of a white male protagonist featured in Western cinema suggests the extent to which Western cultural codes of intimacy have permeated call center life.

Call center owner Laveena echoes Joel's giddy affect when she describes the romances that go on in her call center: "I've got *The Bold and The Beautiful* happening at call centers! I'm telling you!" I2U, focus group interview, 2005). As one of the first soap operas broadcast in India, *The Bold and the Beautiful* became emblematic of American-style intimacies for much of urban India in the early 1990s. At the same time, satellite television imported a new wave of gender representations in India (Malhotra and Crabtree 2002). The show resonated with urban Indian audiences because of its familiar focus on a central extended family, paired with the unfamiliar enticement of characters who quickly swap lovers and partners. Laveena's comment that she has the "*The Bold and the Beautiful* happening at call centers" refers to the dramas (jealousies, love triangles, and gossip) that ensue from agents dating each other, Western-style, within call centers. Her comment gives evidence to the network geography generated by call center labor in which telecommunications and the virtual reorient material conditions. It suggests the extent to which virtual migration extends beyond agents' labor to animate their most intimate ties. Although early in their training agents might have watched *The Bold and the Beautiful* as a training activity, then performed what they learned in their interactions with American callers, here we see the performative force of call center labor spill out to animate their performance of identity and intimacy. The slippage between virtual and material space erupts. Each space mutually produces the other.

The formation of call center communities provides a fulfilling affective site for agents who must negotiate tremendous cultural shifts. For Harish, such intimacies represent agents' internalization of Western culture and a relinquishing of the "normal Indian system":

> And also in terms of other things, in terms of dating and the other social lives that they have. I think that we are almost going very, very close to the Western culture. Living in relationships, dating! It's a common thing. You'll be surprised, you see people very normal when they come in. After some time you realize this girl and this guy, they are living together. You know, they've taken the same apartment and are living [together]. Because they are dating, they are living together. It's probably very common in the West, but it was not definitely something which was normal to the Indian system. It's not direct, but it's like an offshoot. It happens. (Harish, Premier Accounting, focus group interview, 2005)

Harish verbally registers surprise at his own realization that agents are "living in relationships—dating!" He worries over how quickly those very "normal" people are transformed by their proximity to "Western culture" (agents are "very, very close to the Western culture"). This proximity suggests the extent to which the industry's network geography reconstitutes the material and affective terrain of agents' lives. The transformation of their intimate lives is particularly concerning for Harish, especially as their dating moves from the workspace to the domestic sphere, which suggests that it is precisely these cultural, social, and interpersonal upheavals that are most unsettling. The accelerated rhythm of dating (dating like they do in the West) spills outside of the call center into domestic space ("they've taken the same apartment and are living" together). Perhaps most unsettling about this privatized coupling is its failed performance of "normal" (traditional) Indian family life.

Like Harish, Lloyd worries that call center intimacies risk rupturing his previous affective landscape. Perhaps his life as an agent, he muses, will make it impossible for him to "go back to get married":

> I don't know. I hope I don't have to do that. I really don't know. But I know that it is what happens for many people. You have your Bangalore lifestyle and then you go back to your small hometown village, and you have your real lifestyle. So those who go back to get married, good luck! I think there will always be problems there. (Lloyd, I2U, personal interview, 2005)

When Lloyd finds it difficult to imagine a partnership with someone from a "small hometown village" because the cultural difference would be too great. He shifts from the personal "I" to the generic "you," generalizing his concern over the loss of his previous vision of a family to other agents (those who share his "Bangalore lifestyle"). He frames the space of Bangalore as a space of virtuality, in stark contrast to the "real lifestyle" of the "small hometown village." As a timeline, Lloyd places Bangalore in the present and his "hometown village" both in the past and as a potential, almost unimaginable, future. This space-time distance, in turn, generates an unbreachable affective gap that he imagines would confound traditional heterosexual intimacies. Lloyd quips: "So those who go back to get married, good luck! I think there will always be problems there." His comment suggests the distance agents "travel" by virtue of their labor in ways that emulate Indians living in the diaspora. Lloyd's persona mimics that of a diasporic subject, who cannot imagine himself returning home to a traditional lifestyle. Lloyd's "hometown" is both spatially and temporally distant, a place and time to which he cannot—thanks to his new lifestyle—return. Anila marks the affective shift in her life as a "generation gap" that is mapped through new and nontraditional forms of intimacy. Her intimacies shift from her parents to an increased tie with friends, who are often other call center agents:

> Friends do become emotional support. You start sharing with them much more than what you used to. After a certain point of time, you stop sharing with your parents. I am not sure whether that leads to a generation gap, or maybe it happens because of a generation gap. (Anila, I2U, personal interview, 2005)

For Anila, friends become the primary relationship from which she receives "emotional support." Simultaneously, Anila withdraws from, or "stops sharing with," her parents. She marks this shift temporally—"after a certain point of time" she redirects her emotional energies from the previous generation to her own.

Saurabh frames this kind of generational distance as an affective rupture; it arises from a struggle between parents and "kids":

> The biggest thing for me would be the teenagers asking for independence. . . . You have parents trying to find out what your kids up to and kids won't like it. I guess that would be the biggest impact in terms of communication between the parent and the children, more than anything else. (Saurabh, I2U, personal interview, 2005)

As with Laveena's account above, Saurabh positions agents as "kids," "teenagers," and "children," who are prone to rebel against their parents. Agents "are asking for independence," and they "won't like it" when their parents "try to find out" what they are "up to." For Saurabh, agents are presumably "up to" something, which evokes a secretive relationship between the generations and the breakdown of communication and trust. When thought of as a network temporality, Saurabh's comment points to the ways that the industry's network culture strains traditional relationships, again positioning agents to suture India's temporal ruptures.

Harish's narrative provides a concrete sense of the potential loss that animates the uneasy "something" of Saurabh's excerpt:

> It's hard. I would say that sometimes [the call center agents are] a little confused. . . . I very personally believe that there are good value systems there that they would have learnt. India is traditionally very value-driven. You know? That is what your parents teach you all the time. More traditional and conservative. But I think there's a good part of that which one should never lose. . . . Some people have the maturity to kind of balance it out—pick up what is needed and still not forget your base roots. But I've seen some people who get completely carried away. They're like lost. They're like totally confused. (Harish, Premier Accounting, focus group interview, 2005)

The call center agent in Harish's account is "confused" and "lost," at risk of getting "completely carried away" from "tradition" and their "base roots." His metaphors point to the role of time in the formation of agents' identities, underscoring the dizziness of the industry's acceleration. Resonating with Axel's argument that diasporic sensibilities are characterized by loss and return, India emerges retrospectively within Harish's narrative as a repository for "tradition" and "values." Harish's longing is posed not from a spatial sense of distance but rather from a sense of temporal distance. The trope of the parent/child relationship recurs in Harish's story, providing agents with "roots" and opportunities for agents to participate in stabilizing potential temporal ruptures (parents teach you what is "more traditional and conservative"). Alternatively, the excessive stretching of generational time is also mapped through spatial metaphors (agents are "lost," "confused," and "carried away"). The distance agents travel through time is recast as a spatial distance, even as Harish holds out for the possibility that agents might achieve a temporal equilibrium, "the kind of maturity to balance it out." Such a balanced relationship to time would empower agents to balance Westernization with the "good part of that [tradition] which one should never lose." This "good part" is figured through the intimate parent/child tie, which binds agents to India.

For Ganesh, the threat of an intergenerational rupture is one that the call center industry must actively manage. He explains that his company has instituted a host of practices to help agents retain ties to their parents. They offer "family days, where [agents] invite their family to offices. They show them the workplace. They show them, 'This is where your child goes and eats. This is where your child goes and sits. See what a great atmosphere this is? Air-conditioned. This is safe. These are your bosses'" (Ganesh, TechNow, personal interview, 2007). Again the agent emerges as an infantilized subject, whose labor is displayed by the agency for the parents to safely consume: "This is where your child goes and eats. This is where your child goes and sits." The point of the performance is to reassure the parents that their "children" are "safe" in multiple senses of the word. This safety is particularly important for female agents, whose modernization within the industry symbolizes the precarious nature of accelerated development as women's safety is literally at stake when they transgress the space-time of the nightscape (Patel 2010). Thus the practice of call center management bringing agents' parents in to assure their safety underscores the gendered nature, not only of call center labor, but of larger processes of modernization and Westernization. The "great atmosphere" and "air-condition[ing]," in turn, suggest class mobility, while Ganesh's final reference, to the agents' "bosses," frames the affective labor structure of the call center industry as one in which the "bosses" replace the parents in supervising the "children." As stand-in parents, industry leaders are positioned to suture the generational rift between parents and children generated by call center labor. Managers' parental role signifies the gendered nature of call center labor: while female agents are targets of male violence and control in the face of rapid modernization (Hegde 2011), Ganesh does not distinguish between female and male agents as needing protection. In this sense, his comment feminizes, even as it infantilizes, agents as a class in need of protection.

This familial theme emerged within the narratives of most nearly all the managers and CEOs with whom we spoke. Laveena, for instance, draws a parallel between her children and the "youngsters" she employs:

> But at the same time I think it also stands in terms of being a young mother. I have two children, five and seven. I would worry if I had a seventeen-year-old. I would be extremely concerned as to what would happen. And also I think because I spend a long time first meeting with these youngsters and then recognize the troubles that they are going through, and as a result of it, I am not detached. I just believe that would be socially irresponsible if I did not do anything about it. (Laveena, I2U, personal interview, 2004)

Laveena positions herself as a "responsible" mother to her children, and by extension to her agents. As the figurative and in many ways practical "mother" of her agents, she "spends a long time meeting" with agents. These extensive meetings counteract the rapid acceleration of agents' subjectivities, giving Laveena time to "recognize the troubles they are going through." Laveena affectively invests in the younger generation of call center agents in ways that mirror her relationships with her much younger children. The call center agent emerges as an affectively ambivalent figure, one for whom Laveena "worries" and in whom she invests—or at least she is "not detached." Her own children, alternatively, are still protected by their relative youth and class status (it's unlikely that her children would end up working in a call center).

The role of mothering the agents is also gendered as female managers and owners tend to assume responsibility for suturing the affective, psychic, and relational rifts generated by call center labor. Laveena commits to the feminized role of transferring culture to agents, who represent the future of the industry in particular and India more broadly. While Harish and Ganesh share Laveena's concern over the young agents, these male managers do not assume responsibility in these intensely interpersonal ways. In spite of these gendered differences, the positioning of agents as "kids" and leaders as "adults" resonates with Armaan, who shares that he is also a father. Call center managers Armaan and Laveena converge over the theme of parenting:

ARMAAN: I have three kids, it sounds like parenting.
LAVEENA: It *is* like parenting!
ARMAAN: These companies are taking place of what they're getting in the household. Because now they spend more time at work than they do at home. (Armaan and Laveena, I2U, focus group interview, 2005)

As with Laveena's quote above, Armaan's parental relationship with his three children serves as a point of reference for the affective labor Laveena is describing doing. Armaan underscores this arrangement through the imperative of the call center industry's power temporalities. Because agents "spend more time at work" than at "home," companies must take the "place of what they're getting in the household." Thus the call center industry is imagined through a vexed relationship to the family: the company both displaces and then affectively replaces the home. Yet Armaan's parental identification, unlike Laveena's, remains affectively removed. He does not hold himself responsible for cultivating Indianness in the call center agent with his own time and affective labor. In this sense, it seems the affective labor of suturing India falls on women in positions of power.

These passages suggest that the distribution of affective labor not only circulates horizontally among worker/consumers, but also among differently positioned workers and managers. The tremendous reach of the network geographies and temporalities of call center life become apparent in the host of emergent affective ties that are generated by virtual migration. Indeed, agents' affective landscapes are profoundly redistributed by their labor, both within the call center industry and beyond. Their imaginaries of their own identities and the ways in which owners and managers decode those identities are rendered intelligible through a host of affective redistributions. Allegiances shift and are renegotiated between parents and friends, home and the company, India and America. These affective ties, in turn, are framed as a site of struggle over national, transnational, and diasporic belongings. The affective distances and convergences are also often marked through as an anxiety over ruptured intergenerational relationships. At stake in this generation gap is a future potentially unmoored from its imagined foundation in the past. This future is bound up in American consumerism in which agents participate by virtue of their labor, which then animates all aspects of their lives. Agents are figuratively, psychically, and affectively stretched across the globe, occupying multiple modernities even as they continue to invest in tradition.

CONCLUSION: TOWARD A SYNCHRONOUS INDIAN NATIONAL IDENTITY

This chapter explores the convergences between virtual and material space within and outside of Indian call centers. The intimate ties we explore here reveal the affective contours of network geography. These intimacies in turn converge with inverted and accelerated temporalities through which call center labor is organized. Such disparate temporalities converge and collide in the material spaces of India, exceeding the boundaries of the call center industry and generating a host of anxieties over India's future. The power of time to realign material and intimate relations suggests the importance of accounting for the temporalities of network geography. As we explore in previous chapters, the "kids" who work in call centers become increasingly immersed in American culture, accent, and consumer practices.

Those communication and cultural habits in turn come to animate their lived experiences. Agents' virtual assimilation converges with their youth and their accelerated affective ties to create a sense of anxiety for many of our interviewees. The accelerated intimacies that animate call center life are so starkly different from those associated with a pure conception of India that the industry risks rendering India unintelligible.

In part it is agents' class mobility that threatens such a rupture. Young agents make "more than their parents at retirement" (Ganesh), and they use their wealth to go "shopping, buying, clubbing, clubbing, clubbing" (Saurabh). Their earning potential and the way they use their earnings do not conform to a traditional Indian developmental trajectory. Rather, agents are on a developmental fast track: they outearn and outspend their parents. The accelerated rhythms of agents' lives, so the story goes, are so radically different from those of the previous generation that they risk spinning out of control. Above we argue that the rising class status of Indian agents is also tied to the virtual migration they undertake: as agents become upwardly mobile, they also become Americanized. The inverse is also true: agents' virtual migration enables their upwardly mobility. Thus their class mobility is also a form of virtual global travel. Yet the virtual quality of agents' migration also spills over into the daily lives of agents.

Agents' class mobility, as we explore here, reverberates both with previously theorized forms of Indian upward mobility and with diasporic subjects' sense of longing, loss, disorientation, and displacement. As the pseudohybridities that agents cultivate through the production of their labor animate their material lives, agents are recognized as a distinct group and as the source of a host of affective investments: anxiety, disdain, and admiration. The intertwining of their class mobilities and their virtual assimilation animate their material lives. As these transformations reterritorialize both physical geographies and virtual space, India is increasingly interpenetrated by Western zones, forms of belonging, and virtually assimilated subjects. These network geographies provide a productive site through which to explore questions not only of space and nation, but also of time. Indeed, it is India's future that seems to be at stake. The repeated themes that animate the discourses analyzed here are concerns over agents' intimacies, their indulgent lifestyles, their addiction to credit. These preoccupations signal the affective labor each of call center workers—agents and CEOs alike—must exert to synchronize India's disparate temporalities.

Conclusion

Returning the Call

The coolest thing [about call centers] is the infrastructure. We have
access to everything over here. The toughest thing I face is to take
care of my health because of the timing, and on and off. At times we
have to work when we used to sleep and at times you have to, you
know, vice versa.

—YADAV, 365-Call, focus group interview, 2006

The Indian call center industry, as Yadav suggests, is a vexed site of possibility and constraint, of increased access to modern subjectivities and of inverted temporal lives. For agents like Yadav, call center life is both the "coolest thing" (it provides the infrastructure, cultural capital, and labor practices, giving them "access to everything over here") and the "toughest thing" (the health issues caused by the "on and off timing"). Yadav is an agent on whom the long hours have taken a toll. He complains about his health even as he enjoys the material benefits of his job. The center is designed to meet his needs: cafeteria, gym, and recreation rooms. As we've traced over the course of *Answer the Call*, this both/and quality permeates the industry and animates the lives of those who labor within its structures. The labor and technological forms that organize the Indian call center industry are leveraged toward new time-space relations, giving agents "access to everything over here." But they do so at a cost as the agents' bodies mark the limits of the elasticity of virtual globality. The ongoing communication activity of answering the calls of American consumers over the course of the night shift generates a sense of movement and migration, of assimilation and in-between-ness. Our readings of call center workers' stories track the various ways agents turn in response to these repeated hailings. We find that agents are interpellated into a host of global and national power relations, neoliberal disciplinary technologies, and disparate time-space structures. These forces recalibrate and hybridize their already hybrid identities.

The time-space terrain that animates Yadav's account, as with those we've tracked throughout this study, maps the here and the there onto national and transnational geographies and temporalities. The Indian call center industry converges, collapses, and remixes social geographies and the rhythms by which they move. By "here," Yadav references both India and the physical place of the call center; each becomes collapsed into, or is mutually constitutive of, the other. We witnessed this theme in chapter 4 as agents mobilize Indian citizenship through their participation in mediated global interactions: the local and the national are not sacrificed through agents' participation in the transnational but rather enhanced by it. As India becomes increasingly visible on the global stage, so too do call center agents become increasingly audible to faraway others. Thus the neoliberal project of Indian nation building converges with globalized call center labor. This convergence gives agents a sense of participation in neoliberal sites of inclusion while simultaneously fortifying their participation in the project of nation building.

Yet the exportation of American jobs associated with the call center industry, and outsourcing more broadly, produces a sense of anxiety for many Americans. Chapter 1 explores the production and management of such anxieties in reality-based programming. These productions seek to alleviate sensibilities of invasion and loss through the reassertion of clear temporal and spatial distances between here and there, now and then. However, we find in chapter 4 that the compulsion by some American callers to police the virtual borderlands of the call center exchange suggests that such reassurances do not alleviate these anxieties. Rather, they animate the virtual space of the phone call, which becomes a site in which U.S. racism is mobilized in an oral/aural sphere. The unevenness of the exchange is apparent in the fact that while call center agents are expected to attain fluency in the current football and baseball scores in the United States, there is no expectation that American callers would have any knowledge or interest in the latest victories of the Indian cricket team. These arguments suggest that as new information technologies generate virtual transnational connectivities, the layering of mediated and physical spaces with power differentials continues to complicate any easy time-space conflations and crossings.

The here and the there, the territorial boundaries between nations, and the now and the then are no longer (if they ever were) so easily demarcated. Because clear spatial and temporal distinctions territorialize the production of difference, such uncertainties in turn animate new modes of inclusion and exclusion. These dynamics invite cultural critics to attend to the simultaneous blurring and violent reassertions of boundaries as the territorial boundedness of the nation becomes increasingly crosscut by virtual connectivities. Within such a context, the role of the nation-state, citizenship, and neoliberal inclusion commingle in no necessary relationship to one another. For instance, neoliberal citizenship does not necessarily imply a diminished investment in the nation-state. Rather these sources of inclusion and exclusion bump up against one another, generating shifting antagonisms and alignments—sometimes fortifying and other times undermining the capacity of the nation-state to serve as the arbiter of citizenship.

Even as the particular time-space compression generated by the call center industry blurs boundaries and borders, it also in turn stretches the agents' bodily inhabitance thin: the "toughest" thing for Yadav is to care for is his health. This is "because of the timing, on and off," a theme we theorize in chapter 3 as a temporal inversion. Call center labor, as we have argued, enables agents to migrate to America: a migration through time; through the checkered first world and third world zones of the modern call center industry within the developing space of India; and through the virtual spaces its telecommunication processes enable. These converging forms of migration orient agents toward distant sites, even as they enable virtual travel without agents ever actually arriving at a tangible elsewhere. On one hand, virtual migration is part of broader globalizing processes that bring America to India (in Raja's words, "We have the U.S. getting into India"). Call center labor exports agents' labor while their bodies remain bound within the Indian homeland. It is marked by a coninual movement *toward* (agents "are moving toward the Western culture," Sunita explains) that never culminates in an *arrival at.* This is not to say that agents want to migrate to the United States in any other way. Rather, it suggests that as we study the communication processes through which globalization circulates, we must attend to the ways identities and forms of labor migrate without the bodies that produce them.

This migration without bodies does not, however, elide the body from the picture. Rather, as chapter 3 argues, the agents' bodies and the affective ties that animate agents' lives become the condensed sites in which agents carry the freight of the time-space compression. Indeed, the temporally inverted lives call center labor creates reconfigure agents' bodily inhabitance (sore throats, coughing blood, nightmares, insomnia) as well as their affective orientation. "My dad works in a government office, so his shift starts from 8 o'clock A.M.," Mahesh explains. "I would be in a night shift, so when I go back to my home, he won't be there. When he comes back, I won't be there" (Mahesh, 365-Call, focus group interview, 2006). A continual sense of near misses marks call center labor. While Mahesh lives in the same house as his father, neither will "be there" when the other comes home. Dressed in a short-sleeved, button-down shirt and gray trousers, Mahesh hails from a lower-middle-class family and speaks with a thick Indian accent. But since he is a high-tech worker, who e-chats with Western customers who need computer help, his voice doesn't matter. His work in a nonvoice process insulates Mahesh from some of the immediacy of phone work—and the affective labor it entails. Mashesh's body matters not only to the kind of labor he does, but also to the way his particular embodiment positions him in relation to American customers. And his body, or its absence, matters a great deal to his father.

Temporal inversions generate affective distance as agents lose touch with those nearby, even as they cultivate belonging with those faraway others within the virtual space of call center labor. This dynamic of mediated inclusion charts the terrain of chapter 4 in which the call center encounter generates a virtual border zone in which Indian, American, and neoliberal citizenship are negotiated. Thus agents' movement through time converges with their movement through layered space—a network geography that invites us to distinguish between physical and virtual space and to underscore the layering of networked spaces atop physical places. Attending to such layerings enables cultural critics and geographers to complicate critical notions of socially constructed space, which rely exclusively on examinations of physical space. Our study of the various ways call center labor puts agents in touch with distant others raises questions over the limits of strictly space- and place-based approaches to geography, inviting cultural workers to attend to the convergences and divergences between physical and virtual space—always with an attention to the machinations of bodily inhabitance. Further, the force of time in reconstituting the industry's network geography also suggests the importance of excavating the temporal dimensions of such virtual and material upheavals.

A close examination of such convergences of time, space, and virtuality also enable us to theorize the uneven dispersion of globalization's time-space compressions. Our ethnographic interviews within the Indian call center industry provide insights into the ways in which time is drawn out for agents in order to compress time for American callers. "So if my name is Sundarshini Sen Gupta, it'll take two and a half minutes for the American to understand what my name is," Ganesh explains. "So the reason that the nicknames actually happened was for the American to understand." The American caller need not be burdened with the lengthy foreign names of Indian agents; Indian names take too much time. Imperatives of expediency and cultural accommodation compel agents to shorten their names or to change them altogether. As chapter 2 argues, agents make tremendous efforts to accommodate the perceived temporal and affective needs of their callers: they take on pseudonyms, neutralize their Indian accents, and strive to become fluent in the mundane details of American life. In these little and big ways, agents enable time and space to become accelerated for American callers, even as the countless hours of training and answering calls over the course of the night shift forestall time for agents. Our study, then, underscores the danger in universalizing claims about the accelerated or compressed nature of time and space under globalization. Such generalizations stabilize time-space horizons, erasing the uneven conditions that enable time-space compressions in the first place.

For instance, as chapter 3 argues, the bodily and affective labor that agents expend in order to accommodate American callers exposes the limits of how we theorize the category of experience. While agents' bodies remain in India, virtual migration compels them to stretch their consciousness to imagine a host of experiences they have never had. Ganesh explains, "When we speak to the customer, we build rapport. Somebody's calling from Boston, so you say, 'Hey, the Red Sox won finally!'" In Ganesh's account, we see the strategies agents cultivate to build rapport. "That's the way the Americans also feel like they're speaking to someone close to them." So agents' affective labor works to generate affective proximity designed to diminish or overcome the geographic and temporal distances of time arbitrage. A familiarity with the mundane details of American life, like a Red Sox victory, is one of many strategies agents use to create a sense of affective proximity with their callers. At the same time, the temporal inversion of call center labor isolates and insulates the agents' bodily and affective inhabitance from their immediate surroundings. As theorists study the virtual globalizations enabled by new telecommunications technology, then, we might attend to the tensions between bodily inhabitance and virtual travel. The virtuality of various forms of mobility must remain a central nexus of analysis. Further, the uneven distribution of affective labor within such virtualizing processes—the various ways that affect is withdrawn and redistributed—must also be attended to.

The concept of virtualscapes is one productive move this work has revealed to address these tensions that animate this historical moment. The consumer practices cultivated within the call center industry converge with the compulsion for agents to perform Americanness over the course of the night shift to generate a new moment within Appadurai's earlier theorization of globalization's scapes. Iqbal explains this movement, from the 1991 opening of India's media markets to the economic mobility and consumer practices call center labor enables, as converging forces that reconfigure Indian culture:

> The way the culture has changed. I think the major contributor to that is the U.S. media, which has sort of penetrated into the Indian market. And that has helped us because people are now more familiar with the Western culture and how people dress, or lifestyles over there. The major impact this industry is having is lifting the economic lifestyle of people over here. It's giving them more money. It's giving them the ability to go out and do something they were not able to do: buy designer clothes, buy satellite or cable television in their house. (Iqbal, Infofloz, personal interview, 2004)

Agents' "familiarity" with "Western culture" is mobilized as cultural capital, a privileged form of knowledge that helps agents build the Indian call center industry. As we explore in chapter 2, call center training draws on American sitcoms like *Friends* to cultivate this familiarity. They do so not merely for the pleasure of consuming U.S. popular culture, but also in order to hone their skills in the performance of Americanized communication practices. The study of culture within communication-based transnationalisms invites us to attend to the ways that neoliberal subjects might increasingly be valued through the performance of such normative cultural fluencies. Indeed, as we explore in the afterword below, neoliberal pedagogies will continue to animate the project of Indian nation building under transnationalism.

The ways in which the call center industry is transforming the material and daily lives of call center agents is an important consideration. There has been a significant discussion of the cultural shifts in Indian cultural life after liberalization. Our study demonstrates that there are identifiable shifts generated through agents' participation in this industry—shifts that deepen or extend previous research. For this particular group of English-speaking and educated youth, social mobility is enabled through what we've called a temporal inversion. Raja captures this dynamic in his account: "The kind of livelihood that you live, because of the timings—that you go back and sleep during the day when the rest of the world is around, and you actually don't get the time to meet with another circle of people outside" (365-Call, focus group interview, 2006). Because call center life is structured to accommodate the U.S. workday, agents like Raja often work the night shift. This temporal inversion is experienced as affective distance as agents "don't get time to meet with another circle of people outside."

This temporal inversion redirects agents' affective ties. First, as we explore in chapter 3, agents feel a distance from local family and friends, even as they reorient their consciousness and affective labor toward the American caller. And second, as we explore in chapter 4, agents' virtual migration also creates a sense of shared time, space, and culture among agents. As Raja puts it, "Where do you go? For a date?" The answer seems to be: to other agents. Call center agents share the unique experience of becoming Americanized through their ongoing participation in call center labor even as they are aligned through the segregated space-time of the industry. So when agents build intimate ties, almost exclusively with one another, they form a unique subculture. They are recognized as an "immediately identifiable group" (Armaan) who share a diasporic sense of loss and longing for and departure from a pure India. Agents' virtual migration recalibrates how we think about diaspora. Virtual migration is marked by a movement toward America without ever leaving India's shores—and without physically arriving in the West. But the network geographies and temporalities that reconstitute their lived space-time and affective lives are distinctly recast through their labor. Their work in the industry affords agents a high degree of upward mobility. But their orientation toward the West—their Americanized affect and consumer/worker tendencies—produces a nostalgic sentiment like those living in or returning from the Indian–U.S. diaspora. It is their pseudohybridity, to use Raveena's term, that resonates with, but further hybridizes, the positionality of diasporic Indians. Their in-between-ness is virtualized and virtually produced, even as the cultural affects of their labor spill over into their daily lives, cultural practices, and intimate relations. The virtual thus reterritorializes the material, forging agents' subjectivities with a sense of acceleration. As it does so, the industry becomes the source of tremendous anxiety over what the formation of call center subjectivities means for India's future. It is the question of future to which we now turn.

AFTERWORD: FORMING INDIA'S NEOLIBERAL FUTURES

Where is the Indian call center industry today, at the end of the nine-year journey that culminates in *Answer the Call?* On the basis of all that we've learned over the course of this study, this afterword points to some possible futures—not only for the call center industry, but also for the broader changes in Indian culture and the globalization of which the industry is a part. We returned to India in 2009, 2010, 2011, and 2012 to continue to talk to leaders in the call center industry and follow cultural shifts. This research has enabled us to trace new industry and cultural developments and to learn how those in such positions are envisioning the industry's future. Our afterword features our extensive interview with Laveena, who owned I2U, a small, 600-employee call center. Now her company has been bought by a larger international conglomerate. Consolidation is the word of the day, Laveena explains. She sold I2U "primarily because I realized that the BPO business, the call center business is meant for extremely large players [...]. Unless it is tens of, you know, thousands of people it would take a really long time for you to break even" (I2U, personal interview, 2009). Laveena is expanding the training modules she developed in the industry for broader neoliberalizing economic educational projects.

Laveena's choice to sell I2U and her next career move are one woman's life choices. But her choices are also situated within a larger global economy and India's place in it: "India is not becoming a global player," as she insists. "India *is* a global player." What does it mean that India, emphatically for Laveena, is a global player? How might we read her own subject position, her previously formative role in building the call center industry in India, and her current ambitions within such a historical context? Some recent economic indicators are at odds with Laveena's assessment; they suggest that India's GDP growth rate has slowed from its earlier double-digit figures to vacillate in a broad range from 3.9 to 9.8 percent between 2007 and 2012 (WorldBank Data 2012). But there is also evidence that India continues to grow, even if not as rapidly as before given the global economic recession, particularly for the rising middle class. For instance, the Bay Area Council Economic Institute created a report on

India's growth, but the study also indicates new global connectivities between India and the United States. The study finds indicators of economic growth, such as "Levi's has two-hundred outlets in India. Visa has issued more than twenty-million credit cards there and Cisco Systems' second headquarters is located in Bangalore" (Drummond 2009). But perhaps more important for our purposes, the study signals the continuation of a series of space-time convergences between the United States and India that resonate with and extend those we've tracked in this book. First, San Francisco is Bangalore's sister city, so the study is part of a host of investments and development projects that increasingly move both ways. And second, the ongoing importation of Levi's and Visa cards are markers of the products and practices through which agents like Raja come to imagine that "America is getting into India."

The sense of collaboration and relative parity between the United States and India explored in this study also resonates with the observations offered by Ronit in a recent interview. Ronit believes that "high-value end work" and an "ethos of collaboration" are trends in the "next phase of the industry" (Ronit, personal interview, 2012). Ronit explains that this shift entails collaboration at the design stage of production, as opposed to outsourced labor carrying out pink-collar service work. For example, "When the aerospace designers are outsourced right here and sitting here . . . when the molecular engineers and doctors are here," the ethos of collaboration becomes an "area where the call center industry can evolve." Such collaborations would transform the face of the Indian call center industry and outsourcing more broadly, creating multiple contradictory potential outcomes. The forms of labor Ronit envisions are high end, technologically advanced, and lucrative. Further, the positionalities of the Indian workers—doctors, engineers, aerospace designers—are highly educated, well paid, and elite. The shift Ronit envisions extends our findings in chapters 1 and 3, in which we trace India's growth and development vis-à-vis U.S. economic decline. Chapter 1 details the production and management of the anxieties associated with these global shifts in reality programming, underscoring the important role of power temporalities in reasserting American supremacy over India. Although images of call center agents mimicking Thomas Friedman's American accent may reassure watchers that India will always be a step behind the United States, media coverage of a specialized and highly trained Indian workforce doing America's jobs may be even more threatening. Likewise, the anxieties expressed by callers explored in chapter 3 suggest the extent to which some Americans are deeply unsettled by such collaborations and the virtual borderlands and forms of migration they generate.

The formation of checkered geographies and the presence of America in India continue to permeate India's cityscapes. Our travels have taken us to a wide variety of upscale malls, coffee shops, bars, and restaurants. One restaurant on the outskirts of Bangalore offers an exclusive experience of slow cooking, where diners enjoy a seven-course meal specially created for them, based on individual food preferences. Priced at $100 a plate, it is a small fortune by middle-class Indian standards. Another recent trend is popularly referred to as reverse outsourcing, in which India "has actually begun to send jobs back to the U.S." (Drummond 2009). Because the growth in economic zones such as Bangalore has exceeded their current infrastructure, India is drawing on America's "help with everything from waste management to setting up a public health system" (Drummond 2009). This "surprising" trend signals several implications for themes we've traced throughout this study. Although popular representations of reverse outsourcing may potentially alleviate some U.S. anxieties over American job losses due to outsourcing, the representational practices through which the phenomenon is depicted works through an orientalist logic, not unlike that which animates the documentary films we examine in chapter 1. The discourse contains the threat posed by the inversion of power marked by the term *reverse outsourcing* by framing India as in need of America's help and the United States as the central frame of reference.

The reverse outsourcing trend also marks an intervention by the nation-state to extend and deepen the cultivation of what we've called India's checkered geography. It suggests a certain synergy between neoliberalism and Indian nation building, or the degree to which the nation-state participates in the production of such first world zones within the third world zone. Further, this checkering of space, as we have argued, is one condition that contributes to the larger phenomenon of virtual migration. As Indian subjects increasingly move between first world and third world zones, the forms of migration we have documented here will continue to shape their subject positions. The phenomenon of checkered geography will continue to reconfigure Indian geographies, not only in urban but increasingly in rural settings. One new trend in this regard is that as labor and land costs increase in the cities, the call center industry increasingly penetrates rural areas to save money on labor, overhead, and resources. Local spaces will continue to be revamped as the call center industry progressively permeates more traditional spaces, such as working-class and village communities. "A decade ago," one source reports of a sleepy Indian town (Ram 2009), "Gurgaon was little more than a farming community. Then outsourcing boomed, and the town became a preferred location for companies that answer phones, create PowerPoint presentations, and do other business tasks for U.S. clients."

This new trend may well exacerbate the tensions over the accelerated conditions of agents' subject formation that we examine in chapters 2 and 4. America and India increasingly interanimate one another as the reach of the West increasingly extends into rural areas. This move will likely deepen some of the forces and affects of virtual migration we outline above as places like Gurgaon become increasingly animated by the kinds of network geographies and temporalities that reconstitute physical space, affective ties, and local and national culture. India is likely to continue to house major American and multinational corporations, import iconic American commodities, and increase Indian's reliance on credit. It becomes apparent that these practices, which have so intensely reconfigured agents' subjectivities, will continue to remake Indian subjectivities along the lines we have explored here and in new ways we can only begin to anticipate. One difference we may see is the forms of regional migration and new kinds of checkered geography that may follow. The agents in our study often move from small communities, towns, or villages to large city centers, such as Bangalore and Mumbai. Such agents find that regional migration is, in many ways, experienced as a form of global migration. But in this case, the industry itself is migrating. As it moves into these more traditional (less Westernized) sites, the cultural divergences between agents and local community members may become even more acute than those we trace here, even as the infrastructure of these sites may well rapidly develop in order to keep up.

As India continues to offer global corporations new opportunities for growth, it will remain a primary site for outsourcing. As of this writing, India still ranks as the number one destination for outsourced jobs, and the BPO (business process outsourcing) industry is projected to continue to grow.[1] Journalist Amit Tripathi (2009) predicts "that the Indian BPO sector will reach over thirty billion dollars in export revenues by 2012." To do so, India must remain flexible in its services and labor practices while competitive in its pricing. The flexibility of transnational capital continually rewrites cartographies of outsourcing, making out-sourcing a dynamic project.[2] The percentage of global labor exported to Eastern Europe is on the decline, for instance, while outsourcing to the Middle East and Africa has risen significantly. Reports show that "while India, China and Malaysia retain the top three spots they've occupied since the inaugural GSLI in 2004, a fundamental shift in the index has taken place as once strong Central European countries have yielded ground to countries in Asia, the Middle East and North Africa" (PR Newswire, 2009). Trends like these discipline Indian leaders to accommodate these market dynamics.

Unless India continues to shift, grow, and react to the needs of this flex-ible capital, so the story goes, it will lose its place. Call center manager Ganesh describes the competitive threat posed by the Philippines: "They're much more customer-centric. They're less ambitious, so they don't leave the jobs very often. We're much more smart technically. But in customer service, I think they kind of beat us quite a bit." The essentialisms that permeate Ganesh's account reiterate a concern we've traced over India's job-hopping agents. Because Filipinos are "less ambitious," they are more likely to remain in their jobs. Perhaps Indian agents are too flexible, too ambitious, too individuated through their neoliberal enculturation. Ronit reflects on the nuances of ambition that, he suggests, get in their way. "I think we are a caste hierarchy system. We are—we have hierarchy on the brain. I mean, I would interview people, 'where do you want to be in five years?' 'I want to have your job.' Straight answer . . . And I'd say, you know, I'm very, very impressed but I hope to have my job also in five years. But if I leave, yes. I am impressed by your ambition, not so impressed by your motivation" (Ronit, former BigBank executive, personal interview, 2012). So for Ronit, who left the industry to pursue a career in the arts, one must also recognize their placement in the hierarchy. Alternatively, Filipino workers, Ganesh imagines, are "less ambitious" and perhaps more docile and other directed—more "customer-centric." Mapped onto the global market, these individual attitudes and labor practices shape and are shaped by the flexible global flows of the outsourcing industry. But as Ronit's account of increasingly collaborative and high-end connectivities between the United States and India transforms Indian outsourcing, a global shift in pink-collar labor may be absorbed by other developments.

One concern among industry leaders is that a mobile labor force drives up the cost of outsourcing to India: mobile agents make the whole industry less competitive. Labor cost is a central factor contributing to the trend of consolidation within the Indian call center industry that motivates Laveena to sell her company. Indeed, consolidation is tied to the figure of the mobile agent, who skips from one job to the next. This is a "very common thing between call centers," agent Joel explains. "For a higher salary, people keep jumping. Now call centers have agreements between each other to not hire between each other." Indian call centers, as Joel suggests, have always been more organized than their employees. At the time of our research, the industry actively sought to control price inflation by creating cooperatives through which companies would agree not to poach each other's labor. In spite of such efforts, the industry has been relatively unsuccessful at containing agents' mobility, making consolidation a business necessity. Laveena explains: "The cost of retention of talent was high because you just train them and in three, four, five months, just when they are about ready to start producing for you, they have moved on to someone else" (I2U, personal interview, 2009). The larger conglomerates, like the one that purchased I2U, are able to absorb these spiraling costs. Smaller call centers are forced to merge.

Such consolidations have not undermined the global strength of the Indian call center industry. Rather they are seen as a strategic move contributing to its increasing efficiency. Such efficiencies enable India to remain competitive, even as other nations, including the United States, become increasingly competitive. The recession in the United States has generated new investments—both affective and material—in returning jobs to its shores. For instance, there has been a recent surge in home-based labor, where workers do call center jobs from their own homes. Reports suggest that the economic downturn has provided an abundant, "well-educated and mostly female" workforce located "anywhere in the country" (Smerd 2009, 33). Because they work out of their own homes, this labor force saves the company money by reducing overhead and labor costs. This feminized, domestic workforce converges with a series of U.S. anxieties over outsourcing, especially those traced in chapters 2 and 4.

Home-based labor counteracts such anxieties as the exportation of jobs, the security concerns over foreign workers handling sensitive information, and the broader deterritorialization of America. The return of this labor home marks a return both to the U.S. nation-state and to the intimate domestic sphere. Thus the emergence of home-based labor marks a symbolic and material reassertion of the territorial integrity of the nation and of the American dream. The return of call center labor to America thus marks a moment of containment of the very anxieties that so deeply permeate the U.S. production of the Indian call center industry, and outsourcing more broadly, which we have examined in this study. In spite of the affective appeal that animates this retreat from the global, this kind of labor seems to hold little interest for American workers. This trend is evidenced by the high attrition rate within the home-based call center industry. It raises the question of the degree to which this domesticization of labor serves symbolic, more than material, interests.

From the Indian side, Laveena is confident that this relatively small American workforce cannot handle the volume of outsourcing work that companies need. In order to continue to attract foreign investment, she reasons, India needs to provide inexpensive and high-quality labor. The industry must develop its labor pool to minimize the training costs of preparing workers to participate in the globalized labor market while maximizing their capacity to do so. Addressing this conundrum is where her most recent intervention lies. Laveena is currently developing call center industry training practices into teaching modules for middle-class Indian college students. The modules are designed to address what she calls the gap between the level of education students acquire in Indian higher education and the needs and expectations of global employers. This gap became evident to her when she sought to train call center workers to be ready to work the phones. "The gap was really vast, and it really didn't matter what you studied in school," Laveena explains. "But when they came on board, we really had to start from scratch. So it boiled down to the fact that the curriculum mismatch really costs the industry, as a whole, millions and millions of dollars a year" (I2U, personal interview, 2009). There is a gap, then, between liberal Indian education and neoliberal subject formation. The contents that constitute this gap are basic skills that enable Indian workers to produce surplus value in an increasingly service-based global economy: "teaching them how to type, basic grammatically correct English, e-mail etiquette, professionalism" (Laveena, I2U, personal interview, 2009).

The gap Laveena identifies signals the critical role that the call center industry plays in the national project of developing global subjects, even if the industry itself dies or shifts to high-end work. The industry has been formative in extending neoliberal inclusion to middle-class and lower-middle-class young workers. Laveena thinks these same practices—those that bridge the gap—hold tremendous potential for contemporary Indian nation building. The rise of the Indian call center industry marks a particular historic moment in which the mediated, informatics, and telecommunication needs of global circulation and exchange gain tremendous salience within late capitalism. In order to perform such labor, workers must be able not only to speak English, but also to speak a certain kind of English that is globally intelligible: "The biggest, biggest, biggest challenge all around is communication. [. . .] That makes a big difference to a lot of kids when they start to understand how to speak simple, grammatically correct English that makes them feel more confident" (Laveena, I2U, personal interview, 2009). Laveena's sense that such communication skills generate "confidence" among these "kids" resonates with agents' sense of empowerment, a theme we explore in chapter 4. Agents' subjectivities are remade as their identities become mediated through a global politics of recognition and as Indian subjects are increasingly cultivated as neoliberal subjects who perform on a global stage. Laveena is poised to fill this gap through the formation of neoliberal pedagogies that seek to cultivate globally intelligible (Westernized) communication skills among India's youth.

Laveena's project is not to teach English to poor, non-English-speaking youth; nor is she concerned with the first-tier college students, who, she argues, already have access to the kinds of skills she seeks to disseminate. Rather, her project aims to recast the communication practices of working- and middle-class students from second-tier schools within assimilated, Westernized, and neoliberal models of communication and culture. Such pedagogies, she argues, are required to keep India competitive with other outsourcing competitors and to counteract the return of call center labor to the United States:

I don't necessarily see [call center labor] shifting overseas because at the end of the day, India does have the advantage of still having a large, large English-speaking population. Now also from the industry perspective, if you look at the call center industry in the U.S., these are jobs that have one to two hundred percent attrition. People just come in [for] three weeks. They are on a holiday, they want to make some quick bucks, they go in and become a telephone operator. You know, their training is three to four hours and they are good to go, right? So the Indian industry has to get that level of nimbleness. They don't have to have people on their rolls, you know, twenty-four/seven, three hundred and sixty-five days of the year. When they have peaks, they can bring in folks. So there is a hurricane in the U.S. and call centers have to be staffed up—they are getting calls. It's an emergency, right? (Laveena, I2U, personal interview, 2009)

As we have argued, particularly in chapter 2, India is produced and imagined as a primary outsourcing destination—particularly for U.S. and Western call centers—because of its "large English-speaking population." And as we explore in chapter 4, the question of how this large population will be cultivated is central to Indian nation building within transnational capitalism. Within such a context, nimbleness is the word of the day. The cultivation of such a nimble labor force—one that could be trained in "three to four hours"—would leverage the corporation's flexibility over the Indian agents' currently excessive mobility. Indeed, such a labor pool could be hired and laid off not according to workers' economic needs or desires, but rather according to the immediate and capricious needs of global capital. In Laveena's example, a "hurricane in the U.S." would require "emergency" staff to answer the call of Americans in need. The hurricane comes to stand in for a host of possible short-term scenarios in which labor might be temporarily required and then discarded. Within such a formation, America's emergency becomes India's opportunity.

For Indian business leaders like Laveena, the projects of neoliberalism and of nation building converge. Those neoliberal forms of inclusion agents develop through call center labor as they service the needs of global customers are also imagined as communication practices that enable forms of national inclusion. As India emerges onto the global stage—or, as Laveena argues, "*is* a global player"—the formation of neoliberal subjects becomes part and parcel of its nation-building project. "So based on that, even the nation-building part," Laveena explains, "we need youth. We need youth who are educated and trained and employable. So as a result of that, this is a very important part of ensuring that we continue to sustain the global head start that we have now" (personal interview, 2009).

Such nation-building projects require a pedagogical system to cultivate this "educated, trained, and employable youth." As we argue in chapters 2 and 4, India's youth come to stand in for the nation's future. Youth circulate as a site of heavy cultural investment and anxious discipline. Such investments in producing neoliberal subjects invite us to consider the specificities of Henry Giroux's (2004) insight that neoliberalism must be understood as both an economic theory and a powerful public pedagogy

and cultural politics. The economic and cultural manifestations of neoliberalism must be actively aligned. Neoliberal pedagogy becomes the
condition of possibility for the convergence between the economic and
the cultural through which neoliberal formations circulate.

It would follow that Laveena is currently developing those forms of
pedagogy that she acquired and cultivated in the call center industry for
more general pedagogical purposes. Her training modules and workshops
are designed to teach midlevel, middle-class Indian college students the
kinds of communication skills and cultural sensibilities she envisions as
enabling them to be competitive on the global market. "So I am trying
to do a systemic change, trying to go to universities, et cetera. It is going to
be humungous." The "humungous" scope of the project includes online
training modules, workshops, and training sessions. These sessions are
designed to discipline, inform, sensitize, and cultivate students into a host
of neo-liberal sensibilities. The following excerpt is transcribed from the
online training module Laveena played during the interview. It provides
a sense of the ways her online training modules operationalize these learning outcomes. The screen shows animated figures, and the voice-over orients the viewer to the teaching session by developing the characters of
three students:

> Raja, Shree, and Manoj decided to attend the presentation made by PREPS.[3]
> The presentation started at 10 A.M. sharp. Anyone who was even a minute
> late was not allowed to come in. During the presentation, Shree and his
> friend made a lot of noise and tried to distract the PREPS career advisor by
> asking stupid questions. At [one] point, the PREPS career advisor threw the
> boys out. The boys saw that the PREPS career advisor meant business, and
> Shree and the usually noisy guys decided to keep quiet and ensured that
> they were not thrown out. (Laveena, I2U, personal interview, 2009)

The audio text is performed by young male and female animated Indian
students enacting this and similar scripts. One aim of the film is to cultivate students as self-managing subjects: the "usually noisy" friends had
to show up on time and "decided to keep quiet" to "ensure they were not
thrown out." The pedagogy of Laveena's scripts leverages the boundaries of neoliberal inclusion through local sites of participation in forums
of neoliberal subject formation. The first step in becoming a neoliberal
subject is to "ensure" one's inclusion within the structures of neoliberal

pedagogy. The power of the training is contingent on the students submitting themselves to being trained. They are compelled to invest in the disciplinary project through the circular logic the narrative outlines: "the PREPS career advisor meant business." The metonymic power of this ascription is presumably sufficient to warrant self-disciplining as business comes to stand in for a host of inclusions and exclusions circumscribed by the bounds of the training session.

One strategy Laveena has developed to encourage students to invest in their training is to require them to pay a nominal fee in order to participate. The fee serves more of a symbolic than material function. Because students pay to participate, she explains, they learn to invest in their education and are more likely to complete the program of study. Last year her team administered tests to "about 10,000 kids for free." Because the tests were free, Laveena reasons, they undercut the value of the testing and ensuing training: "Everybody came and took the test, wasted our time, paper, and money—and then didn't show up, or were not qualified, or didn't really care about it." Students failed to provide returns on her firm's output. Thus she opts for a different tactic: "So this year I want some skin in the game from them, right? So we said, 'Let's charge them 200 rupees.' And interestingly, the resistance from them was, 'Oh my god, no way. Why should we pay?' But our conversion numbers are like 70 to 75 percent because only the people who are really interested in a job come for a job" (Laveena, I2U, personal interview, 2009). The line between the "skin in the game from them" and the fee students pay blurs here, students' "resistance" seeming to reaffirm this reading: skin is a function of the tangible and metaphoric investment students are compelled to make. The training project teaches students to invest in these two senses of the term (materially, and by extension affectively). These investments are designed to cultivate their "interest" in employment within global circuits of power.

This disciplinary logic in turn permeates the online training modules to generate synergies and identifications between the students' lived experiences and their consumption of the online texts. In the following excerpt from the training module, the animated students perform the themes outlined by Laveena above. Manoj illustrates an appropriate response to neoliberal pedagogy:

"Dude, don't be so oversmart. These people have already tested thousands of students like us in India. Less than 10 percent got jobs. Don't be thinking that PREPS is trying to make fools of us. Actually, don't you read [the] papers? Everywhere they are saying that people are losing jobs. Who is saying that getting jobs is easy? You may know all the local *gundas* [goons] and politicians. I need a job, and I need a job badly. And why should it be free? Will PREPS employees take home the salary we make? All of us have no problem in paying 200 rupees for a movie ticket, but no chance we will pay these people for a job?" Raja and Shree realized Manoj was right, and they both decided to take the PREPS assessment and competency tests. (Laveena, I2U, personal interview, 2009)

The character of Manoj leverages horizontal affective power as a neoliberal logic to interpellate Raja and Shree. By virtue of its representation in the film, his speech is designed to hail the students who are invited to identify with the group's wise choice to invest the 200-rupee fee. These rhetorical choices both engage and then undercut student resistance. They are strategically incorporated across mediated and material training practices. Neoliberalism's multiply mediated pedagogies are leveraged to guide students to the right answer: pay the fee, roll the dice, invest in your success, get a job.

For diasporic subjects like Laveena, the project of Indian nation building entails the active cultivation of network geographies: leveraging the virtual in order to cultivate neoliberal subjects, practices, and sites at home. The middle-class youth she targets do not necessarily, as we argue in chapter 4, have the opportunities or even the desire to live abroad. Yet their formation as virtually diasporic subjects is a critical component of their capacity to serve global capitalism. One prong of Laveena's vision is to "make them aware of what is going on in the world":

For example, I want an assignment saying go to NPR, listen to a piece that has been put in there. Put on NPR, download it, listen to it. Now suddenly they get exposure to NPR to an American accent, they get exposure to world news. Then get them to go to BBC, get them to do an assignment on who the world's classical musicians are. Because I think that's really what makes someone aware of multiple, different things—to become a rounded personality and be better at jobs. It's not really book knowledge that makes someone really good as a long-term, high-potential employee, right? (Laveena, I2U, personal interview, 2009)

In the absence of traveling the globe, the rising middle-class student is invited to participate in a virtual cosmopolitanism by consuming the West through the Internet: to download and listen in order to become aware. The cultivation of a cosmopolitan sensibility is not merely for the pleasure of consuming these texts, but rather, as we argue in chapter 3, to cultivate the performance of a global subject. Just as agents must become fluent in a host of experiences they do not have, students are trained to become fluent in those "different things" that mark a worker as a "long-term, high-potential employee." Laveena's ambitious project aims to retool the technologies productive of the Indian call centers' virtualscapes in order to democratize them, making them available to a wider population of college students. Her selection of NPR and BBC, as opposed to CNN or local news, marks the particular intellectual constellation that she seeks to cultivate in her students and that would be intelligible to other cosmopolitan subjects as such.

Giroux's (2005) argument might categorize Laveena's training regimen as part of "virulent" neoliberalism's "vast educational propaganda machine" (1). Her emphasis on producing students who are fluent in Western classical and intellectual discourses might also be seen as preparing them for engaged citizenship and inclusion into a nation-building development vision. But the production of neoliberalism in India must not be collapsed into neoliberal formations in the United States. For example, Laveena wants to teach students about issues of gender and religious diversity: "So now I have put two girls into it. One is a Muslim girl and one is a Christian girl. So there is Christian–Muslim thing," she explains (personal interview, 2009). The function of the inclusion that the "Christian–Muslim thing" signifies allows us to explore such convergences and divergences. On the one hand, such efforts to sensitize students to issues of diversity are complicit with imperialistic discourses of tolerance. On the other hand, it serves to lubricate the affective terrain of India's neoliberal nation-building project.

Wendy Brown (2006) underscores the troublesome undercurrents of tolerance projects. Because tolerance is mobilized to produce Western exceptionalism, it also becomes a standard by which nontolerant difference is coded as barbaric. For Brown, tolerance circulates as a multivalent form of govermentality that functions "less as a strategy of protection than a telos of multicultural citizenship"—particularly in a post-9/11 historical context in which the "enemy of tolerance is now the weaponized radical Islamicist state or terror cell rather than the neighborhood bigot" (5–6).

This is not to flatten the distinctions between U.S. and Indian nation-building projects, but rather to consider what might be at stake in pedagogies of tolerance for Indian national identity. Indeed, as we argue in previous chapters, Indian agents are often the target of post-9/11 U.S. American racism. Further, terrorism takes on different meanings in the United States and India. The November 2008 Mumbai terrorist attacks occurred just over a month before this interview, yet Laveena never linked her vision of diversity to this event. Whereas the 9/11 attacks provoked just such a response from the West, the Indian response to the Mumbai attacks[4] was forged through a host of more subtle and vexed negotiations with otherness. Responses to the Mumbai attacks reverberated with America's strategy of othering, even as they were permeated by Mahatma Gandhi's pacifist political stance.[5] India has not responded with military aggression toward Pakistan as the United States did toward Afghanistan, and later Iraq.[6] The production of tolerance in India departs from its American counterpart as India's nation-building project seeks economic, not necessarily military or imperial, modes of power.

So while tolerance might function in a U.S. context to leverage imperialist militarisms, India seems to have a different interest in its production. These nationally situated productions of tolerance might be said to converge through neoliberal forms of inclusion and exclusion. As we explore in chapter 3, agents' immersion in American culture and accent training invariably includes a diversity piece, giving agents a value-added function. Such convergences reveal the production of tolerance as a marker of both neoliberal inclusion and exclusion: Indian agents gain status within global circuits of communication-based exchange through their capacity to master such discourses of multicultural inclusion. Yet agents seem to recognize that it is they who are included or excluded at the whims, economic needs, and affective investments of more powerful American business leaders and, at times, consumers.

The production of tolerance in Indian neoliberal pedagogies, then, generates the kinds of virtual migration we examine throughout this study. Through demonstrations of civility, tolerance, and global knowledge, the Indian subjects Laveena seeks to cultivate might productively participate in virtual globality. Yet tolerance also implicitly teaches them that they too may become its objects if their inclusion threatens those with more power, real or imagined. The forms of neoliberal inclusion that Laveena's project aims to generate are in many ways limited before they even begin. In a post-9/11 historical context, in which American borders will remain vigilantly protected, virtual connectivities will continue to serve as the terrain through which such subjects migrate. Although they may not become tangibly diasporic or cosmopolitan, the Indian subjects of neo-liberal inclusion may succeed in becoming virtually so.

As we consider the larger project of the call center industry and its potential to shape India's development, growth, and national identity, Laveena's neoliberal pedagogical project serves as an example of the kinds of new formations we might anticipate. Ronit concurs, stressing the "important impact" the industry has had, both economically and culturally. The call center industry, he contends, is "the starter drug for many people in this country. It's the marijuana of globalization" (Ronit, personal interview, 2012). By this, Ronit underscores the ways in which the industry's network geography has spilled over to animate people's lived experience, "from the way they dress, to the way they eat, the way they communicate, the way they travel, the way they aspire and the way they dream. The call center will be that first port of call for a dreamer who has acquired a command of a new language, and a new set of skills, through an education system and then commences to put it to immediate effect while getting feedback all the way on how they're doing" (Ronit, personal interview, 2012). Call center labor has a tremendous capacity to reconfigure every aspect of agents' lives, from their dress to their dreams to the food they eat—not to mention *when* they dress, eat, and dream. Ronit's metaphors for the Indian call center industry—the "marijuana of globalization," new forms of travel, the "port of call for a dreamer"—crystallize the psychic quality of virtual migration. Call center labor is a gateway of sorts, a portal through which agents traverse time and travel the globe, never to return home to the way things were.

Notes

Introduction

1. A *salwar kameez* is a traditional North Indian form of dress, which consists of loose pajama-style pants and a long, flowing top that goes down to midthigh or even the knees. It is often worn with a *dupatta,* a long, broad scarf.

2. Outsourcing practices are neither unique nor new to transnational flows of capital and production. The outsourcing practices that we consider here are just one part of this continuing trend. Ross (2009) traces historical and contemporary migration of capital and labor across the globe. He notes that while in uneven power relations, both capital and labor move in response to opportunities. Corporations seek increasing profits and move across the globe to facilitate them while simultaneously relying on a controllable workforce. Although historically workers have shifted their living practices to coincide with the location of labor in order to stabilize their long-term work efforts, in the contemporary moment, what we see is a "new geography of livelihoods" wherein workers increasingly define themselves as more flexible and mobile (3). This involves the potential to move across industries and companies as well as location. We see this phenomenon in the call center industry as the industry moving to India and workers' movement in the industry seeking higher wages, contributing to accelerated attrition rates.

3. This study builds on previous studies of the transnational migration of workers that relies heavily on Indian labor. Xiang's (2006) study of the "body shopping" industry describes the ways in which multinational corporations set up shop in places like Australia and the United Kingdom and employ and bring in Indian workers in short- to long-term employment in the technology industry. Workers themselves are transported back and forth from India to the job site, while some seek permanent residency. Xiang considers the interconnections of transnational labor and migration with cultural practices and standing. Though the work is difficult, workers do enjoy social and transnational mobility through their placement in the industry. Xiang's study highlights the significant changes and mobility that this industry practice affords some

workers, but the call center industry is different in important ways. In this industry, the agents remain within India and within the industry process that moves across borders. Further, whereas in other industries workers provide back-office support, in the call center industry, there is direct communication between agents and consumers. Our consideration is to look into the experiences of agents when the conditions of their labor bring them into direct communication with other nations while physically remaining in their own.

4. Aneesh (2006) describes virtual migration as the processes of multinational corporations that transfer information across high-speed connections that connect workers in one country with consumers in another without direct physical contact and simultaneously circumventing immigrant policy and practice. However, he argues, "Workers based in India may be governed by local practices, including labor and tax laws, yet like traditional immigrant workers, they do cross national boundaries and directly occupy some employment space in sectors of American economy. In short, they migrate without migration" (2).

5. Upadhya and Vasavi (2008) argue that the I.T. industry has reconstituted the terrain of workers' lives. Information technology, they argue, recasts the workforce in Bangalore through the creation of the I.T. workforce, as well as the new forms of labor, employment, and management it enables. As a result of these significant shifts, their participation in the industry redefines the workers' lifestyle, identities, and sociality. The idea of the worker transforms from previous incarnations of Indian labor to a model of flexibility, mobility, and reinvention of self. The unpredictability of the industry demands this kind of flexibility: workers must continually reinvent themselves to adapt to the rapidly shifting needs of the industry. Upadhya and Vasavi's study reveals that because this industry so dramatically shifts workers' lives, it produces a sense of separation from family and friends—a loss of the traditional model of the extended family, reconstituted through this labor as child-care providers. The construction of their identities as workers generates a sense of nostalgia for their previous lives. Although their compelling study insightfully reveals the deeply transformative nature of I.T. labor, our development of virtual migration departs from theirs, both in terms of the depth with which the call center agents of our study are fully immersed in and transformed by this migration and in terms of the point of global contact (the United States as opposed to Europe) with which workers engage. Our attention to virtual migration as a layered process (as agents migrate through time, virtual space, and checkered geographies) extends their work by considering the ways in which agents' subjectivities are recast through their immersion within the virtual borderlands between India and the United States. This focus on the United States is of particular salience for call center agents; Upadhya and Vasavi focus on the role of the workers in the Netherlands, Belgium, and Germany.

6. Three notable recent books that have been published on Indian call centers are Patel (2010), Mirchandani (2012), and Nadeem (2011). We reference these books throughout our text. Earlier productive conversations in this area that include specific

work on Indian call centers are Mirchandani (2004), Pal and Buzzanell (2008), and Shome (2006). Studies on call centers in other parts of the world include Cameron (2007), Castilla (2005), Fernandez and Sosa (2005), Holborow (2007), Stevens and Lavin (2007), and Winiecki (2007).

7. Homi Bhabha has been a seminal figure in theorizing processes of colonial hybridity, mimicry, and ambivalence. Hybridity is the creation of transcultural forms within colonial histories and relationships (Ashcroft, Griffiths, and Tiffin 1998). The term has been associated with Bhabha's analysis of the relations between colonizer and colonized. Bhabha argues that cultural identity and cultural systems are constructed in the "Third Space of enunciation" ([1994] 2003, 37), wherein the ambivalence and interdependence of the colonizer and colonized construct hybrid cultural identities (Ashcroft, Griffiths, and Tiffin 1998, 118). What's interesting about call center labor in extending this rich theoretical debate, however, is that the material practices through which hybridity is traditionally theorized are displaced, or reterritorialized, through the virtualscapes of call center labor. The virtual quality of call center labor produces a hybridity of hybridity.

8. Ong (2006) argues for an attention to the uneven production of space. Ong's productive theorization of "flexible sovereignty" explores the ways in which "special spaces" get carved out of developing countries to achieve the strategic goals of regulating groups in relation to market forces, to attract foreign investment, technology transfer, and international expertise to zones of high growth. These strategies lead to spatial fragmentation and diverse categories of human capital, creating "graduated" or "variegated sovereignty" (7). As we argue on the basis of the interviews we conducted with call center workers, India's developing status is a condition of this country's call center industry's existence. Its poverty serves as what Ong calls the "hinge" of neoliberal inclusion and exclusion. Ultimately, agents' job-hopping mobility risks raising the costs of Indian call center labor, compelling Western interests to invest elsewhere; transnational capitalism's flexibility is thus continually leveraged against agents' mobility. We draw on Ong's notion of flexible, variegated, or graduated sovereignty to consider the ways in which agents migrate across what we call checkered space.

9. "Understanding internet globalization is not simply a matter of tracking linear geographical diffusion," Abramson (2002, 198) argues, but rather "the geographies of infrastructures are networked spaces atop physical places; in the interplay between these, territory is configured and inequalities are remapped."

10. Call centers and other centers that conduct back office operations for multinational corporations are often referred to within economic literature as BPOs, for business process outsourcing.

11. India has led other outsourcing destinations in customer service and has remained the top destination of U.S. corporate outsourcing since 2007 (Kearney 2009). India's top spot as a highly desirable location is situated in a postcolonial context. Throughout its history, India has long attracted foreign capital interest, including material resources and trade routes to consumer-workers (Bardhan and Patwardhan

2004). It was as a British colony that India's long-standing contact with Western culture began, and it was the institution of English as the national language in 1837 that anchored a familiarity with the West (Ma-Rhea 2002). Since India's 1991 economic liberalization policies took effect, U.S. corporations have invested heavily in the Indian economy, and the U.S. government has approved a record number of foreign worker visas to Indian workers (Walton-Roberts 2004). There were and remain multiple reactions to foreign capital; it is primarily the middle and upper classes who benefit the most (Sridharan 2004). Given this history, when the Indian economy was liberalized in 1991, there was considerable debate in the Indian press about the possibility of being recolonized by the West. Because of the Indian experience with the British first coming to India as traders, the story went, India was at risk of being recolonized through new economic means. Now, more than a decade later, the rhetoric sometimes frames India's colonization by the British in celebratory terms. Because of the English-speaking masses that this history has produced, India is well poised to attract foreign capital. India now prides itself on its ability to compete on a global stage, to be the source of technological innovation and service to the West. India's liberalization policy, which opened its markets to foreign investment, saw its workers become highly desirable global laborers, which has generated a rapidly growing middle class (Chopra 2003; Sridharan 2004; Walton-Roberts 2004). The labor pool of Indian call center workers is culled from this English-speaking population. The industry does not train agents to speak English but to speak American English. Call center managers and CEOs often comment on the good fortune of being colonized by the British because they recognize that this colonization is the source of their marketable labor pool.

12. One of the reasons call center work in India is so cost-effective for U.S. corporations is that technology has enabled companies to use the Internet, rather than traditional transnational phone lines, to route their calls. Whereas transnational phone lines charge by the number of calls made or the number of minutes per call, VoIP (Voice over Internet Protocol) allows for calls to be made through modems that are connected to the Internet. The connections between India and the United States are possible through multiple networks linked to each other—that is, smaller networks connect to larger networks, which then connect to national networks, which then connect to the Internet's so-called backbone, or the very high bandwidth networks run by giant companies like Cisco. These backbones build redundancy so that a continuous network experience is assured. For further discussions of the Internet, see Carpenter (1996) and Abramson (2002).

13. "In mid-2003 the annual cost of an experienced call center agent in the U.S. was about $43,000. In India, the direct equivalent was about $6,200. The full cost of the U.S. employee was of the order of $58,500, but the 'full' comparative person in India cost $12,000" (Davies 2004, 41).

14. Since India's liberalization in 1991 dramatically shifted its global status and economic standing, the communication and trade channels between the United States and India have become increasingly important means of exchange within late

capitalism. India's double-digit GDP growth in the past few years has been cast within contemporary rhetoric as evidence that India is emerging as a "new global superpower" (Bhandare 2007), even threatening to take up a new position of dominance in relation to the West. Although India's success represents a tremendous threat to American workers, business leaders find this new Indian positionality to be of particular interest in terms of possible new markets and access to new labor pools. India's complex relationships with foreign national corporations remain ambivalent, but India's postliberalization policies indicate their permanence (Bardhan and Patwardhan 2004; Chakravartty 2004). Postliberalization U.S. corporations have been on the rise in India, and as time goes on, more and more corporations outsource their business to India.

15. A *kurta* is a long, flowing shirt worn by both men and women, usually over loose pants. However, a popular hybrid style of wearing it is over jeans, thus mixing traditional wear with Western wear.

16. Orientalism, Edward Said (2003) theorizes, is that production of difference between the West (the United States) and the East (India) that mobilizes physical distance as a lack of contact and familiarity—an exoticization of the East and a simultaneous production of Western superiority. This trope of the exotic, dangerous, and feminized East is reengaged in contemporary U.S. productions of the Indian call center industry as the physical distance that is virtually overcome becomes a trope of the uncanny return of the colony repressed.

17. See Vijay Prashad (2000) for a discussion of Indians in the United States and subsequent productions. He argues that the primary relations between U.S. populations and Indians are mediated through images of an orientalized spectacle. These include the foreign and exotic guru at the World's Fair through the highly visible figure of Deepak Chopra. These images construct Indians through the tropes of suspicion, the premodern, and mysticism. We see these tropes echoed throughout interactions of call center agents with American consumers.

18. When the industry began, the training sessions were even longer, but as a result of less stringent secrecy codes, sessions have become shorter over time.

19. Women currently account for a little over 30 percent of the workforce in the I.T. industry (Murthy 2009). However, there has been a 60 percent increase in the number of women employed by BPOs over the past two years, leading to a projected 45 percent participation rate in call center work for women in the near future("Number of Women" 2009).

20. According to their website, the NASSCOM Foundation seeks to "leverage information and communication technology to empower and transform the lives of the underserved" (http://www.nasscomfoundation.org/).

21. Hegde's (2011) insightful reading of popular coverage of the case in which a young female agent was raped by a man posing as a driver exposes the gendered dynamics the industry confronts. The details of the case, Hegde argues, "sent tremors around the country. The Indian media went into high gear with the coverage, calling into question both the conditions of call center work and the responsibility of multinational

corporations for employee safety. It was a highly charged case that drew sharp responses from across the social spectrum evoking discussions about sexuality, violence, modernity, and the erosion of tradition, all of which were embedded within the binary of the national and the global" (180). Through her reading of this discourse, Hegde reveals the ways in which "the body of the 'globalized' woman is constructed as sexually transgressive" and in need of discipline.

22. Foucault ([1977] 1990) describes total institutions as those in which its subjects are completely identified and from which they cannot move away. For example, prisons are total institutions in which prisoners are almost completely cut off from the rest of culture and therefore can have little influence on it. Thus, members of total institutions form their own culture as the institution and its structural norms form their subjectivities. Tracy (2000) extends total institutions to other, more voluntary types of organizations, such as the cruise ship. On a cruise ship, one cannot leave, and therefore something happens. In call centers, the conditions of employment intersect with those of globalization and technology to produce this industry. Agents come and go, but the timings and the outward orientation of agents' lives constitute a form of a total institution that produces subjectivities in motion.

23. High attrition in the industry is an ongoing problem. Workers struggle with the physical and sociofamilial effects of night shift work; there is also the monotony and stress of the nature of the work. Work conditions couple with the ability of experienced workers to move within the industry seeking higher wages. For more on the industry and attrition rates, see Budhwar et al. (2009).

24. At stake in such examinations is the apprehension of "the ways in which rhetoric, space, and power inflect one another to produce differentiated (im)mobilities, opportunities, and levels of (un)safety for differently racialized, classed, gendered, and sexed subjects" (Carrillo Rowe 2004, 118). See also Grossberg (1997) and Shome (2003).

25. Freeman (2000) argues that the global assembly line is extended into the realm of computer-based work as young Barbadian women are increasingly employed in high-tech informatics jobs. These workers are simultaneously produced as consumers through the enactment of professionalism in their dress, labor practices, and the industry's reward systems, which position them as active consumers in the global economy—for example, high-performing workers might win a trip abroad. As such, informatics workers distinguish themselves from factory workers as a new class of pink-collar workers, who earn the same amount as factory workers but gain social status through their capacity to participate in the global economy, both as workers and consumers.

26. Feminist philosophers have underscored the importance of theorizing the body, especially to challenge philosophy's traditional preoccupation with the mind. "The body as animal, as appetite, as deceiver, as prison of the soul and confounder of its projects," Bordo writes; "these are common images within Western philosophy" (1993, 3). Contemporary globalization theorists attending to questions of virtuality

also risk eliding the centrality of embodiment: "Embodiment has been systematically downplayed or erased in the cybernetic construction of the posthuman in ways that have not occurred in other critiques of the liberal humanist subject, especially in feminist and postcolonial theories," argues Hayles (1999, 4). Our analysis here seeks to extend such important insights by retaining a focus on embodiment within the context of virtual migration.

27. Anzaldúa (1987) sees borderlands as sites of contradiction, confusion, and ambivalence. Although the borderlands is traditionally imagined as the southwest territory of the United States–Mexico border, the space of call center labor creates a deterritorialized borderlands that exists both in virtual space and in the material terrain of people's lived experience.

28. "The image, the imagined, the imaginary—these are all terms that direct us to something critical and new in global cultural processes: *the imagination as a social practice*," Appadurai argues ([1996] 2000, 31). On the basis of this insight, he offers a series of "scapes" that serve to connect people imaginatively, even across tremendous distance. The ethnoscape is the landscape of persons who constitute the shifting world in which we live, such as tourists, immigrants, refugees, exiles, guest workers, and other moving groups and individuals. Such groups "constitute an essential feature of the world and appear to affect the politics of and between nations to a hitherto unprecedented degree. . . . The warp of these stabilities is shot through with the woof of human motion, as more persons and groups deal with the realities of having to move or the fantasies of wanting to move" (33). The technoscape is the global configurations of fluid technology that moves across previously impervious boundaries; financescape is the movement of global capital, which moves across nations rapidly, impacting and impacted by currency markets, national stock exchanges, and commodity exchanges. Mediascapes refer to the distribution of electronic capabilities necessary to produce and disseminate information; these capabilities are now available to a growing number of private and public interests throughout the world, as are the images of the world created by these media. Ideoscapes are those images that are "directly political" (36) and frequently have to do with the ideologies of states and the counterideologies of movements explicitly oriented to capturing state power or a piece of it. These scapes converge within call center labor to generate a new scape: virtualscape. What is distinctive about the virtualscapes that call center agents engage is that they mobilize and participate in these previous scapes through a compulsory performance of Americanness, consumed through mediascapes and ideoscapes within the virtual space of the phone call (a technoscape). One may participate in a form of assimilation within an ethnoscape while remaining within the homeland.

29. India's adoption of economic liberalization policies in 1991 opened the door for Western products and media to proliferate—which they did, within a very short period of time. Indians thus quickly went from having access to a limited state-run television system to suddenly being able to access and watch tens of channels in a privatized satellite television universe. The sudden media presence of networks like MTV,

CNN, Discovery, and NBC led to a newfound fascination with the West, as well as many debates about how the new media and product exposure would affect Indian culture. Would traditional ideas of Indian femininity be trumped by images of working women on *L. A. Law,* for example, or of Madonna wearing a spiked bra and performing on stage? More and more images of independent women who worked outside the home also proliferated, providing role models for young girls, particularly in urban India. At the same time, Indian markets were being flooded with Western products: Nike and Puma shoes, the fast food chains McDonald's and KFC. Most Western brands were highly coveted even though they were often priced outside the earning power of much of the Indian middle class. The 1990s thus opened the floodgates to the emergence of a much more Western-oriented society in India than had existed in the four and a half decades after India won independence in 1947.

30. We draw on Louis Althusser's (1998) notion of interpellation to account for the ways in which subjects are "hailed" by discourses of power. Althusser notes that at the moment the subject turns in response to the hailing—that is, the moment in which the subject recognizes that it is he or she who is being hailed—is the moment in which the subject is formed as a subject in discourse. Althusser's example is of a cop who calls out, "Hey, you there!" The subject recognizes him- or herself in the hailing as a response to power. This example provides a productive way into the function interpellation that we seek to evoke in our title—*Answer the Call*. We read Althusser through Judith Butler's (1997) notion of performance as the repetition of activities through which the subject becomes stabilized. Butler's productive extension of Althusser reads the role of law (i.e., the example of the cop, Althusser's ideological state apparatuses) through communication, voice, and performance. It is the "voice of the law" and the responsiveness of the one hailed that constitutes a successful interpellation. "To become a 'subject'" within an Althusserian frame "is thus to have been presumed guilty, then tried and declared innocent. Because this declaration is not a single act but a status incessantly *reproduced,* to become a 'subject' is to be continuously in the process of acquitting oneself of the accusation of guilt. It to have become an emblem of lawfulness, a citizen in good standing, but one for whom that status is tenuous, indeed, one who has known—somehow, somewhere—what it is *not* to have that standing and hence to have been cast out as guilty" (Butler 1997, 118). In this book we unpack this repeated activity of Indian call center labor, in which agents continually turn to the hailing of the American caller.

31. Grewal (2005) examines how the circulation of people, goods, social movements, and rights discourses during the 1990s created transnational subjects shaped by a global American culture. The United States functions for Grewal not as an imperialist nation-state that imposes unilateral political power in the world, but rather as the source of a compelling notion of America: a nationalist discourse that moves beyond the boundaries of the United States by disseminating an ideal of democratic citizenship through consumer practices. America functioned "as a discourse of neo-liberalism making possible struggles for rights through consumerist practices and

imaginaries that came to be used both inside and outside the territorial boundaries of the United States" (2). We explore the multiple ways in which transnational America is produced in India through call center labor as agents participate in the American dream through their capacity to serve Americans, consume American or Americanized goods, and perform American culture and accents within and beyond the confines of the call center industry.

32. The commercial success of the film *Slumdog Millionaire* in the U.S. market is one more demonstration that the rhetoric surrounding India is beginning to resonate within the United States. *Slumdog Millionaire*'s eventual sweep of the 2009 Oscars became a source of great celebration and pride, but it also sparked debate about the slum-focused image of India it portrayed in the Indian national press.

33. Also known as the Festival of Lights and considered the Hindu New Year, Diwali is one of the biggest festivals of the Indian cultural calendar, comparable in scale to Christmas in the United States.

34. Globalization theorists often identify the current historical moment and the mid-nineteenth century as historical periods in which time-space compressions occurred. These moments are marked by both an "acceleration in the pace of life" and a "collapse of spatial coordinates" that converge to generate a "radical restructuring in the nature and experience of both time and space" (May and Thrift 2001, 7).

35. For instance, Paul Virilio (in Decron 2001, 71) writes that "we are entering a space which is a speed-space," and Harvey (1990, 284) announces, "I want to suggest that we have been experiencing, these last two decades, an intense phase of time-space compression that has had a disorienting and disruptive impact upon political-economic practices, the balance of class power, as well as upon cultural and social life."

36. This concept builds on Batty's (1997, 339) statement that computer-mediated communication technologies are "generating an entirely new dimension to geography," which Batty calls virtual geography. Virtual geographies "include virtual technologies but are also constituted by the social relations, discourses, and sites in which these technologies are embedded," Crang, Crang, and May (2004, 2) argue. Thus, technologies "cannot be considered in isolation from the 'landscapes of translation' in which they are encountered, used and for which they may be designed." Rather, they must be seen as "socialized . . . in an ongoing process throughout the circuits linking technological production distribution, and usage."

37. "The culture of real virtuality is a culture in which many of our cultural representations/ideas/beliefs depend on images/sounds processed in/by the electronic hypertext. It is virtual (electronically produced/transmitted images). It is real because it forms a substantial part of our reality" (Castells and Gerstner 1999).

38. In describing the qualities of the contemporary historical moment, Bauman (2000) deploys the metaphor of liquidity: mobile, difficult to pin down, molecules in constant motion that must be contained by a structure if they are to stand still at all. He uses this metaphor to account for shift from preexisting social forms seen as solid (fixed, stagnant, enduring, impenetrable) to contemporary social relations, which are

marked by their fluidity. The communication processes through which call center labor is mediated enable the industry's services in liquid form as agents' labor is exported while their bodies remain bound within the homeland. Yet their bodies are quite material and solid; in many ways, they are limited in their capacity to be endlessly pliable. As with theorists of space-time, Bauman's conception threatens to erase the body.

39. "Because information had lost its body," this construction implied that embodiment is not essential to human being. Embodiment has been systematically downplayed or erased in the cybernetic construction of the posthuman in ways that have not occurred in other critiques of the liberal humanist subject, especially in feminist and postcolonial theories" (Hayles 1999, 4). The move to the virtual risks the erasure of the body, but we follow Hayles's efforts to retain the centrality of the body within the virtual. As the virutal interanimates the material, the network geographies the body inhabits recalibrate embodiment, but they do not erase them. Here we also invoke the important work of Nakamura (2002), who troubles the oft-celebrated seamless virtuality and transcendence of the body and identity politics in virtual culture. Rather, through her studies of online sites and gaming worlds she finds that communicators both reproduce racist and sexist tropes and mobilize neoliberal constructions of colorblind rhetoric in the exchanges they engage in online. Although telephone communication differs from online communication in that the engagement is aural, we find that similar invocations happen in this situation.

40. Mosco (1996) productively theorizes the intersections between political economy and communication to offer a political economy of communication that aims to work against the essentialisms that often circulate within orthodox Marxist approaches to capitalism: "Communication is a social process of exchange whose product is the mark or embodiment of a social relationship. Broadly speaking, communication and society are mutually constituted. The tendency within political economic and forms of institutional analysis is to concentrate on how communication is socially constructed, on the social forces that contribute to the formation of channels of communication, and on the range of messages transmitted through thee channels" (72). Following Mosco, our communication-based approach enables us to deconstruct some of the essentialisms and universalisms that circulate within current globalization theory.

41. Again, following Mosco (1996), a rhetorical approach enables us to "reconstitute epistemology by shifting from analytic methods that have guided science for three hundred years to a range of communication-based approaches centering on rhetoric and a set of standards to be found in rules of discourse. From this point of view, the rhetoric of convention, as much as the logic of inquiry, should provide the standards of science" (71). Our rhetorical approach enables us to tease out the ways in which certain categories of analysis get reified. We thus leverage agents' voices with and against cultural theory to cultivate such rhetorical methods and epistemologies as those imagined by Mosco.

42. Clifford Geertz (1977), James Clifford (1988), and Kamala Visweswaran (1994) have provided rich analyses of the linguistic and reflexive turn within anthropology. "Detachment is neither a natural gift nor a manufactured talent," Clifford Geertz writes in his initial foray into anthropology's ensuing reflexive turn. "It is a partial achievement . . . [that] comes not from failing to have emotions or neglecting to see them in others, . . . [but] from a personal subjection to a vocational ethic . . . to combine two fundamental orientations toward reality—the engaged and the analytic—into a single attitude" (in Marcus 1997, 111). Geertz ventures out to the edge of the anthropological envelope only to be folded back in, hailed by the guarantee of the epistemic frame inscribed onto the figure of rapport (Marcus 1997). This is to suggest that the ethnographers who strive to situate themselves within their texts, to produce decolonial ethnographic texts, and/or to build alliances with their subjects, are continually foiled in their efforts. Yet the linguistic turn, in which the constitutive role of language emerged as a central paradigm within critical theory and philosophy, marks a moment when such endeavors become both politically fraught and necessary.

43. Lal (1996) encounters a similar conundrum in her efforts to ally herself with women factory workers in India. In spite of their allegedly shared identity as Indian women, Lal is consistently confounded in her efforts to conduct research that might empower her subjects. Lal concludes that identity is inadequate to apprehend the positionality of the researcher "because one is constantly being situated into it by the micropolitics of the research interactions and the macropolitics of societal inequality" (197). To illustrate this fault line, Lal describes how a male manager humiliates a woman worker as he calls her into the interview room to exhibit a "slow" worker. Particularly troubling is Lal's (in)capacity as native researcher to achieve insider status. Like Lal, our efforts to ally ourselves with agents may have been challenged by family and interpersonal ties to owners and managers, while our structural positions placed us in the all too familiar positionality of the American caller.

1. The Rhythm of Ambition

1. See Harvey (1990) and Ong (1999) for analyses of the flexible quality of late capital. Harvey (1990) argues that in the wake of Fordism's spatially bound relationship to production, flexible accumulation generates divisions among spatially disparate laboring classes as global capital's ability to move challenges traditional forms of resistance such as organizing labor. Flexible accumulation works through a fluid relationship among labor processes and markets, products, and patterns of consumption, enabling newly globalized sectors of production that is constitutive of the time-space compression (147). Ong (1999) examines this kind of global flexibility in relation to transnational subject formation. Her notion of flexible citizenship refers to the transnational practices and imaginaries of the "nomadic subject," the Chinese citizen who holds multiple passports, to refute the notion that transnationalism does not displace nation-states but rather exists in complex relationships to them. This chapter

extends these arguments in two ways. First, whereas both Harvey and Ong attend to the spatial components that enable this flexibility, they do not tease out the complexities of its temporalities. A second and related point is that of the power temporalities through which contemporary flexible accumulation unevenly distributes and manages modern time.

2. The *NOW* segment frames and produces the politics of outsourcing through its broadcast on Labor Day, which asserts U.S. nationalism and belonging through its "threatened" labor force.

3. Neoliberalism is a form of economic organization that is based in a suspicious relationship to government control instead favoring a free-market economy. This economic form gained particular status under the Reagan administration, in conjunction with Thatcherite rule in Britain, in ways that combined the rollback of government services and spending with the strategic opening of developing markets in ways that tended to benefit wealthy nations at the expense of poorer nations through global agencies, such as the World Bank and the IMF, and policies such as strategic adjustment lending (see Bello 1999). Ong (2006) underscores the ways in which neoliberalism reconfigures the relationship among governing, sovereignty, and territoriality: "Neoliberalism can be conceived as an economic doctrine in negative relation to state power, but it's also a new relationship between government and knowledge through which governing activities are recast as non political and non ideological problems in need of technical solutions" (3). For our purposes in this book, we attend to the ways in which neoliberalism, as a representational practice constituted through outsourcing, reconfigures the relationship between the U.S. American imaginary of its global hegemony and the politics of territoriality that are destabilized by outsourcing.

4. The rhetorical force of these debates from multiple political platforms functioned ironically in that they located the "problem" of outsourcing U.S. jobs elsewhere while simultaneously downplaying the United States' heavy reliance on foreign labor.

5. This text departs from the others in its postmodern aesthetic and its critical politics, even as its uptake in the United States compels us to excavate the politics of its reception. See Mani (1990).

6. Hogarth (2006) argues that documentary's attachment to public service values tends to make it a stubbornly place-bound genre, a quality that tends to work against the postnational formation of contemporary television production more broadly. Yet documentaries are increasingly "produced and exchanged for profit within and across borders" and so may be regarded as a "transnational commodity" (8). Worldwide documentary channels, such as the Discovery network (which distributes the Friedman video), may function as duty offerings (9). Yet the Friedman production was well funded and well circulated; the PBS film *1-800-INDIA* funded and relied on a female director to get the gendered angle on the call center industry; *30 Days* was an FX-funded production; and *John and Jane* was a shoestring Indian production that now finds global and U.S. circulation through film festivals and HBO distribution. These components of the films' production and circulation, read with and against

their United States–centered framing, provide productive sites through which to interrogate these tensions. They point to a formation that simultaneously goes global even as it is bound to the domestic. Indeed, our analysis suggests that these films fold the globalization of capital and the formation of neoliberal subjectivity into U.S. national identity.

7. Ong's (2006) notion of postdevelopmentalism teases out the unevenness of development within Southeast Asia not as a uniform phenomenon but as a process of strategic, market-driven collaboration between nation-states and corporate interests that creates asymmetrical zones within the nation-state. Within this process, space becomes unevenly classed and developed according to neoliberal calculations in which some areas and populations are seen as advantageous to the global market, constituting a "checkered geography" (77).

8. Alexander (2005) distinguishes among colonialism, neocolonialism, and neoimperialism as distinct practices and temporalities that get scrambled within palimpsestic time. Colonialism is a political category that marks a set of practices, occurring within the height of European imperialism, that limit a people's self-determination; neocolonialism attends to the classed relations of ruling during anticolonial struggles; and neoimperialism refers to the new relations emerging from global capitalism, operating in conjunction with the G8 countries and multinational corporations. Alexander attends to the ways in which "processes of heterosexualization as a way of narrating these simultaneous histories . . . are often positioned as distant and separate, occupying a linear temporality in which tradition ostensibly displaces the neocolonial and modernity displaces the neo-imperial as preferred terms" (183). Alexander's project thus provides a productive framework for decoding how heterosexuality mediates and creates links among these disparate temporalities that enable new relations of ruling and belonging.

9. As Silverman (1983) explains, suture is the cinematic work necessary to overcome the anxiety the viewer experiences upon encountering an image framed by the camera's reduced point of view by stitching images together into a reliable series, structured through the narrative expectations of the viewer. This process of stitching provides the viewer a positionality through which to apprehend his or her relationship to the image by framing the point of view that constructs a subject position for the viewer. Suturing works through the 180-degree rule, which limits the range of a shot to the viewer's seeing capacity, leaving the visual field that the camera occupies unexplored. "Thus it derives from the imperative that the camera deny its own existence as much as possible, fostering the illusion that what is shows has an autonomous existence, independent of any technological interference, or any coercive gaze" (201). Although the viewer will temporarily adhere to this imperative, Silverman explains, he or she will soon "demand to know whose gaze controls what it sees" (202). This demand is met through a series of shot/reverse shots, which orient the viewer to the camera's gaze through the character or object from whose perspective the viewer is invited to see. Thus, the filmic strategies through which this positioning is managed,

produced, and crafted suture the viewer into the film's movement and look, and hence its time-space qualities, sometimes through fairly straightforward identifications and other times by generating multiple and even competing identifications or structures of feeling.

10. Filmmaker Jill Godmilow describes documentary film's "unspoken promise" to its audience through which the genre "knits" viewers into an imagined community through a shared notion of social awareness and compassion. Viewers are invited to identify as good subjects through the belief evoked: "I learn from this film because I care about the issues and people involved and want to understand them better; therefore, I am a compassionate member of society, not part of the problem described, but part of the solution" (Shapiro 1997). The documentary film thus constitutes a "we" joined through a sense of moral authority.

11. Alexander's (2005) notion of palimpsestic time relies on the metaphor of the palimpsest, "a parchment that has been inscribed two or three times, the previous text having been imperfectly erased and remaining therefore still partly visible" (190). Here we explore how palimpsestic time bridges disparate time-space dynamics in outsourcing discourse in order to consider the ways in which neoliberalism gains traction through the rhetorical force of previous rescue narratives.

12. "Implicit within this tradition/modernity position is a conception of time that is linear and hierarchical. . . . This formation of time itself is ideological in that it props up an investment in the political and psychic economies of capitalism which ground modernization and provides the conditions in which it thrives" (Alexander 2002, 190).

13. The work of queer and feminist theorists such as Grosz (2005), Freeman (2007), and Halberstam (2005) excavate the complexities and political possibilities at stake in a careful attention to gendered, heterosexed, and queer temporalities. Grosz (2005) argues that by attuning feminist and culture politics to a future "that is unattainable and unknowable" in the present, we might displace the presentism within contemporary feminist thought in favor of an indeterminate present based in questions of "becoming-art of politics" (1–2). This move enables her to reconfigure the relationship between time and subjectivity: "It is we who are in time, rather than time that is in us" (3). Freeman (2005) proposes the notion of erotohistoriography to open horizons of a "politics of unpredictable, deeply embodied pleasures that counters the logic of development," attending to the ways in which queer relations "complexly exceed the present" (59). This attention to the productive work of time vis-à-vis subject formation, pleasure, and development attunes us to the politics at stake in eliding temporalities and provides a point of entry into newly attending to the ways in which power temporalities mediate the formation of global subjectivities.

14. "The socially oriented film maker is thus the almighty voice-giver (here, in a vocalizing context that is all-male), whose position of authority in the production of meaning continues to go unchallenged, skillfully masked as it is by its righteous mission" (Minh-Ha 1990, 84).

15. The structure of the suture organizes time-space relations into a seamless narrative by stitching together disparate images into a reliable series and positioning the viewer within that structure. It takes the dizzying and anxiety-producing phenomenon of the Indian call center industry and renders it neatly intelligible to the U.S. viewer. The visual and temporal work that the figure of Spurlock and his Indian replacement conducts gestures toward the temporal quality of suturing within globalization. Although Silverman (1983) underscores the shot/reverse shot sequence as suturing viewers into the film, here we see the suture work arranged through the temporal structure of the mimetic gesture, which positions the viewer both spatially and temporally.

16. We borrow this term from Freeman's (2005) compelling articulation of "time binds": "At the simplest level, 'binds' are predicaments: like Frankenstein's monster, we cannot reproduce little queers with sperm and eggs, even if we do choose to give birth or parent: making other queers is a social matter. In fact, sexual dissidents must create continuing queer life worlds while not being witness to this future or able to guarantee its form in advance, on the wager that there will be more queers to inhabit such words: we are 'bound' to queer successors whom we might not recognize. 'Binds' also suggests the bonds of love, not only attachments in the here and now but also those forged across both spatial and temporal barriers: to be 'bound' is to be going somewhere. . . . Binding, we might say, makes predicament into pleasure, fixity into a mode of travel across time and space. Like 'dissemination,' it counters the fantasy of castration that subtends melancholic historiography, for it foregrounds attachments rather than loss" (61). In the work of marking, the binding work of time comprises the articulation between certain identities and the temporalities through which they are imagined become more apparent. Freeman also invites us to consider the forms of intimacy that are forged across disparate time-space relations. This move reverberates with the question of newly mediated intimacies that are the condition of call center labor and that bind Americans and Indians through mediated labor in the uneven dispersion of affective labor.

17. If colonial mimicry is marked by its inherent ambivalence—mimicry "must continually [produce] its slippage, its excess, its difference" (Bhabha [1994] 2003, 86)—progress narratives that define the West over and against the third world serve to reassure the Western subject of his or her superiority through a temporal and spatial placement in the developed world, which serves as the telos of the developing world.

18. Keating (2008) deploys a "fraternalist approach to colonial rule" that emphasizes a "racial kinship among the colonizers and the colonized elite," a bond that serves to consolidate power and control over women and the family. She argues that such an attention to fraternalism reveals one of the important components of Indian anticolonial nationalism, which capitulated to a form of "compensatory domination in which consent to colonial authority is engendered by countenancing, structuring, and enabling forms of inter-group and intra-group rule" (23). This homosocial dynamic reproduces itself in 30 Days as Chris is positioned as a big brother to Raja, showing him the path to modern masculinity, particularly in relation to the gendered dimensions of

home life. In this scene, we see how this fraternalism generates class solidarity that supersedes national boundaries to both allow the audience to feel for the poor with the reassurance that the native (Raja) can translate the subaltern inscription and also be unsettled by it.

19. The reterritorialization of America depicted through the documentary's representation of outsourcing simultaneously operates through the power temporalities that maintain U.S. centrality as daytime "here" frames the rhythm of work life "there." These power temporalities invite U.S. viewers, sutured into the text through the authorial gaze of the white male figures they feature, to arbitrate the moral worth of the figure of the call center agent. Ong (2006) explains that neoliberalism extends, retracts, and denies citizenship not through nation-states but through economic or classed forms of citizenship, adjudicated by "a moral system of distributive justice" (16) and operating under a veil of power that is imagined as nonpolitical and nonideological. The market, she argues, confers value on those individuals whom its sees as having capital value, despite their national citizenship status, and for whom it accordingly makes exceptions. Although Ong's insightful argument assigns evaluative agency to neoliberalism and the market, these films locate the moral agency to determine the worth of the call center agent within the U.S. American viewer.

20. Colonial mimicry is a term Bhabha ([1994] 2003) theorizes as the performative repetition (in body, language, affect, visibility) of a colonial presence. The force of the performance, of the internalization of colonial power relations, remains in the body and psyche of previously colonized populations even after colonial occupation. Though the performance references the colonial culture, it is, however, a fraught and anxious project marked by its inherent ambivalence for the colonizer. Though performances of colonial mimicry invoke a harnessing of progress narratives for Indians, they do so unevenly: depictions of the third world in relation to the West reassure the Western subject of his or her superiority through a temporal and spatial placement in the developed world, which serves as the telos of the developing world.

21. Here we focus on the spatial reconfiguration of transnational America as opposed to other first world neoimperial formations, as the films we examine are designed for the U.S. consumer/viewer.

22. Whiteness, as many scholars in the field of critical whiteness studies have argued, gains its power through its presumed invisibility (see Dyer 1998). As Frankenberg (1993) writes in her founding text within this field, *White Women, Race Matters:* "Naming 'whiteness' displaces it from the unmarked, unnamed status that is itself an effect of dominance" (6). We argue that U.S. racial formation positions people of color in a relation marked by a temporal lag behind whites as whiteness serves as the unmarked center within U.S. racial formations (Morrison 1992).

23. "We shall use heteropatriarchy as the pivot on which to make these moves, the chart to help us navigate the various ways in which it is at once intimate to modernity and its intersecting practices—the very practices through which nation and state are mediated and produced" (Alexander 2005, 195).

24. This progress narrative also traffics in a 1950s nostalgia of unfettered white male control. Sally Robinson (2000) writes of the "painfully pleasant nostalgia for the days when higher education was the exclusive white male club, and the classroom a space for homosociality animated by sublimated sexual desire" (79). This critique also layers the temporal aspirations at work in the documentaries under investigation in this chapter. Under globalization and within the context of outsourcing, the white male figure Robinson writes of is increasingly under siege.

25. *Pooja* is the rituals of worship.

26. Sentimentalism's "'touching' register," Greyser (2007) writes, "constructs shared feeling out of social distance, so that the resulting formations become *affective geographies*: palpable emotional connections among subjects that often emerge across boundaries of race, class, and gender" (277). Indeed, the affective geography at work within this touching scene moves the Western viewer through the bodily encounter between the idealized U.S. American citizen-subject and the abject Indian woman, momentarily collapsing the temporal and geographic distance that divides disparate subjects.

27. Alexander (2005) argues that while tradition and modernity are deployed to designate distinct temporalities, they are also highly interested practices that gain their purchase through the production of this very distinction. And yet, she observes, these temporalities are neither distinct nor inert, which brings her to the question of how they come to matter, and what work sexuality does in affixing these temporal distinctions: "Does heterosexualization occupy a civilizing nexus in the neocolonial state's imperative of distancing itself from tradition in order to be counted as modern, that is, 'civilized,' and accorded the 'benefits' of modernity?" (193). Her analysis invites us to interrogate the ways that heterosexuality serves as a hinge that verifies the temporal divide, affixing tradition to a distant and distinct time-space, allowing the modern to come to recognize itself as such and thus to gain its attendant benefits.

2. "I Used to Call Myself Elvis"

1. We know where we are, she explains, even if we are in a dark room, by reaching out, touching the objects that surround us, and thus inferring "which way we are facing" (Ahmed 2006, 7). Orientation, then, attends to the ways we occupy space that provide us with a sense of direction, of being in place, and a certain "intimacy of co-inhabiting spaces with other things" (111). Yet this intimacy and the capacity to be grounded in relation to the spaces we inhabit are disrupted for the racialized subject by a racial scheme that "'stops' black bodies inhabiting space" by orienting the world as "white space" (111). Ahmed's argument presumes a contiguous and proximate relationship between objects and bodies that is interrupted and recast in the labor of call center workers.

2. Space gains meaning through processes of communication that are embedded in power relations, and space in turn gives meanings to the bodies that inhabit and move unevenly through space. Space is arranged in ways that facilitate the movement

of those who hold power and seek to immobilize and/or forcibly move those who are dominated (Carrillo Rowe 2004; Shome 2003).

3. Grosz (2005) describes prostheses as "an opening up of actions that may not have been possible before, the creation of new bodily behaviors, qualities, or abilities rather than the replacement of or substitute for missing or impaired organs" (147). Although her argument presumes prosthetic objects designed to enhance the body's capacities, we extend her considerations to interrogate the ways in which some bodies are forged as prosthetic objects to others. This shift not only places racialized and imperialist power relations in the center of our analyses of the reach of power, but also enables us to consider the prosthetic formulation from the other side. That is, while we in the West become accustomed to the ways that others around the globe extend our reach, we often do not consider what it means for those others who are conducting the labor of that extension.

4. Agents who are working technical support will often request remote access to control the caller's computer desktop so that they can see what the caller is seeing and help them troubleshoot the technical issues at hand.

5. In her study of imperial geographies, Jacobs (1996) argues that the space that one group previously thought of as home becomes unrecognizable because another force animates it.

6. Hardt (2003) describes capitalism within this historical moment as marked by its increasing reliance on immaterial labor—labor that produces no material product but rather circulates in affective labor necessary within the service, information, and communication industries. This era of postmodernization and informatization, Hardt argues, is one in which biopower might be leveraged for subversive, anticapitalist purposes. Hardt's account of postmodernization, in which information and communication services become increasingly valued in the global economy, situates call center labor within a broader historical context. Yet here we find that neoliberal biopower is not leveraged against the expansion of capital but rather in the service of the transnationalization of capitalism within the neoimperial formation of the outsourcing of assimilation. That is, the affective labor produced by the call center agent, which is demonstrated in a fluency in American life in order to make American customers comfortable, is structured through a set of disciplinary technologies that rely on a continual suppression of the immediate and engagement with the faraway.

7. Appadurai ([1996] 2000) opens his book with a vignette of his own encounter with modernity, a shift he marks through his sensual encounter with America within the spatial terrain of Bombay: "Reading life and American college catalogs at the United States Information Service Library, seeing B-grade films (and some A-grade ones) from Hollywood at the Eros Theatre, five hundred yards from my apartment building" (1). He describes his gradual disenchantment with all things British—that while these cultural forms equipped him well for his emersion into American education and culture, there was something distinctly modern about his unfolding relationship with America. This account charts an imagined migration that, now some forty

years later, ushers Indian call center agents into a different moment of modernity as an imagined community with America is formed not through physical migration but via the daily encounter with Americans on the telephone.

8. Appadurai's ([1996] 2000) treatment of mediascapes presumes a passive relationship between media and audiences, characterized by the subject's consumption of such media forms as "newspapers, magazines, television stations, and film-production studios" (35) and electronic media, including (without differentiation of the quality of interaction) computers and telephones.

9. Aneesh (2006) argues that because the Indian worker's body remains in India while their labor is exported through information technologies, they do not undergo any psychic migration. What is distinct about call center labor's contemporary constellation and convergence of scapes in this instance is that the two moments in Appadurai's account of modern subject formation (media and migration) become collapsed in the activities of call center labor. It is precisely the convergence of two media forms—images, story lines, meanings, and cultural capital associated with television and film as well as the daily, performative, interactive encounter enabled by the Internet and in particular the telephone—that reterritorializes the conditions under which the agent migrates.

10. Biopower, Foucault ([1977] 1990) argues, is a modern form of population management that both enables and constrains human activities—disciplining humans to form them as subjects of the modern state. As with call center labor, the "body as machine" (139) becomes a central preoccupation of modern power. This focus generates a host of "technologies of power" through which to integrate subjects into "the machinery of production and the adjustment of the phenomena of population to economic processes" necessary to the formation of both capitalism and the nation-state (141). Attending to the postmodern and global forms of disciplinary power in the call center industry, we deploy and extend Foucault's productive concept.

11. Foucault's concept of biopower can be Eurocentric and statecentric. It has limits when we try to stretch it to account for call center labor. When race, nation, ethnicity, and multiple modernities become central to how we theorize biopolitical processes of subject formation, this contradictory function emerges as a formative social force. Further, when we examine governmentality within a communication- and information-based transnational economy, we detect significant historical shifts from modern theories of biopower. See Spivak (1998) for a detailed critique of Foucault's Eurocentrism. Some productive work in the Foucauldian tradition takes race and nation as central disciplining forces (Grewal 2005; Stoler 1995). Foucault's focus on population, Grewal (2005) argues, cannot be demarcated spatially or temporally in ways that account for the uneven encounters and disciplinary processes that occur within geopolitical power relations: "We also seek an understanding of how populations are judged in relation to each other—differences are produced between populations on the basis of territory, culture, gender, race, nation—and technologies of governments are devised, applied, adjudicated in relation to these differences" (18). Grewal's theory

of transnational connectivities allows us to theorize the uneven connections to the global available to differently located subjects. For instance, the call center agent is cultivated from the middle-class and lower-middle-class populations who have a basic mastery of English. Our analysis of the discourse of call center agents, however, enables us to explore the neutralizing processes necessary to the production of the call center agent as a neoliberal subject. That is, the assimilation of this subject into transnational America occurs simultaneously through the cultivation of the unmarked subject and the suppression, rejection, and negation of difference.

12. Winiecki (2007) develops the concept of shadow boxing to account for the ways in which U.S. American call center agents and managers resist disciplinary processes of their labor by manipulating data in ways that produce statistics of their labor within regimes of maximization, even as workers carve out space and time, and refuse managerial overtures of control.

13. A common term used for those who labor in Indian middle- and upper-class homes, even today, is *servants*. This term, which connotes those who serve, describes the housemaids, cooks, gardeners, chauffeurs, and nannies who comprise the help in an Indian home.

14. Ahmed (2006) comments on "the otherness of things" as a quality that "allows me to do things 'with' them. What is other than me is also what allows me to extend the reach of my body. Rather than othering being simply a form of negation, it can also be described as a *form of extension*. The body extends its reach by taking in that which is 'not' it, where the 'not' involves the acquisition of new capacities and directions— becoming, in other words, 'not' simply what I am 'not' but what I can 'have' and 'do'" (115). Linking this concept with Grosz's (2005) theorization of prosthetics enables us to turn the phenomenology that presumes the location of the Western subject on its head. Rather, we become attuned to the ways that call center agents cultivate, discipline, and suppress their own lived experience, consciousness, and labor in order to do that work of extending.

15. This echoes Ahmed's (2006) argument about extending the reach of whiteness. As the production of transnational America within call center labor generates zones of American performativity, "the familiarity of the 'white world' . . . 'disorients' black bodies such that they cease to know where to find things—reduced as they are to things among things" (111).

16. Kruks (2001) notes that many postcolonial readings of Fanon (1967) overlook the "role that existential phenomenology plays in his work." She notes that "Fanon's approach has strong affinities with Sartre's account of 'existential' psychoanalysis, in which neuroses are explained not at the level of the unconscious but as fundamental choices made in responses to concrete situations" (90). Following Kruks's move to read Fanon phenomenologically, we find that the very grounds of phenomenology— experience—are productively called into question. Hansen (2006) also conducts a phenomenological reading of Fanon, arguing that the objectification constitutive of the visual encounter unravels in the virtual contact: "By decoupling identity from any

analogical relation to the visible body, online self-invention effectively places everyone in the position previously reserved for certain raced subjects: everyone must mime his or her identity" (145). Yet the power-free zone that Hansen envisions within the virtual encounter is certainly called into question by the call center exchange as the terms of the performance of identity are deeply embedded within postcolonial power relations.

17. Mohanty (2003) finds that experience becomes the problematic foundation for universal sisterhood. She argues, rather, that "historicizing and locating political agency is a necessary alternative to formulations of the 'universality' of gendered oppression and struggles" (107). Moya (2002) argues that experience is "the fact of personally observing, encountering, or undergoing a particular event or situation," noting that experience should be theorized "in its mediated form [which] contains an epistemic component through which we can gain access to knowledge of the world" (38). Scott (1998) is critical of the ways that experience is deployed to shore up nondiscursive notions of subject formation. Rather, Scott argues, "It is not individuals who have experience, but subjects who are constituted through experience" (60). Although Scott's poststructuralist orientation certainly departs epistemologically from Mohanty and particularly Moya's realist orientation, all of these notions of experience presume a simultaneity of experience and knowledge formation. Here we wish to consider what happens to the category of experience when knowledge and lived reality become decoupled.

18. Affective labor, Hardt and Negri (2004) argue, "is labor that produces or manipulates affects. . . . One can recognize affective labor, for example, in the work of legal assistants, flight attendants, and fast food workers (service with a smile). One indication of the rising importance of affective labor, at least in the dominant countries, is the tendency for employers to highlight education, attitude, character, and 'prosocial' behavior as the primary skills employees need. A worker with a good attitude and social skills is another way of saying a worker adept at affective labor" (108). When we factor in the extent to which call center workers must reconfigure their relationships to time, space, culture, the performance of identity, and local affective encounters, the cost of affective labor is contextualized beyond the immediacy of the encounter in which positive affects are produced. This is to suggest the importance of contextualizing affective labor within broader sociocultural and historical sites of its production, and in this case disparate consumption.

3. "I INTERACT WITH PEOPLE FROM ALL OVER THE WORLD"

1. Many contemporary political, feminist, and globalization scholars have begun to theorize the range of contestations constitutive of contemporary citizenship in ways that depart from previous concepts of national citizenship. With the emergence of universal human rights and economic globalization, such shifts usher in new forms of subjectivity beyond, within, and outside of nation-states (Mouffe 1992). New sites of belonging, often imagined as postnational and oriented around sexuality, diasporic

experience, social movements, and cosmopolitanism, are emerging alongside of—and at times in contestation with—traditional notions of citizenship (Grewal 2005; Isin and Wood 1999).

2. These notions of citizenship have been contested by feminist and political theorists as exclusionary on the basis of gender, race, and class (Orkin 1999; Pateman 1998; Eisenstein 1996).

3. As Turner (1993) points out, following Durkheim, the tension between the notion of citizenship as a national identity or as a human identity situates the questions of belonging surrounding citizenship within a moral terrain. Further, Turner argues, citizenship understood within a strictly legal and political framework is too limiting. Rather, citizenship considered as a social phenomenon opens us to the problems of the social within modern societies. For instance, he writes, following the Marxist tradition on citizenship, "Citizenship, once inscribed in the institutions of the welfare state, is a buffer against the vagaries of the marketplace and the inequalities of the class system, because citizenship is a method of redistribution of resources to those who are unable to provide for their own needs" (xi). This function of citizenship is undercut by the globalization, individuation, and neoliberalization of citizenship: as the benefits of inclusion increasingly become tied to one's capacity to gain value within the global market, the responsibility of some collective governing body through which such notions of citizenship have formerly been defined become hollowed out. Sassen (2002) maps the tensions between deterritorialized citizenship and traditional notions of citizenship onto different ways of theorizing citizenship: ways that attend to the "historicity and embeddedness" of citizenship and ways that attend to its "formal features" (42). Our account attends to the different investments that differently located social actors place on these often competing features and the ensuing contestations that arise within their communication practices.

4. Deleuze and Guattari ([1972] 1983, [1980] 1987) productively theorize the relationship between place and culture as processes of deterritorialization and reterritorialization. These concepts enable culture workers to examine shifting relationships between place and culture across historical contexts. Under globalization, places are deterritorialized (previous objects, sensibilities, subjectivities, or organizational structures are lost or removed) and reterritorialized (new ideas, connectivities, conditions of subject formation, or organizational structures reconstitute those spaces). Our specific concern in this chapter is the relationship between place and national identity. Globalizing processes displace earlier articulations between national territory (nation imagined as a bound geographical space) and citizenship (the rights and benefits associated with national belonging). National territories are increasingly crosscut by diverse populations and cultural formations. Further, as we argue above, the "place" of America becomes increasingly bound and unbound through such free-market practices as outsourcing. Such displacements disrupt a national imaginary based on clearly defined boundaries.

5. For instance, Appadurai's ([1996] 2000) account of the postnational frames it as an accomplishment as opposed to an ongoing contestation. Although the transnationalization of markets, people, media, and finances creates new modes of belonging and social, cultural, and political organization, the nation-state, particularly the U.S. nation-state, is often reasserted as a legitimate site of sovereign rule. Just as the "national" is contested within globalization, so too is citizenship. Contemporary citizenship theorists often fall into a similar trap, eliding the impulse of those forces invested in previous notions of citizenship to reclaim its benefits and entitlements for those traditional, privileged members of normative inclusion.

6. Indeed, the India Shining campaign that the Bharatiya Janata Party (BJP) organized in the 2004 elections was intended to draw on the sense of optimism in India around the tech boom and the plentiful rains of the preceding year. Having spent approximately $20 million on a massive advertising campaign promoting this vision of India as shining, or coming into its own under their leadership, the BJP lost the general elections because the slogan was perceived as hollow, given the lack of basic services (like water and electricity) in many parts of the country. The perception that its claims lacked substance led to a backlash against the BJP, particularly for those who felt disenfranchised from India's prosperity, for whom India was hardly shining at all. This suggests the importance of a double movement in Indian national identity: that it is increasingly emerging as a global player, but in doing so, its economic disparities are often overlooked. Thus call center agents and other middle- and upper-middle-class global players come to represent India, while the poor are pushed to the side of the national imaginary.

7. Particularly for upper- and rising middle-class Indians, Indian national identity gains traction within globalization, while for a declining class of Americans, U.S. national identity loses ground. Even though the United States is still imagined as the dominant global player, its status is challenged at the same time that India's gains momentum and recognition. India rises as neoliberalism generates a rising class of global professionals, while America sinks as the American dream becomes increasingly illusive to average educated Americans. U.S.-based multinational corporations outsource labor (increasingly middle-class jobs) to manage production costs, even as American citizenship is still imagined, especially by aspiring U.S. American subjects, through the promise of sociopolitical inclusion, economic security, and the belief that a college education should translate into a good-paying job.

8. When India was subjected to U.S.-led sanctions, it defended its right to develop and test such weapons by challenging the inherent disparity in the American argument around nuclear arms: we're developed, logical, and controlled so we can have the bomb; you're not civilized, so you don't deserve such power. This challenge had the effect of bringing India to the global table, increasing its recognition as a legitimate nation-state (Bhagwati and Calomiris 2008).

9. This shift in the production of Indian national identity raises a compelling point for the politics of recognition. As India emerges onto the global stage, its national

identity is increasingly constructed and imagined through the gaze of the West. The politics of recognition, according to Taylor (1994), challenges liberal notions of human identity, arguing that human identity gains meaning through interactions with and recognition by significant others. Thus, according to Taylor, subject formation is a function of whose gaze, judgments, and assessments the subjects value or consider to be significant. As a nation that once oriented its identity through protectionism and isolationism, previous articulations of Indian identity might be understood as emerging through an inward-facing politics of recognition. For India to emerge on the global stage marks a radical shift in its identity production by virtue of the nation performing itself for a global and largely Western/American audience.

10. "When other countries are seen as 'threatening' to the United States, politically or economically, racialized individuals who look like 'the enemy' to sections of the majority group are subjected to higher levels of discrimination and hate" (Purkayastha 2005, 42).

11. "Americanness as a concept shifted by location and place and historical context, as well as factors such as race, gender, class, nationality, and religion, producing different kinds of subjects. This shifting and changing national subject could be, as with immigrants, transnational, moving across nations and national boundaries to produce American identities imbricated within a consumer citizenship that exceeded the bounds of the nation to become transnational. While the American dream has been an essential aspect of consumer culture in twentieth century America, producing the 'American way of life' as a primary component of nationalism formed through a conceptualization of liberal democracy, it came to signify a variety of affiliative practices of belonging on the part of many migrants within the U.S. by the end of the century" (Grewal 2005, 7–8).

12. Aneesh (2006) argues that technology renders the U.S. border fraught in a number of ways: "As a system of enclosures, it [the nation-state] has the necessary force to stop or to allow the physical flow of goods or labor across its heavily guarded boundaries. However, physical borders are less useful against virtual mobility. Although walls can be raised even against virtual mobility by disallowing material anchors like computers . . . such measures . . . reduce the power of the state by robbing it of the possibility to govern virtual flows and hence reap financial gains. Thus technologies of virtual mobility . . . increasingly require the fine-tuning of existing institutional organization if the nation-state is to retain its power of governance" (34).

13. Not only does the declining American dream generate resentments against foreign others, but also, as Castronovo (2001) argues, U.S. citizenship functions through a particular nativism, a rejection of nonnational others: "Citizenship is a state technology that kills non-national cravings for more complexly lived subjects. The death of non-national possibilities satiates the state's political longing for people dressed up in the unremarkable off-the-rack garb of generic personhood. But it does not follow that specific racial, gender, economic, and sexual identities are somehow free of regulation" (6). The previous chapter considered the ways in which Indian call center

agents' participation in the American dream circulated through a particular kind of sociocultural, experiential, and affective death.

14. Journalist Mira Kamdar (2007) shares the account of her encounter with a New York film producer. "Who needs the American audience?" he asks. "There are only 300 million people here [in the United States]. India, by comparison, has crossed the one billion people mark some years ago." Although Kamdar's book leans toward hyperbole, it is one of a spate of books published in the popular press since 2000 that increasingly spotlight the Indian growth "miracle."

15. See Butler's (1993) well-known argument on the repetition of performance as constitutive of identity.

16. Grewal (2005) describes "transnational connectivities" as those global circuits of power "within which subjects, technologies and ethical practices were created through transnational networks and connections of many different types and within which the 'global' and the 'universal' were created as linked and dominant concepts" (3).

17. "At this historical juncture," argues Puar (2007, 38), "the invocation of the terrorist as a queer, nonnational, perversely racialized other has become part of the normative script of homophobic-racist images (reactivated from the 1991 Gulf War, the Israel–Palestine conflict, and eighteenth-, nineteenth-, and twentieth-century Orientalist histories) of terrorists since September 11, 2001." This perverse racialization was in turn mapped onto the bodies of South Asian citizens and noncitizens, both residing within the national boundaries and beyond.

18. Bhatia (2008) argues, on the basis of his study of New England South Asian Indians, that his subjects perceive themselves as having assimilated to the extent that before 9/11, they saw themselves and imagined that others also saw them as others as part of the nation.

19. Maira (2008) argues that in the post-9/11 moment, the notion of flexible citizenship must be thought more explicitly through the machinations of empire. Although South Asians, especially those whose class status affords them mobility and certain relationalities, have established themselves as model minorities and therefore gain access to normalized American citizenship, there are ways in which racial discourses can cast them suspect. Particularly Muslims in the United States have been understood in the post-9/11 moment as suspect and outsiders, which is especially consistent with U.S. scapegoating practices in the wake of any national crisis that is posed from without or from within. "Flexibility in national loyalty is viewed as potentially threatening when national security is perceived to be at risk, and there is a fear that this threat is both from without—from foreigners who oppose the United States— and from within—from treacherous immigrants or 'un-American' citizens" (716–17). Although flexible citizenship has been theorized to understand a certain degree of mobility and relationality among nations, organizations, and people, "after 9/11 . . . flexible citizenship can be a tenuous or even politically dangerous strategy for Muslim immigrant youth, for transnational ties and shifting national allegiances are precisely

what have come under scrutiny for Muslim Americans by the state in the era of the PATRIOT Act" (712). This accounts for the ways in which alliances and belongings to organizations are now suspect, ties to home and people are under acute scrutiny, and "flexibility . . . is always in tension with *control*, and it is a strategy that is in practice constrained by the state and by ideologies of who can and cannot move or waver" (714). So again, in the post-9/11 moment, we need to return and rethink South Asian, especially Muslim, subjectivity and national (non)belonging.

20. An Indian call center worker with a university degree might earn under $8,000 a year, while her American counterpart earns $50,000. Additionally, operation costs are significantly higher in the United States than in India. The combined savings to companies are over 50 percent (Ong 2006, 167). This dynamic, in the wake of the dot-com boom that brought thousands of high-tech Indian workers to the United States, is responsible for a dot-com reverse brain drain, where Indians are moving back to India from the United States to leverage their American education or work experience and to pursue opportunities to form their own companies, thus taking advantage of the economic realities of outsourcing.

21. Mohanty's (2003, 228) "Two-Thirds World" is a term used in financial markets describing the practice of buying low in a market and selling high elsewhere. Arbitragers exploit price discrepancies between money markets for profit. An outsourcing company coined the term *labor arbitrage* to mean "'the ability to pay one labor pool less than another labor pool for accomplishing the same work, typically by substituting labor in one geography for labor in a different locale.'" (Ong 2006, 158). Ong explains that "the ethnicization of high-tech workers, the reverse brain drain, and the rise of low-wage cybercenters in Asia have converged, making global labor arbitrage a relentless logic in knowledge-based industries" (167).

22. See Kennedy's (1996) reading of the power of the figure of the white male victim to generate a backlash against civil rights advances for women and people of color. In the contemporary global context, this backlash gets recast onto the faraway body of the call center agent.

23. See Friedman's (2005) thesis that the world is flat and shrinking through technology, and that the United States will not hold its leadership position without reinventing itself and using its imagination to innovate and compete globally.

24. The relationship between the emergence of neoliberalism and the remasculinzation of America has not been fully explored. In this chapter we seek to examine this exchange. Although the historical unfolding of events suggests that the remasculinzation of America may have ushered in neoliberalism, this historic moment seems to be marked by a resurgence of masculine U.S. nationalism against the forces of neoliberalism that dilute the nation-state.

25. Transnational feminist theorists such as Alexander (2002, 2005) and Mohanty (2003) account for their formation as women of color through their encounter with U.S. third world feminism. In particular, Cherrie Moraga and Gloria Anzaldúa's *This Bridge Called My Back: Writings by Radical Women of Color* (1983) stands out as a

politicizing text, vision, and movement in the formation of radical women of color as both an identity and a politics of survival.

26. In an effort to situate questions of race in relation to those more recognizable discourses of caste in India, Reddy (2005) argues that although race and caste are comparable formations, we might productively think of these modes of power through the category of ethnicity. The move to ethnicity, Reddy argues, "highlights two important and intimately related features of caste in contemporary India: its fluidity, in contrast to its presumed doctrinally-given rigidity, and therefore its capacity to strategically deploy established, essentialized notions of itself in a movement that seeks less to undermine caste than to restore dignity to re-claimed caste identities" (547). Reddy analyzes the Indian government's refusal to consider caste as synonymous with race in the 2001 U.N. World Conference Against Racism, Racial Discrimination, Xenophobia, and Related Intolerance (WCAR), held in Durban, South Africa. One goal of these gatherings was to explore the various conflations and refusals of caste and race, and the ways in which caste is at various points in history and globally brought into discourses of race. The primary group making these claims within this context was the Dalits in South India, who were protesting the Indian government's refusal to consider caste as part of the conference on the basis of the premise that race and caste are not synonymous. This type of comparison or reliance on a recognizable global rhetoric is not new: she notes the ways in which it circulated especially in post-independence movements where Marxist groups formed following African American groups fighting for civil rights, specifically the Dalit Panthers formed in 1972 as well as for those making the comparison between caste and race for global solidarity. Whether there is race in India is a continuously contested idea. She argues that in the current discussions, race and caste are often constructed retroactively to meet the political and theoretical needs of the groups that are advancing or eliding the link between caste and race.

27. Reddy (2005) argues that the British introduced the notion of race into India as an organizing mechanism: "H. H. Risley's use of late-nineteenth century European race science in anthropometric research aimed at categorizing and enumerating the castes of India" (543). In the context of the call center encounter, race is reimported as the reinvigoration of an older imperial script, but agents, it seems, have little language or consciousness through which to resist or make sense of their subordination.

28. Caste is sometimes mapped onto education in India, partially because caste was originally a system of division of labor, with scholars (who studied the religious texts) considered to be the highest castes in a hierarchical system. A parallel assumption, then—and one almost unconsciously articulated in Ganesh's comment—is an association of ignorance with a lack of education and the lower castes.

29. Part of Reagan-era economics was the idea that prosperity for the wealthy would translate to prosperity for the masses—that is, the idea that the rising tide lifts all boats (see Blumenthal 1986 for a longer discussion). Sometimes conflated with

supply-side economics and the assumption of a trickle-down effect, this old saying was evoked by the Reagan administration to justify their economic policies.

4. "I'm Going to Sing It the Way Eminem Sings It"

1. Fernandes (2006) argues that the emergence of the Indian middle class is not necessarily a new phenomenon, but rather a continuation of the changes in India's postliberalization economy. Whereas the initial material changes tended toward privatization of the economy, as India became more of a global player, this practice rapidly trickled down through the individual practice through consumption and lifestyle changes in the upwardly mobile. While the middle class is marked through their materiality, Fernandes argues, that the notion of the middle class is a discourse that extends from postliberalization. The discourse of the middle class provides the illusion of attainability and access to the middle class through consumption and materiality for those who are not economically suited toward it. She insists that "outsourcing is an extension of earlier processes of liberalization, rather than a cause of the restructuring of the Indian middle class" (116), but here we attend to the temporal dimensions of the process coupled with outsourcing's production of subjectivities that do indicate alternate aspects of mobility and identity.

2. Raveena's sense that call center agents develop a pseudohybridized identity makes them difficult to define according to the categories of cultural studies: they are not quite diasporic, nor are they completely middle class.

3. This framework calls attention to the ways in which the boundaries of time and space are narratively produced in ways that naturalize distinction—the here/there and now/then—to reify power relations. Massey's (2005) argument rather reveals the illusion of distinction and questions: "What might it mean to reorient this imagination, to question that habit of thinking of space as a surface? If, instead, we conceive of a meeting-up of histories, what happens to our implicit imaginations of time and space?" (4). We interrogate here not just space as surface but also space as layered phenomenon.

4. Fernandes (2006) notes the emergence of private clubs, upscale theaters with one pricing level, and new neighborhoods and gated communities to argue that these are all not necessarily new formations. Rather, colonialism established such private spaces, which also were extended into the postindependence era. However, the rising middle class is generating a new contestation over urban space that, through spatial practices, seeks to map space in ways that reinforce class distinctions. Although squatters, hawks, and lower-class people have always coexisted in upper-class spaces, mostly as service providers, emerging spatial practices work to segregate such populations altogether. India's rising middle class is thus a unique formation, reterritorializing postcolonial and late industrial Indian spaces that distinguish them from gentrification in places like the United States or Europe.

5. Edelman (2004) argues that constructions of the future are bound to the force and focus of heterosexual/heteronormative reproduction and the ever-present figure

of the child. The child, as the center and repository of the future, structures the present in its service. Whereas for Edelman this serves as the impetus for queers to reject the future, here we see the mobilization of anxiety and disciplinary gestures in order to recuperate the agent back into normativity.

6. Axel (2002) argues for a move away from place as a defining marker of diaspora within diasporic studies. Rather, he poses a turn to the "diasporic imaginary" as the social force through which a group comes to congeal as a diaspora through recognition of a common history and a shared future that is marked through particular embodied figures. He writes that this imaginary "is not an adjective that describes or qualifies the diaspora, its 'people,' or 'community' as illusory or as a mere figment of some misguided imagination. Rather, the *diasporic imaginary*—used as a noun— indicates a precise and powerful kind of identification that is very real" (424). Axel proposes this category as a "corrective to the primacy that diaspora studies has awarded to the construction of place, the diasporic imaginary shifts the emphasis to temporality and corporeality—their centrality to relations of recognition and their negotiation through discourses of purity and origin. Neither drawing from a common-sensical notion of illusions and mirages nor engaging in a recuperation of Benedict Anderson's (1991) 'imagination,' I am rather looking toward the analytic of subjectification" (424). This framework is useful to theorize the group identification emerging around the figure of the Indian call center agent as it provides a rhetorical account for the ways in which "homeland" is narratively produced over and against the construction of "America" as markers of identity and as processes of temporal subjectification. That is, the power temporalities through which call center labor is organized and the economic gain it affords its workers converge to create new conditions for subject formation that have no necessary relationship to time, space, and nation. Rather, it is in the scrambling of these social forces and their reconstitution within the imaginary of the subject that these processes of subjectification constitute new sites of belonging and recognition. This frame enables us to "account for the creation of the diaspora, not through a definitive relation to place, but through formations of temporality, affect, and corporeality" (412). Indeed, the category of diasporic imaginary suggests that the notion of a homeland is produced retrospectively through narratives of belonging and recognition, thus compelling us to attend to the temporal, corporeal, and affective dimensions of subject formation.

7. ABCD stands for "American-Born Confused Desi," often a derogatory term used for second- and third-generation Indian Americans. *Desi* draws on the Sanskrit word for homeland *(des)* to refer to people of Indian descent living in the United States. The "confusion" associated with the ABCD references the cultural hybridity of second- and third-generation Indians born in the United States. It refers to their loss of cultural authenticity and assimilation (Prashad 2000).

8. For instance, the first two of Robin Cohen's nine criteria of diaspora define the category through such movement. A diaspora is either "dispersal from an original homeland" or "the expansion from a homeland in search of work, in pursuit of trade

or to further colonial ambitions" (Fludernik 2003, xii). The term *diaspora* circulates across disciplinary boundaries "to describe the mass migrations and displacements of the second half of the twentieth century, particularly in reference to independence movements in formerly colonized areas, waves of refugees fleeing war-torn states, and fluxes of economic migration in the post World War II era" (Braziel and Mannur 2003, 4).

9. The term *Bangalored* has been discussed recently in the *Bangkok Post*, the *Times of India*, and other Asian newspapers. A search suggests it was in use in the United States during the year 2011 but began to appear in print later, starting in 2012. It refers to people who have been laid off from a multinational corporation because their job has been moved to India. Bangalore is cited in particular because of its reputation in the United States a high-tech city, the Indian equivalent of Silicon Valley, which has benefited significantly from such outsourcing. When this term first appeared, in a newsletter, many subscribers immediately connected it with the so-called Bangalore torpedo, a tube packed with explosive used by troops for blowing up wire entanglements, which got its name because it was invented in that city. One website is selling T-shirts with the slogan, "Don't Get Bangalored." It is odd for a place-name to become a verb, but there are precedents, such as Sodom from the Bible.

10. The reference to the future, figured through the trope of what Edelman (2004) describes as the sacred child, animates Raja's discussion. This figurative child, produced through and necessary to heteronormative nation building, becomes a trope through which affect gets temporally and spatially mapped.

11. See Ong's (2006) notion of graduated sovereignty and Massey's (1994) notion of power geometries.

12. Grewal (2005) argues that globalization's circulation of ideas, images, people, and goods creates a context in which an "American" subject may be formed outside of the territorial bounds of the United States. Through the export of multicultural nationalism, neoliberal democracy, and consumer culture, America comes to signify globally through the circulation of an idealized form of democratic citizenship. Here at the conjuncture of a host of apparently competing discourses and material practices (multicultural inclusion, neoliberal democracy, consumerism, nationalism, and transnationalism) arises a convergence of these forces to constitute a promise. "America was important to so many across the world," Grewal writes, "because its power enabled the American nation-state to disseminate the promise of democratic citizenship and belonging through consumer practices as well as disciplinary technologies" (2).

13. Leela Fernandes (2006) argues that the Indian middle class is emerging in ways that depart from the previous state-managed economy. The formation of the new Indian middle class is marked through attitude, lifestyle, and consumption as the media details the spread of consumer items such as cell phones, rising wage levels, and choices for consumers. The new Indian middle class is defined through their mastery of English and their education, and the formation is constructed through its potentially expansive reach and inclusion. Fernandes notes the rhetorical production of

rural and lower-class aspiration that is materialized through consumer practices. The reconstitution of urban space (new private clubs, upscale theaters, gated neighborhoods) usher in new spatial practices designed to maintain class distinctions by segregating space. Thus, the formation of the new Indian middle class might be understood as a set of discursive and material processes that both extend (through the promise of upward mobility) and retract (through the checkering of urban space) a promise of class mobility. Fernandes argues that the state and the middle class collaborate in forming an idealized vision of India that has been transformed by the idealized image of the global city, providing a point of entry to theorize this reconstitution of national space and the imaginary of the nation-state through the formation of the new Indian middle class as a distinctly transnational, global, or Americanized process that is marked through new time-space relations. We would like to distinguish the kinds of regional migrations, coupled with class mobility, that reconstitutes agents' subjectivities from those Fernandes theorizes. Although her framework does account for their class mobility, it does not account for the ways in which their subjectivities become Americanized through the production of their labor.

14. *Baba* is a sign of reverence when used for an elder. It is often used in combination with the person's first name. However, when used for a child, it is form of endearment combined with respect. *Guddi* is a form of endearment used for a female child. *Guddu* is the male equivalent.

15. Freeman's (2000) ethnography constructs the Barbadian pink-collar worker through her emphasis on and internalization of the industry's professionalism, figured through the trope of high heels as a marker of feminized and classed identity production. Through the cultivation of a professional identity for these female workers, the informatics industry gains a loyal and relatively inexpensive workforce as the women invest in a fetishized construction of class privilege in the forms of dress, company parties, and gifts of travel to reward good workers. In this sense, Freeman attends to the ways in which the informatics worker is simultaneously produced as a worker and consumer—indeed, that the consumer identity is the condition of possibility for the production of the informatics laborer. Here we explore the implications of her insights to attend to the ways in which the call center industry also produces the laborer as a consumer. Further, we attend to the specifically Americanized form that this consumerism is articulated to in an effort to consider this production itself as a form of migration.

16. Hardt (2003) marks the shift in subject formation as a function of economic organization—from agricultural to industrial to informatics—through the metaphor of the soul. That is, he sees the production of the soul as inextricable from the means of production and consumption that define economic exchange within a given historical moment. "Where the production of soul is concerned," he writes, "we should no longer look to the soil and organic development, nor to the factory and mechanical development, but rather to today's dominant economic forms, that is, to production defined by a combination of cybernetics and affect." How, then, does the call center industry generate specific conditions for the formation of the agents' soul?

CONCLUSION

1. This position is in tension with the conditions of, and rhetoric surrounding, the U.S. recession and the subsequent demand for job creation.

2. Other trends of the Indian outsourcing industry include a growing proportion of work that is now shifting from BPO to KPO (knowledge process outsourcing). This is the higher-value work that requires knowledge-based skills other than English. This is one of the fastest-growing segments of the Indian outsourcing industry, which is rapidly moving toward high-value jobs, including doing work for consulting firms, legal firms, and medical institutions. Globally, the KPO pie was estimated to reach $25 billion by 2010, and India is expected to command 60 percent of its market share ("Number of Women Working" 2005). Although this trend is important to the broader picture of global outsourcing, it does not directly relate to the viability of the call center industry and is thus beyond our scope here.

3. PREPS is a term used for the training modules/courses that Laveena is developing.

4. Or, for that matter, to the 2001 attacks on the building housing the Indian Parliament in New Delhi. The Mumbai attacks consisted of a series of coordinated terrorist aggressions directed at symbolic sites that Pakistani extremists carried out for three days from November 26, 2009, until they were finally contained on November 29, killing 173 and injuring at least 300 (Magnier and Sharma 2008). Although Pakistan initially denied that the attackers were Pakistani (Waraich 2009), Pakistan only officially accepted the nationality of the surviving gunman as Pakistani at about the time of this interview (Zaidi 2009).

5. Popular talk shows, such as *We the People* on NDTV, held hotly contested discussions on what India's response should be to the attacks. Should India be guided by the Gandhian principles that have provided an idealized moral compass for the nation since independence, setting up the parameters of a civil society, or should India be engaging Pakistan militarily? A 2008 statement on the website for the show reads, "War or even a state of suspended hostility between India and Pakistan will blight the whole region's future. It is a collective issue. We are facing a common enemy and we must join hands to defeat this enemy. Caught amidst this commotion of what's right and wrong, this week on *We the People*, we ask, can civil society make any real difference?" (ndtv.com).

6. By "relatively passive," we mean that although the United States invaded two countries after the 9/11 attacks without any evidence linking the attacks to these nations, India provided evidence that the Mumbai attackers were Pakistani (Sengupta 2009); and although India considered military strikes against Pakistani terror camps, it instead has relied on the U.N. and NATO to mediate the conflict.

Bibliography

Abramson, Bram Dov. 2002. "Internet Globalization and the Political Economy of Infrastructure." In *Critical Perspectives on the Internet,* edited by Greg Elmer. Lanham, Md.: Rowman & Littlefield.

Agamben, Giorgio. (1978) 1993. *Infancy and History: The Destruction of Experience.* Translated by Liz Heron. New York: Verso.

Ahmed, Sara. 2006. *Queer Phenomenology: Orientations, Objects, Others.* Durham, N.C.: Duke University Press.

Alexander, M. Jacqui. 2002. "Remembering Bridge." In *This Bridge We Call Home: Radical Visions for Transformation,* edited by Gloria Anzaldúa and AnaLouise Keating. New York: Routledge.

———. 2005. *Pedagogies of Crossing: Meditations on Feminism, Sexual Politics, Memory, and the Sacred.* Durham, N.C.: Duke University Press.

Alexander, M. Jacqui, and Chandra Talpade Mohanty, eds. 1997. *Feminist Genealogies, Colonial Legacies, Democratic Futures.* New York: Routledge.

Althusser, Louis. 1998. "Ideology and the Ideological State Apparatuses." In *Cultural Theory and Popular Culture: A Reader,* edited by John Storey. Athens: University of Georgia Press.

American Jobs. 2004. Produced and directed by by Greg Spotts. Spotts Films.

Anderson, Benedict. 1991. *Imagined Communities: Reflections on the Origin and Spread of Nationalism.* London: Verso.

Aneesh, A. 2006. *Virtual Migration: The Programming of Globalization.* Durham, N.C.: Duke University Press.

Anzaldúa, Gloria. 1987. *Borderlands: La Frontera.* San Francisco: Aunt Lute.

Appadurai, Arjun. (1996) 2000. *Modernity at Large: Cultural Dimensions of Globalization.* Minneapolis: University of Minnesota Press.

Ashcroft, Bill, Gareth Griffiths, and Helen Tiffin. 1998. *Key Concepts in Post-colonial Studies.* London: Routledge.

Axel, Brian Keith. 2001. *The Nation's Tortured Body: Violence, Representation, and the Formation of a Sikh "Diaspora."* Durham, N.C.: Duke University Press.

———. 2002. "The Diasporic Imaginary." *Public Culture* 14 (2): 411–28.

Baldwin, Elaine, Brian Longhurst, Scott McCracken, Miles Ogborn, and Greg Smith, eds. 1998. *Introducing Cultural Studies*. Athens: University of Georgia Press.

Bardhan, Nilanjana, and Padmini Patwardhan. 2004. "Multinational Corporations and Public Relations in a Historically Resistant Host Culture." *Journal of Communication Management* 8 (3): 246–63.

Batty, Michael. 1997. "Virtual Geography." *Futures* 29 (4/5): 337–52.

Bauman, Zigmunt. 2000. *Liquid Modernity*. Malden, Mass.: Blackwell.

Bello, Walden. 1999. *Dark Victory: The United States and Global Poverty*. Oakland, Calif.: Food First.

Bhabha, Homi K. (1994) 2003. *The Location of Culture*. New York: Routledge.

Bhagwati, Jagdish N., and Charles W. Calomiris, eds. 2008. *Sustaining India's Growth Miracle*. New Delhi: Stanza.

Bhandare, Namita, ed. 2007. *India: The Next Global Superpower?* New Delhi: Roli.

Bharucha, Rustom. 2004. "Muslims and Others: Anecdotes, Fragments, and Uncertainties of Evidence." *Inter-Asia Cultural Studies* 5 (3): 472–85.

Bhatia, Sunil. 2008. "9/11 and the Indian Diaspora: Narratives of Race, Place, and Immigrant Identity." *Journal of Intercultural Studies* 29 (1): 21–39.

Bhattacherjee, Debashish. 1999. *Organized Labour and Economic Liberalization; India: Past, Present and Future*. Geneva: International Institute for Labour Studies.

Blumenthal, Sidney. 1986. *The Rise of the Counter-establishment: The Conservative Ascent to Political Power*. New York: Crown.

Bordo, Susan. 1993. *Unbearable Weight: Feminism, Western Culture, and the Body*. Berkeley: University of California Press.

Braziel, Jana Evans, and Anita Mannur. 2003. *Theorizing Diaspora: A Reader*. Malden, Mass.: Blackwell.

Brown, Wendy. 2006. *Regulating Aversion: Tolerance in the Age of Identity and Empire*. Princeton, N.J.: Princeton University Press.

Budhwar, Pawan S., Arup Varma, Neeru Malhotra, and Avinandan Mukherjee. 2009. "Insights into the Indian Call Centre Industry: Can Internal Marketing Help Tackle High Employee Turnover?" *Journal of Services Marketing* 23 (5): 351–62.

Butler, Judith. 1993. *Bodies That Matter: On the Discursive Limits of "Sex."* New York: Routledge.

———. 1997. *The Psychic Life of Power: Theories in Subjection*. Stanford, Calif.: Stanford University Press.

Cameron, Deborah. 2007. "Talk from the Top Down." *Language and Communication* 28:143–55.

Carpenter, B. 1996. *Architectural Principles of the Internet*. RFC 1958. community.roxen.com.

Carrillo Rowe, Aimee. 2004. "Whose America? The Politics of Rhetoric and Space in the Formation of U.S. Nationalism." *Radical History Review* 89:115–34.

Castells, Manuel. 1989. *The Informational City: Information Technology, Economic Restructuring, and the Urban–Regional Process*. Oxford: Blackwell.

Castells, Manuel, and John Gerstner. 1999. "The Other Side of Cyberspace: An Interview with Professor Maneul Castells." *Communication World,* March.

Castilla, Emilio J. 2005. "Social Networks and Employee Performance in a Call Center." *American Journal of Sociology* 110 (5): 1243–83.

Castronovo, Russ. 2001. *Necro Citizenship: Death, Eroticism, and the Public Sphere in Nineteenth-Century United States.* Durham, N.C.: Duke University Press.

Chakravartty, Paula. 2004. "Telecom, National Development and the Indian State: A Postcolonial Critique." *Media, Culture and Society* 26:227–49.

Chatterjee, Partha. 1993. *The Nation and Its Fragments: Colonial and Postcolonial Histories.* Princeton, N.J.: Princeton University Press.

Chopra, R. 2003. "Neoliberalism as *Doxa:* Bourdieu's Theory of the State and the Contemporary Indian Discourse on Globalization and Liberalization." *Cultural Studies* 17 (3/4): 419–44.

Clifford, James. 1988. *The Predicament of Culture: Twenthieth-Century Ethnography, Literature, and Art.* Cambridge, Mass.: Harvard University Press.

Crang, Mike, Phil Crang, and Job May, eds. 2004. *Virtual Geographies: Bodies, Space, and Relations.* New York: Routledge.

Davies, Paul. 2004. *What's This India Business? Offshoring, Outsourcing, and the Global Services Revolution.* London: Nicholas Brealey.

D'Cruz, Premilla. 2006. "Unionisation of Indian Call Centre Agents: The Role of Professional Identity." In *Bi-national Perspective on Offshore Outsourcing: A Collaboration between Indian and U.S. Labour,* edited by Centre for Education and Communication et al. Jobs with Justice. www.jwj.org.

Decron, Chris. 2001. "Speed-Space." In *Virilio Live.* Edited by John Armitage. London: Sage.

Deleuze, Gilles, and Félix Guattari. (1972) 1983. *Anti-Oedipus: Capitalism and Schizophrenia.* Paris: Les Editions de Minuit/University of Minnesota.

———. (1980) 1987. *A Thousand Plateaus.* Paris: Les Editions de Minuit/University of Minnesota.

Destination Bangalore. 2007. Directed by Jim Kerns. Cinequest.

Drummond, Tammerlin. 2009. "Tammerlin Drummond: Bay Area Looks to India for Economic Boost." *Oakland Tribune,* November 29.

Dyer, Richard. 1998. *White.* New York: Routledge.

Edelman, Lee. 2004. *No Future: Queer Theory and the Death Drive.* Durham, N.C.: Duke University Press.

Eisenstein, Zillah. 1996. *Hatreds: Racialized and Sexualized Conflicts in the 21st Century.* New York: Routledge.

Fanon, Franz. 1967. *Black Skin, White Masks.* New York: Grove Press.

Fernandes, Leela. 2006. *India's New Middle Class: Democratic Politics in an Era of Economic Reform.* Minneapolis: University of Minnesota Press.

Fernandez, Roberto M., and M. Lourdes Sosa. 2005. "Gendering the Job: Networks and Recruitment at a Call Center." *American Journal of Sociology* 111 (3): 859–904.

Fludernik, Monika. 2003. *Diaspora and Multiculturalism: Common Traditions and New Developments.* New York: Recopy.

Foucault, Michel. (1976) 1990. *Discipline and Punish: The Birth of the Prison.* Translated by Alan Sheridan. New York: Random House.

———. (1977) 1990. *The History of Sexuality: An Introduction.* Volume 1. Translated by Robert Hurley. New York: Vintage Books.

Frankenberg, Ruth. 1993. *White Women, Race Matters: The Social Construction of Whiteness.* Minneapolis: University of Minnesota Press.

———. 1996. "When We Are Capable of Stopping, We Begin to See: Being White, Seeing Whiteness." In *Names We Call Home: Autobiography on Racial Identity,* edited by Becky Thompson and Sangeeta Tyagi. New York: Routledge.

Fraser, Nancy. 2000. "Rethinking Recognition." *New Left Review* 3 (May–June): 107–20.

Freeman, Carla. 2000. *High Tech and High Heels in the Global Economy: Women, Work, and Pink-Collar Identities in the Caribbean.* Durham, N.C.: Duke University Press.

Freeman, Elizabeth. 2005. "Time Binds, or Erotohistoriography." *Social Text,* no. 84–85 (Fall-Winter): 57–67.

———. 2007. Introduction to *GLQ: A Journal of Lesbian and Gay Studies* 13 (2–3): 159–76.

Friedman, Thomas L. 2005. *The World Is Flat: A Brief History of the Twenty-First Century.* New York: Farrar, Straus & Giroux.

Geertz, Clifford. 1977. *The Interpretation of Cultures.* New York: Basic Books.

Giddens, Anthony. 1990. *The Consequences of Modernity.* Stanford, Calif.: Stanford University Press.

Giroux, Henry. 2004. *The Terror of Neoliberalism: Authoritarianism and the Eclipse of Democracy.* Boulder, Colo.: Paradigm.

———. 2005. "The Terror of Neoliberalism: Rethinking the Significance of Cultural Politics." *College Literature* 32 (1): 1–19.

Grewal, Inderpal. 2005. *Transnational America. Feminisms, Diasporas, Neoliberalisms.* Durham, N.C.: Duke University Press.

Greyser, Naomi. 2007. "Affective Geographies: Sojourner Truth's *Narrative,* Feminism, and the Ethical Bind of Sentimentalism." *American Literature* 79 (2): 275–305.

Grossberg, Larry. 1997. *Bringing It All Back Home.* Durham, N.C.: Duke University Press.

Grosz, Elizabeth. 2005. *Time Travels: Feminism, Nature, Power.* Durham, N.C.: Duke University Press.

Halberstam, Judith. 2005. *In a Queer Time and Place: Transgender Bodies, Subcultural Lives.* New York: New York University Press.

Hall, Stuart. 1996. *Critical Dialogues in Cultural Studies.* New York: Routledge.

Hansen, Mark B. N. 2006. *Bodies in Code: Interfaces with Digital Media.* New York: Routledge.

Hardt, Michael. 2003. "Affective Labor." Presented at the Make World Festival. make worlds.org.

Hardt, Michael, and Antonio Negri. 2004. *Multitude: War and Democracy in the Age of Empire*. New York: Penguin.

Harvey, David. 1990. *The Condition of Postmodernity: An Enquiry into the Origins of Cultural Change*. Cambridge, Mass.: Blackwell.

Hayles, N. Katherine. 1999. *How We Became Posthuman: Virtual Bodies in Cybernetics, Literature, and Informatics*. Chicago: University of Chicago Press.

Hegde, Radha S. 2011. *Circuits of Visibility: Gender and Transnational Media Cultures*. New York: New York University Press.

Hogarth, David. 2006. *Realer Than Real: Global Directions in Documentary*. Austin: University of Texas Press.

Holborow, Marnie. 2007. "Language, Ideology, and Neoliberalism." *Journal of Language and Politics* 6 (1): 51–73.

"India Becomes Trillion Dollar Economy." 2007. *Times of India*, April 26. timesof india.indiatimes.com.

Isin, Engin, and Patricia Wood. 1999. *Citizenship and Identity*. London: Sage.

Jacobs, Jane M. 1996. *Edge of Empire: Postcolonialism and the City*. New York: Routledge.

Jeffords, Susan. 1994. *Hard Bodies: Hollywood Masculinity in the Regan Era*. New Brunswick, N.J.: Rutgers University Press.

Jeffords, Susan, and Laura Rabinovitz, eds. 1994. *Seeing through the Media: The Persian Gulf War*. New Brunswick, N.J.: Rutgers University Press.

John and Jane Toll-Free. 2005. Directed by Ashim Ahluwalia. Produced by Shumona Goel. Television program. HBO, India, November 13.

Kamdar, Mira. 2007. *Planet India: How the Fastest-Growing Democracy Is Transforming the World*. New York: Scribner.

Keating, Christine. 2011. *Decolonizing Democracy: Transforming the Social Contract in India*. University Park: Pennsylvania University Press.

Kennedy, Liam. 1996. "Alien Nation: White Male Paranoia and Imperial Culture in the United States." *Journal of American Studies* 30 (1): 87–100.

Kruks, Sonia. 2001. *Retrieving Experience: Subjectivity and Recognition in Feminist Politics*. Ithaca, N.Y.: Cornell University Press.

Lal, Jayanti.1996. "Situating Locations: The Politics of Self, Identity, and 'Other' in Living and Writing the Text." In *Feminist Dilemmas in Fieldwork*, edited by Diane L. Wolf. Boulder, Colo.: Westview.

Lowe, Lisa. 1996. *Immigrant Acts: On Asian American Cultural Politics*. Durham, N.C.: Duke University Press.

Luce, Edward. 2007. *In Spite of the Gods: The Rise of Modern India*. New York: Doubleday.

Magnier, Mark, and Subhash Sharma. 2008. Terror Attacks Ravage Mumbai: At Least 101 Die; Americans, Britons Apparently Sought as Hostages." *Los Angeles Times*, November 27, A1.

Maira, Sunaina. 2008. "Flexible Citizenship/Flexible Empire: South Asian Muslim Youth in Post-9/11 America." *American Quarterly* 60 (3): 697–720.

Maitra, Srabani, and Jasjit Sangha. 2005. "Intersecting Realities." *Women and Environments International Magazine,* April 1, 40–42.

Malhotra, Sheena, and Robbin D. Crabtree. 2002. "Gender, Inter(nation)alization, Culture: Implications of the Privatization of Television in India." In *Transforming Communication about Culture: Critical New Directions,* edited by Mary Jane Collier. Thousand Oaks, Calif.: Sage.

Mani, Lata. 1990. "Multiple Mediations: Feminist Scholarship in the Age of Multinational Reception." *Feminist Review* 35:24–41.

Marcus, George E. 1997. "The Uses of Complicity in the Changing Mise-en-scene of Anthropological Fieldwork." *Representations* 59: 85–108.

Ma-Rhea, Zane. 2002 "The Economy of Ideas: Colonial Gift and Postcolonial Product." In *Relocating Postcolonialism,* edited by David Theo Goldberg and Ato Quayson, 205–16. Malden, Mass.: Blackwell.

May, Jon, and Nigel Thrift. 2001. Introduction to *TimeSpace: Geographies of Temporality.* New York: Routledge.

Massey, Doreen. 1994. *Space, Place, and Gender.* Minnesota: University of Minnesota.

———. 2005. *For Space.* Thousand Oaks, Calif.: Sage.

Minh-Ha, Trinh T. 1990. "Documentary Is/Not a Name." *October* 52 (Spring):76–98.

Mirchandani, Kiran. 2004. "Practices of Global Capital: Gaps, Cracks and Ironies in Transnational Call Centers in India." *Global Networks* 4:355–74.

———. 2012. *Phone Clones: Authenticity Work in the Transnational Service Economy.* Ithaca, N.Y.: Cornell University Press.

Mohanty, Chandra. 2003. *Feminism without Borders: Decolonizing Theory, Practicing Solidarity.* Durham, N.C.: Duke University Press.

Moraga, Cherrie, and Gloria Anzaldúa. 1983. *This Bridge Called My Back: Writings by Radical Women of Color.* San Francisco, Calif.: Kitchen Table, Women of Color Press.

Morrison, Toni. 1992. *Playing in the Dark: Whiteness and the Literary Imagination.* Cambridge, Mass.: Harvard University Press.

Mosco, Vincent. 1996. *The Political Economy of Communication: Rethinking and Renewal.* Thousand Oaks, Calif.: Sage.

Mouffe, Chantel. 1992. "Democratic Politics and the Question of Identity." In *Dimensions of Radical Democracy: Pluralism, Citizenship, Community,* edited by Chantel Mouffe. London: Verso.

Moya, Paula. 2002. *Learning from Experience: Minority Identities, Multicultural Struggles.* Berekely: University of California Press.

Murthy, N. R. Narayana. 2009. "The Indian IT-BPO Industry Aims to Bridge the Gender Divide." Address delivered at the NASSCOM IT Women's Leadership Summit, June.

Nadeem, Shehzad. 2011. *Dead Ringers: How Outsourcing Is Changing the Way Indians Understand Themselves.* Princeton, N.J.: Princeton University Press.

Nakamura, Lisa. 2002. *Cybertypes: Race, Ethnicity, and Identity on the Internet.* New York: Routledge.

Nalini by Day, Nancy by Night. 2005. Directed by Sonali Gulati. Women Make Movies.

"Number of Women Working in IT-BPO Sector up 60%." 2009. *Economic Times,* May 13.

NOW with Bill Moyers. 2003. Produced by Brenda Breslauer. Television program. PBS, August 29.

Office Tigers. 2005. Directed by Liz Mermin. BBC.

Omi, Michael, and Howard Winant. 1994. *Racial Formation in the United States: From the 1960s to the 1990s.* New York: Routledge.

1-800-INDIA. 2006. Directed by Safina Uberoi. Produced by A. Carter. Television program. PBS.

Ong, Aiwha. 1999. *Flexible Citizenship: The Cultural Logics of Transnationality.* Durham, N.C.: Duke University Press.

———. 2006. *Neoliberalism as Exception: Mutations in Citizenship and Sovereignty.* Durham, N.C.: Duke University Press.

Ono, Kent, and John Sloop. 2002. *Shifting Borders: Rhetoric, Immigrant, and California's Proposition 187.* Philadelphia, Pa.: Temple University Press.

Orkin, Susan Moller. 1999. "Is Multiculturalism Bad for Women?" In *Is Multiculturalism Bad for Women?,* edited by Joshua Cohen, Matthew Howard, and Martha C. Nussbaum. Princeton, N.J.: Princeton University Press.

The Other Side of Outsourcing. 2004. Produced by Thomas L. Friedman. Television program. Discovery Channel.

Pal, Mahuya, and Patrice Buzzanell. 2008. "The Indian Call Center Experience: A Case Study in Changing Discourses of Identity, Identification, and Career in a Global Context." *Journal of Business Communication* 45 (1): 31–60.

Pateman, Carole. 1988. *The Sexual Contract.* Cambridge, Mass.: Polity Press.

Patel, Reena. 2010. *Working the Night Shift: Women in India's Call Center Industry.* Stanford, Calif.: Stanford University Press.

Prashad, Vijay. 2000. *The Karma of Brown Folk.* Minneapolis: University of Minnesota Press.

PR Newswire, 2009. "Geography of Offshoring Is Shifting, According to A.T. Kearney Study." *PR Newswire,* May 18.

Puar, Jasbir. 2007. *Terrorist Assemblages: Homonationalism in Queer Times.* Durham, N.C.: Duke University Press.

Purkayastha, B. 2005. *Negotiating Ethnicity: Second-Generation South Asian Americans Traverse a Transnational World.* New Brunswick, N.J.: Rutgers University Press.

Reddy, Deepa. 2005. "The Ethnicity of Caste." *Anthropological Quarterly* 78 (3): 543–84.

Robinson, Sally. 2000. *Marked Men: White Masculinity in Crisis.* New York: Columbia University Press.

Ross, Andrew. 2009. *Nice Work If You Can Get It: Life and Labor in Precarious Times.* New York: New York University Press.

Said, Edward. (1978) 2003. *Orientalism*. New York: Vintage Books.

Sassen, Saskia. 2000. "New Frontiers Facing Urban Sociology at the Millennium." *British Journal of Sociology* 51:143–59.

———. 2002. "The Repositioning of Citizenship: Emergent Subjects and Spaces for Politics." *Berkeley Journal of Sociology* 46:41–66.

Scott, Joan W. 1998. "Experience." In *Women, Autobiography, Theory: A Reader*, edited by Sidonie Smith and Julia Watson. Madison: University of Wisconsin Press.

Sedgwick, Eve Kosofsky. 1985. *Between Men: English Literature and Male Homosocial Desire*. New York: Columbia University Press.

Sengupta, Somini. 2009. "Dossier from India Gives New Details of Mumbai Attacks." *New York Times*, January 6, 2009.

Shapiro, Ann-Louise. 1997. "How Real Is the Reality in Documentary Film? Jill Godmilow, in Conversation with Ann-Louise Shapiro." *History and Theory* 36 (4): 80–101.

Sharma, Ruchir. 2009. "India's Bulging Middle Goes Shopping," *Newsweek*, August 31, 12–23.

Shome, Raka. 2003. "Space Matters: The Power and Practices of Space." *Communication Theory* 13 (1): 39–56.

———. 2006. "Thinking through the Diaspora: Call Centers, India, and a New Politics of Hybridity." *International Journal of Cultural Studies* 9 (1): 105–24.

Silverman, Kaja. 1983. *The Subject of Semiotics*. New York: Oxford University Press.

60 Minutes. 2004. "Out of India." Produced by A. Bourne. Television program. CBS, January 11.

Smerd, Jeremy. 2009. "Outsourcing on the Home Front." *Workforce Management*, May 18, 33.

Spivak, Gayatri. 1988. "Can the Subaltern Speak?" In *Marxism and the Interpretation of Culture*, edited by Cary Nelson and Lawrence Grossberg. Urbana: University of Illinois Press.

Sridharan, E. 2004. "The Growth and Sectoral Composition of India's Middle Class: Its Impact on the Politics of Economic Liberalization." *India Review* 3:405–28.

Stevens, Andrew, and David. O. Lavin. 2007. "Stealing Time: The Temporal Regulations of Labor in Neoliberal and Post-Fordist Work Regime." *Democratic Communique* 21 (2): 40–61.

Stoler, Ann. 1995. *Race and the Education of Desire*. Durham, N.C.: Duke University Press.

Sudhakar, Ram. 2009. "How India's Next Outsourcing Wave Can Help the U.S." *Business Week Online*, September 28.

Taylor, Charles. 1994. *Multiculturalism: Examining the Politics of Recognition*. Princeton, N.J.: Princeton University Press.

30 Days. 2006. "Outsourcing." Produced by Todd Lubin. Television program. FX, August 2.

Tracy, Sarah. 2000. "Becoming a Character for Commerce: Emotional Labor, Self-Subordination, and Discursive Construction of Identity in a Total Institution." *Management Communication Quarterly* 14 (1): 90–128.

Tripathi, Amit. 2009. "India's Offshoring Share Is Just 25%." *DNA: Daily News and Analysis*, November 19. www.dnaindia.com/money/1313504/report-india-s-off shoring-share-is-just-25pct.

Turner, Bryan S. 1993. Preface to *In Citizenship and Social Theory*, edited by Bryan S. Turner. London: Sage.

Upadhya, Carol, and A. R. Vasavi. 2008. "Outposts of the Global Information Economy: Work and Workers in India's Outsourcing Industry." In *In an Outpost of the Global Economy: Work and Workers in India's Information Technology Industry*, edited by Carol Upadhya and A. R. Vasavi. New York: Routledge.

Visweswaran, Kamala. 1994. *Fictions of Feminist Ethnography*. Minneapolis: University of Minnesota Press.

Walton-Roberts, Margaret. 2004. "Globalization, National Autonomy and Nonresident Indians." *Contemporary South Asia* 13 (1): 53–69.

Waraich, Omar. 2009. "Pakistan Continues to Resist India Pressure on Mumbai." *Time*, January 7.

Winiecki, Donald. J. 2007. "Subjects, Subjectivity, and Subjectification in Call Center Work: The Doings of Doings." *Journal of Contemporary Ethnography* 36 (4): 351–76.

WorldBank Data. 2012. "GDP Growth." data.worldbank.org.

Xiang, Biao. 2006. *Global "Body Shopping": An Indian Labor System in the Information Technology Industry*. Princeton, N.J.: Princeton University Press.

Zaidi, Mubashir. 2009. "Surviving Gunman's Identity Established as Pakistani." *Dawn* .com. January 8. archives.dawn.com/archives/142073.

Index

AIMEE CARRILLO ROWE is associate professor of communication studies at California State University, Northridge. She is author of *Power Lines: On the Subject of Feminist Alliances* and coeditor of *Silence, Feminism, Power: Reflections at the Edges of Sound.*

SHEENA MALHOTRA is professor of gender and women's studies at California State University, Northridge. She is coeditor of *Silence, Feminism, Power: Reflections at the Edges of Sound.*

KIMBERLEE PÉREZ is a doctoral candidate in the Hugh Downs School of Human Communication at Arizona State University.